The New Eve in Christ

The New Eve in Christ

The Use and Abuse of the Bible
in the Debate about Women in the Church

MARY HAYTER

WILLIAM B. EERDMANS PUBLISHING COMPANY
GRAND RAPIDS, MICHIGAN

Library of Congress Cataloging-in-Publication Data
Hayter, Mary.
The new Eve in Christ : the use and abuse of the Bible
in the debate about women in the church/Mary Hayter.
p.   cm.
Bibliography: p. 172.
Includes indexes.
ISBN 0-8028-0325-3
1. Woman (Christian theology) — Biblical theology.   2. Ordination
of women — Biblical teaching.   3. Bible — Hermeneutics.   4. Bible-
Criticism, interpretation, etc.   I. Title.
BS680.W7H39   1987   262'.14—dc19

Contents

Preface

In discussion about women's ministry reference is often made to scriptural teaching pertaining to the subject. Frequently, texts are misappropriated – both by those who think it right to restrict women to lay ministry and by those who would endorse decisions to ordain women to diaconate, priesthood and episcopate. For example, verses from the Old Testament are adduced to show that since God is masculine he must be represented by a male priesthood. Again, it is claimed that Scripture teaches the divinely decreed and permanent subjection of woman to man, the inherent sinfulness of female nature, the unsuitability of Eve's daughters for positions of authority in the Church. Or again, many advocates of women's ordination quote with approval passages like Galatians 3.27f, but fail to give adequate account of their principle of interpretation and simply ignore or dismiss 'problem' passages like Genesis 3.16 and 1 Corinthians 11.2–16.

It is my belief that such views betray a misunderstanding of biblical teaching about God, priesthood, the *Imago Dei*, human sexuality, the effects of Christ's redeeming work upon men and women and the nature of the Bible and its authority. Not only is the full involvement of women in ministry impeded, but the balanced and integrated re-expression of the doctrines of God, man, church and ministry for our age is also jeopardized. I have endeavoured, then, to reassess the contribution of Scripture – particularly of the oft-neglected Old Testament material – to the debate about women's ministry. When careful attention is devoted to resolving the complex hermeneutical problems surrounding the texts, the various misuses of the Bible are exposed and the way is clear for a fresh apprehension of the liberating power of God to lead the Church to a new and deeper understanding of the status and function of women in the Christian community.

The various issues raised by this study have been discussed with several teachers and colleagues. Especial thanks are due to Professor Ernest Nicholson, Professor John Macquarrie, Dr

John Barton, and Colin and Veronica Bennetts in Oxford; to Dr John Muddiman, and to the Principal, staff and friends at Ridley Hall, Cambridge. I am particularly grateful to Dr Michael Sansom, Dr Douglas de Lacey, Jeremy Begbie and Penny West, John Barr and Bobbie Coe: without their endless patience and practical encouragement this book would never have emerged. I cannot be thankful enough to my father, the Reverend Ronald Hayter, who remains the most constant and inspiring mentor. It was from him that I learnt my first theology and through his ministry that I have found the vision for my own. This book is dedicated to him.

Ridley Hall, Cambridge   Mary E. Hayter
Passiontide 1986

List of Abbreviations

AB	*Analecta Biblica*
ACCM	The Advisory Council for the Church's Ministry
AJSL	*American Journal of Semitic Languages and Literature*
AKJV	Authorized King James Version of the Bible
ANET	*Ancient Near Eastern Texts* (2nd edn, J. B. Pritchard)
An Or	*Analecta Orientalia*
AP	*Aramaic Papyri of the Fifth Century BC* (ed. A. C. Cowley)
ATR	*Anglican Theological Review*
BAR	*Biblical Archaeology Review*
BASOR	*Bulletin of the American Schools of Oriental Research*
BCC	British Council of Churches
BCP	*The Book of Common Prayer*
BJRL	*Bulletin of the John Rylands Library*
CBQ	*Catholic Biblical Quarterly*
CD	*Church Dogmatics*, (K. Barth)
CHB	*Cambridge History of the Bible*
CQR	*Church Quarterly Review*
ER	*Ecumenical Review*
ERE	*Encyclopaedia of Religion and Ethics*
ET	English translation
E et T	*Église et Théologie*
Exp T	*Expository Times*
GS	General Synod
HT	*History Today*
HUCA	*Hebrew Union College Annual*
IBD	*Interpreter's Bible Dictionary*
JAAR	*Journal of the American Academy of Religion*
JBL	*Journal of Biblical Literature*
JES	*Journal of Ecumenical Studies*
JJS	*Journal of Jewish Studies*
JSOT	*Journal for the Study of the Old Testament*
JTS	*Journal of Theological Studies*
LTQ	*Lexington Theological Quarterly*

LXX	Septuagint
MOW	Movement for the Ordination of Women
NTS	*New Testament Studies*
PG	*Patrologia Graeca* (ed. J.-P. Migne)
PL	*Patrologia Latina* (ed. J.-P. Migne)
RB	*Revue Biblique*
RSV	Revised Standard Version of the Bible
SJT	*Scottish Journal of Theology*
SN	*Supplements to Numen*
St Ev	*Studia Evangelica*
SVT	*Supplements to Vetus Testamentum*
TB	*Tyndale Bulletin*
TDNT	*Theological Dictionary of the New Testament*
TDOT	*Theological Dictionary of the Old Testament*
TEV	Today's English Version: *Good News Bible*
TS	*Theological Studies*
TWB	*Theological Word Book of the Bible* (ed. A. Richardson)
VT	*Vetus Testamentum*
WCC	World Council of Churches
ZAW	*Zeitschrift für die Alttestamentliche Wissenschaft*

Introduction

Those who plead recklessly for the ordination of women should be urged to turn back to their Bibles, and ask themselves how they are able to reconcile their cherished but ill-regulated enthusiasm with the clear teaching which they find there.[1]

Bishop Kirk's admonition presupposes that scriptural teaching is firmly opposed to women's ordination – a presumption which continues to be made by many people today. R. Beckwith, for example, believes that 'one cannot fail to see that, according to biblical teaching, men and women can no more cease to be in a relationship of authority and subordination than they can cease to be creatures of God'. Ministry always involves some exercise of authority and therefore 'the exclusion of the subordinate partner in the human race from the principal offices in the Christian ministry . . . is as inevitable today as it was in the first century'.[2]

It is not only traditionalist or conservative writers who hold such opinions about the Bible. Most radical feminists would share the assumption of Kirk and Beckwith about the *content* of biblical teaching on women. Disagreement between the two groups occurs over the *value* of this teaching. Assuming that the Bible perpetuates belief in a male deity, which endorses patriarchy, radical feminists regard Scripture as the *fons et origo* of much of the 'sexism' which bedevils society; therefore, far from directing twentieth-century men and women back to this biblical teaching, they denounce it.[3]

In response to all this, some fundamental questions must be raised. Is it true to say that the God of the Bible is a male deity who demands to be served by a male priesthood? Is the patriarchal ordering of Church, society and family absolutely concomitant with the expression of biblical faith? Is it correct to assume that the Bible clearly and consistently casts woman in the role of the 'subordinate partner' and permanently excludes her from the exercise of ministerial authority?

As more and more books about women's ministry are published it becomes increasingly obvious that many writers have misappropriated the biblical material. Two factors, particularly, have provided the specific orientation of my study. The first is the misuse or, frequently, the non-use of the Old Testament. The fact that the Old Testament itself is ignored or treated superficially leads to a misunderstanding of New Testament references to the Hebrew Scriptures – references like Paul's mention of Eve in 2 Corinthians 11.3. Furthermore, as E. L. Mascall points out, it is inadequate simply to say that Jesus appointed an all-male apostolate because the Jewish Church knew nothing of priestesses and it would have been too revolutionary an action to begin to make them in the early Church. Mascall cites with approval a remark of F. C. Blomfield that 'the absence of priestesses in Israel has itself to be explained, before this can be used as an argument for changing the plan'.[4] I have endeavoured, then, to elucidate the Old Testament contribution to Christian thought on issues raised by the debate about women's ministry.

Secondly, in much recent writing on this topic the authors have given way to the temptation to play off one text against another without resolving problems of biblical authority and interpretation. There are, of course, some who assume that the ancient Near Eastern writings which constitute the Bible have little authority over or relevance for twentieth-century men and women in the Western world. I have attempted to counter this radical relativist position. In the main, however, my concern has been to challenge the methodology and the conclusions of those who take a more orthodox view of the authority of Scripture but whose mishandling of the complex hermeneutical problems surrounding the text undermines the credibility of the Bible in the modern world.

If the Bible is to be authoritative in matters of faith and conduct it must be the Bible rightly interpreted.

> The Bible is not a rule book or a dictionary. It cannot, therefore, be used as if it were no more than a vast collection of proof texts which one may call upon at discretion in order to support one's own arguments or confute those of one's opponents. That is a misuse of the Bible's authority.[5]

Nor should a legitimate return to Scripture for guidance on

women's place within the Church's ministry simply expect to find a blueprint which may be applied, detail by detail, to our twentieth-century situation in slavish imitation of a situation in the past. 'This type of return to sources, which is more biblicizing than biblical, is neither healthy or realistic'.[6] Rather, individual texts must be carefully analysed, and the conditions of the times which gave rise to particular statements or formed their background must be borne in mind. Any interpretation and application which is not controlled by the historical context of the passage misrepresents the Bible.

I have not set out to write a general treatise 'for' or 'against' women's ordination. Some of the biblical and doctrinal factors and many of the historical, philosophical, psychological and sociological questions which such a treatise must encompass have been deliberately omitted from this book (though not ignored in the reading which lies behind it). My purpose has been in one sense narrower yet, in another, wider than such a general treatise would allow. It is narrower in that I have focused upon *the use of the Bible* in the debate about women's ministry. It is wider in that I have tried to conduct my study of this specific issue in such a way that its results might have relevance to Christian thought far beyond the question of women's ordination.

Misunderstanding of biblical teaching relevant to the subject of women's ordination involves a misconstruction of biblical teaching about God, priesthood, the *Imago Dei*, sexuality, the effects of Christ's incarnation and redeeming work upon men and women, as well as a misconception of the nature of the Bible and its authority. It is my hope that this book will play some part in the expunction of such misconceptions – not only so that the full involvement of women in ministry might be facilitated but also in order that progress might be made towards the balanced and integrated re-expression for our age of biblical teaching pertinent to the doctrines of God, man and ministry.

NOTES

1. K. E. Kirk, 'The Ordination of Women' in *Beauty and Bands* (London 1955), p. 188.
2. R. Beckwith, 'The Bearing of Holy Scripture' in *Man, Woman, and Priesthood,* ed. P. Moore (London 1978), p. 62.

3. Cf. M. Daly, *Beyond God the Father* (Boston 1973), *passim*.
4. E. L. Mascall, 'Women and the Priesthood of the Church', *Why Not?* ed. R. T. Beckwith (Abingdon 1976), p. 102. He quotes F. C. Blomfield, *Wonderful Order* (London 1955) pp. 26–7.
5. J. Bright, *The Authority of the Old Testament* (London 1967) pp. 41, 47.
6. M. Thurian, *Priesthood and Ministry* (London 1983), p. 2.

Part One

Sexuality in God and the Nature of Priesthood

1
God and Goddess

'Women priests could be a step towards a new religion.'[1] This is a powerful line of argument taken by people who would have us believe that the ultimate reason for the maleness of the Judaistic and Christian priesthoods is the maleness of the God whom they represent. Following the biblical revelation, we worship neither a 'Parent God' nor the 'Great Mother', but 'Our Father'. It is claimed that the ultimate objective of advocates of women's ministry, whether or not all of them are conscious of the fact, is the destruction of belief in the Fatherhood of God and the establishment of a religion based on feminist principles, in which a pantheon of gods and goddesses or a 'God/ess-head' comprising a male and female deity is ministered to by male and female priests.

Certainly, W. Oddie is able to quote from several sources which seem to confirm that he and others are right to claim that feminism is engaged in the demolition of traditional Jewish and Christian beliefs.[2] Oddie points to the alarming resurgence of Goddess worship evidenced, for example, in feminist attitudes towards Scripture and liturgy. And, indeed, R. R. Ruether, one of the less extreme and more reputable feminist theologians, appears to approach the Old Testament and ancient Near Eastern religion in general with the intention of revitalizing and reinterpreting ideas about the Goddess. Broadly speaking, the main thrust of the feminist attack as it concerns the Old Testament is that, contrary to the impression which the Hebrew Scriptures now give, originally the Hebrew faith deified both masculinity and feminity; and that partriarchal male monotheism engineered the final form of the Old Testament so that Goddesses are anathematized by the male God and women are subjugated to men. 'Male monotheism reinforces the social hierarchy of patriarchal rule through its religious system in a way that was not the case with the paired images of God and Goddess.'[3] A recovery of feminine deity not only restores the balance, currently weighted heavily in favour of masculinity, on divine scales; it is also concomitant with the process whereby women rise to leadership positions in society and religion.[4]

It is my contention that Scripture is abused not only by those who approach the Old Testament with the intention of demonstrating either that it is irredeemably sexist or that it may, after all, when stripped of patriarchal accretions, be used to justify (or, at least, may not be used to condemn) modern versions of Goddess worship and the priestesses of the Great Mother. Scripture is also abused by anti-feminists who seek to counter both radical feminism and moderate movements for women's ministry (the two are frequently treated as one homogeneous evil) in vitriolic attacks which stress the maleness of God and priesthood, purporting to derive this emphasis from the Old Testament. Both groups rest their arguments upon two questionable assumptions:

i) the assumption that the God of the Bible is, in so far as the divine can be defined in terms of sex, an exclusively male deity;

ii) the assumption that the maleness, or otherwise, of the deity has an immediate and practical effect upon the maleness, or otherwise, of the priesthood. In the following four chapters these assumptions will be submitted to objective analysis.

As a necessary precursor to this, some clarification must be offered of the terms 'priest' and 'priesthood'. Many people think that, whatever the reason for the exclusively male character of the Judaistic priesthood, it has no bearing upon the Church's ministry because Christian ministry is not 'priesthood' in the Old Testament sense. Others maintain that the catholic view of priesthood has its basis firmly in the Old Testament and that 'a Christian equivalent of the levitical priesthood had to emerge.'[5] It is beyond the scope of this book to re-examine the vexatious questions surrounding the sacerdotalizing of ministry in Cyprian's church.[6] I myself do not believe that Christianity has 'priests' in the Old Testament sense of a cultic sacrificial priesthood, but I have deliberately bracketed out this aspect of the doctrine of ministry so as to meet on their own terms those who assume a close identity between Israelite and Christian priesthood. I hope to show that even those people who equate Judaistic 'priest' and 'high priest' with Christian 'presbyter' and 'bishop' have no justification for holding that priests must be male in order to reflect the maleness of God. Once this assumption is shown to be false, the foundation is removed from the argument that the concept of 'women priests' destroys something intrinsic to Christian religion and essential to faith in the God and Father of Jesus Christ.

A Male God?

First, we must remind ourselves of the beliefs of those who seem to affirm that God is male and that in him is no femaleness at all. The popular image of God is often that of an aggressively masculine figure with flowing beard and stern countenance, seated on a kingly throne and exuding the 'masculine' qualities of power, wisdom, strength. On a cursory reading, the Old Testament texts readily lend themselves as elements in this picture of a thoroughly 'manly' deity who performs 'male' functions. For example, he leads an army (Amos 5.27) and dispenses judgement (Judg. 11.27); he may be compared with a husband (Isa. 54.5), a father (Ps. 68.5), a king (Mal. 1.14).

Several scholars have acknowledged the power of language to influence theology. P. Trible recognizes that although grammatical gender decides neither sexuality nor theology, these distinctions are exceedingly difficult to maintain in our hearing and understanding. 'Consequently, masculine pronouns reinforce a male image of God, an image that obscures, even obliterates, female metaphors for deity.'[7] R. Patai reminds us that in the Hebrew language most nouns have either a masculine or a feminine gender (only a few can take either). Since the two biblical names of God, Yahweh and Elohim, are masculine, since the masculine pronoun, 'he', is used of God, since verbs used in connection with God take the masculine form, Patai infers that 'every verbal statement about God conveyed the idea that he was masculine'.[8]

In recent years, there has been a reappraisal of biblical material. Many scholars now acknowledge that a substantial list of references to so-called 'feminine' aspects of God's nature and activities may be compiled. Yet, with the exception of numerous feminist extremists (many of them American) seeking biblical support for the Women's Liberation Movement, few theologians (with a particular paucity of British scholars) have undertaken to elucidate the implications of this for our total understanding of the doctrine of God.

It is, therefore, not hard to see why many people have constructed a portrait of a 'male God' using evidence drawn from Scripture; consideration must now be given to the question of how this has affected thinking about priesthood. Theologians who take it to be a fundamental tenet of the scriptural revelation that God must be envisioned in terms of masculine imagery will not allow the masculine religious symbolism of the Old Testament to be relegated to the realms of socio-cultural influence; they believe that the 'maleness' of God determines the 'maleness' of the priesthood, so the fact that the Old Testament knows nothing of priestessess of Yahweh cannot be dismissed as a product of a patriarchal society. The maleness of the priesthood is part of the 'eternal order' that God intends for the world; it is a reflection not of human whim but of divine nature and order, for, by his very 'maleness', a priest represents the qualities of the 'male God' to his people.

Mascall does not wish to suggest that there is in the triune Godhead anything crudely corresponding to the biological characteristics of sex. Yet he thinks it is significant that when Genesis 1.27 states that male and female are created in God's image, it is *his* image, not *hers*, to which reference is made. This leads Mascall to remark:

> if it is suggested that the use of masculine terms is a mere accident of language or that the analogical application of terms to God is so remote that their gender is of no significance, it will, I think, be sufficient to remark that our belief in God would be different from what it is if the Trinity was described as consisting of . . . Parent, Offspring and Spirit simply . . . The female sex has its own peculiar dignity . . .; but we can hardly imagine it exercising the Fatherhood of God.[9]

Mascall's argument may be summarized thus: the Christian priest is to exercise fatherhood and not motherhood to God's family, because his office is a participation in God's own relationship to his people, and God is our Father in heaven and not our Mother.

Several Christian thinkers share these views. For example, Lewis wrote:

Christians think that God Himself has taught us how to speak
of Him. To say that it does not matter is to say either that all
the masculine imagery is not inspired, is merely human in
origin, or else that, though inspired, it is quite arbitrary and
unessential. And this is surely intolerable: or, if tolerable, it is
an argument not in favour of Christian priestesses but against
Christianity.[10]

Other writers accuse supporters of women's ordination of being
heretical feminists. They are labelled 'feminist', because they will
not accept the dominance and superiority of a male God who is
represented by male priests; they are branded as 'heretics',
because they dare to suggest that the idea of a male God is more a
product of socio-cultural influences than a 'given' truth of the
Judaeo-Christian revelation.[11]

'Female priesthoods belong to Earth-Mother religions'; so
state G. Russell and M. Dewey in their examination of the
psychological aspects of the question of whether women priests
would distort the Christian doctrine of God. They believe that
Christians are bound, by the dictates of Scripture, to encounter
and to envisage God as male, and that this fact must bear on the
ordination of women; women priests would activate 'the dark side
of the Mother, that which is, in the last analysis, hostile to
growth'.[12] That women priests would change the face of the
Christian God from the heavenly Father to the Earth-Mother is
also the fear of V. A. Demant: the Christian Church has without
question adopted a male priesthood because, as the history of
comparative religion teaches us, none but male priesthoods
belong to monotheisms, in which a male God is Lord over nature
and history. 'Therefore to have a twin priesthood of males and
females could be more disruptive of the Christian Church than
any doctrinal heresy or moral deviation.'[13]

The fear that the ulterior motive of those who advocate
women's ordination is something far more sinister – namely, the
destruction of the Christian faith as we know it – seems to be
substantiated when one samples feminist literature. Some alarming statements appear in the following extract from Goldenberg's
book, *Changing of the Gods*:

How could women represent a male God? Everything I knew
about Judaism and Christianity involved accepting God as the

ultimate in male authority figures. If enough women claimed to
represent 'His' authority . . . congregations would have to stop
seeing God as male, God would begin to look like 'His' female
officials . . . 'God is going to change', I thought. 'We women are
going to bring an end to God' . . . I found this line of thought
most satisfying. I had no great tie to God anyway . . . there was
a magnificence attached to the idea of watching Him go . . . The
feminist movement in Western culture is engaged in the slow
execution of Christ and Yahweh. Yet very few of the women
and men now working for sexual equality within Christianity
and Judaism realize the extent of their heresy.[14]

Even the writings of more moderate 'Christian' feminists
would meet with grave disapproval from people like Mascall and
Demant. Ruether is adamant that the male image of the deity
which dominates the Judaeo-Christian tradition has caused many
women to experience a deep sense of alienation from God and his
Church. She does not regard the absence of the feminine as the
icon of God in all divine fullness as a facet of Old Testament
revelation. Instead, she blames it upon the patriarchal society in
which Hebrew theology fermented. Many people would doubtless recoil in dismay from Ruether's admonitions to Christians
that they should seek an image of God/ess beyond patriarchy and
admit that the male has no special priority in imaging God/ess.[15]

This survey of the fracas between feminists and reactionaries
shows all too clearly that amongst the varied uses of Scripture in
recent theology one of the most contentious is its usage in
discussions about sexuality in God and woman's admissibility to
priesthood. The matter is no trivial one – although it has often
been trivialized or besmirched by over-emotional and irrational
treatment. Far from being the preserve of feminists and male
chauvinists, the topic merits the attention of serious theologians
since it involves discussion of issues as crucial as the nature of
God and the authority of Scripture.

Yahweh's Consort?

So far I have outlined the views of two opposing groups, both of
whom refer to the Old Testament in their arguments about the
question of sexuality in God and the nature of priesthood. On the

one hand, there are those who interpret the Old Testament as teaching that the true God is male and that any form of Goddess worship is quite wrong. On the other hand, there are those who feel that it is right and good to venerate a female deity and that Old Testament writer's were behaving like male chauvinists when they rejected Goddesses. In order to see how both groups have misunderstood the Old Testament it is necessary to summarize the available evidence about Hebrew attitudes towards Goddess worship.

Goddesses feature prominently in ancient Near Eastern religions. Recently there has been much scholarly debate about how far Hebrews were influenced by their contemporaries to venerate a female deity alongside their God.[16] Since the beginnings of Yahweh-worship are shrouded in the mists of antiquity, no one can say with absolute certainty that a female consort was or was not venerated beside Yahweh in mainstream Hebrew piety.[17] The evidence which is available – from archaeological research and historical criticism of the Old Testament documents – suggests that, in certain times and locations at least, it was normal and commonplace to associate Yahweh with a consort.

Such acceptance of Goddess worship, however, is accorded only negative significance in the Old Testament. It is the opinion of Deuteronomic and priestly redactors, with their fierce denunciations of kings who allowed people to serve Baal and Asherah, which has prevailed against those who did not see the worship of Yahweh and a Goddess as mutually exclusive. Information about Hebrew devotion to Yahweh's consort is valuable to our understanding of the religious development of Israel, but it may not be twisted to imply that the Old Testament justifies, or does not condemn, the veneration of God–and–Goddess. From a theological point of view the message of the Old Testament is consistently clear: orthodox believers must eschew all association with Asherah, the queen of heaven, or any other female deity (see, for example, Deut. 16.21; 2 Kings 23.4; Isa. 17.8, 27.9; Micah 5.13f; Jer. 7.18, 17.2, 44.17).[18]

In answer to the question 'What does the Old Testament, as Holy Scripture, teach about Goddess worship?', it must be said that the whole tenor of the Old Testament attitude towards this subject is one of open hostility. The Old Testament includes no passage which may legitimately be used to support the resurgence of Goddess worship. On the contrary, it contains much material which may be incorporated in a denunciation of the Goddess revival. The next stage of our study, then, is to ask *why* the Old Testament says such an uncompromising 'no' to the worship of Yahweh-plus-consort.

Reasons for Rejecting the Goddess

According to both radical feminists and conservative writers, the reaction in the Old Testament against Goddess worship was based upon suspicion of the feminine and the female. Rejection of the Goddess was motivated by anti-feminism or, at least, by the conviction that prosperous, healthy living involved the veneration of a masculine deity who was served by a male priesthood in the context of a patriarchal society. Feminists argue that this suspicion is totally unfounded, a product of male chauvinism; conservatives maintain that it is a suspicion which we do well to share with the Old Testament. It is necessary, therefore to ask whether the attack on the Goddess was the result of anti-feminist tendencies or whether some other explanation lies behind it.[19] I would suggest, in the light of theories propounded by several scholars about Israel's theological development, that the answer lies in *the tension between the increasing denaturalization of Israelite religion,* concomitant with *the transcendentalization of Yahweh,* on the one hand, and, on the other hand, *the irrevocable association between the Goddess and the fertility cult.* To put it more simply, the Hebrews realized that their Lord was not like the fertility deities; they came to see that Yahweh was above the conditions of human sexuality and was not a male God who needed a female consort.

The nature religion of Israel's neighbours, such as the Canaanites, betrays a preoccupation with fertility rites typical of ancient agrarian peoples who believed that the fecundity of plants, animals and man was dependent upon divine sexual activity.[20] It should be remembered that the whole fertility cultus concerns not just one particular religion nor specific deities like Baal and Asherah; rather, it involves a widespread and persistent way of looking at the life of both Gods and men. In the elaborate myths of the ancient Near East, the divine archetypes are masculine and feminine – divine couples – because the life of the world was thought to depend on its relation with the eroticism of the Gods. Kaufmann describes the view of the sexuality of the deity which is produced by the fertility cult ethos:

> male and female deities . . . desire and mate with each other. The cycles of nature are commonly conceived of as the perennial mating and procreating of the gods. Thus, the gods are subject by their nature to sexual needs. At the same time they are involved in the processes of time. They gestate and give birth, they die and are resurrected . . .[21]

Human, no less than divine, sexuality was conceptualized and manifested in a distinctive way under the influence of the fertility cultus. Religious festivals could become occasions for sexual libertinism, as men and women imitated divine orgies – perhaps hoping to force or bribe the deity by the process of sympathetic magic to assure the fecundity of crops, flocks and human beings, perhaps finding a convenient excuse for sexual indulgence.

In contrast to this, the Old Testament documents reveal a radically different outlook on both human and divine sexuality. It was not that the Hebrews took a 'low' or 'negative' view of sex; they regarded it as God-given and good, but within marriage not in '(sacred) prostitution', between husband and wife not between God and Goddess. Von Rad observes that in the Canaanite cult, copulation and procreation were mythically regarded as a divine event; consequently the religious atmosphere was saturated with mythic sexual conceptions. But Israel did not share in the 'divinization' of sex; it was a phenomenon of the creature.[22]

Whatever similarities it may seem possible to find between Yahweh and the sky and storm gods of other religions, the Old Testament compilers cannot be said to have regarded him as the spouse of the Great Goddess. As we have seen it is probable that at one time certain Hebrews saw nothing amiss in worshipping Yahweh and a consort, just as they did not think it wrong to transfer fertility cult imagery – such as the bull symbol – from Baal to Yahweh.[23] As the Hebrews' understanding of the character of their religion grew, however, theologians came to regard such imagery as unsuitable. The rejection of the Goddess was part of a powerful theological development in Israel's thinking about God, man and the world.

Prophetic preaching in the late pre-exilic and early exilic period distanced God from the world and stressed his radical transcendence of his creation. Commentators are impressed, for example, by Deutero-Isaiah's concentration upon the greatness and majesty of *the one God* (44.6, 8; 45.5, 6, 21; 41.4; 43.15; 46.4; 48.12).[24] Yahweh is not to be identified with nor represented by anything in the world (Isa. 40.18; 46.5f). As Creator and Saviour, he demands exclusive allegiance from his people (43.1, 10f; 44.6f, 24f), for beside him 'there is no God' (45.14, 18). His care and concern for his people is everlasting (41.8ff). But it is made clear that this is the compassion of the Creator for the creature (42.5f), of the Redeemer for the poor and needy (41.17), of the Maker for the earthen vessel (45.9f), of the Holy One of Israel for the worm Jacob (41.14). This does not resemble the relationship between the divine and the human as envisaged in cosmogonic religions, where the Deity, who was thought to permeate the world, could be manipulated or cajoled into action by sorceries and sympathetic magic (cf. 47.12f). Thus, the relationship between divinity and humanity is denaturalized, demythologized, disenchanted in the prophetic proclamation, which illustrates the essential contrast between Yahwism and the fertility cult ethos and shows the impropriety of the view that Gods and Goddesses, men and women can together act out and conjure up the seminal energy necessary for the maintenance of the cosmos.

This concentration upon the exclusiveness, the incomparability and the transcendence of Yahweh doubtless had antecedents in earlier times, but it was greatly intensified from the later pre-exilic period onwards. As scholars from Wellhausen to the present day have recognized,[25] the increasing transcendentalization of God and denaturalization of Israelite religion received vital impulses from the prophets, and from the breakthrough in the understanding of God's relationship with the world amongst the majority of the people (not simply in prophetic circles) which was accelerated by covenant theology. The covenant concept dwelt upon the exclusiveness and oneness of Israel's God and forbade his people to associate him with other divine beings. Under the influence of prophetic and covenant theology, then, earlier traditions, which referred to Hebrew worship of the Goddess, were reworked, abridged or excised altogether, so that, in the final form of the Hebrew canon, she always appears as an undesirable phenomenon. The Deuteronomistic historians and the post-exilic redactors believed Yahweh to be the absolute sovereign and omnipotent creator of the universe and its processes; he needed no female partner to perform the sex act with him and give birth to the earth and its inhabitants.

As writers like S. Sapp make clear, one of the key factors which distinguished Israelite religion from other contemporary religions was 'the separation of sexuality from divine creation – that is, the demythologizing of fertility'.[26] It was by his will alone that Yahweh created in the natural order the processes by which vegetable, animal and human fecundity was assured. Agricultural success and human fruitfulness, therefore, could not be coerced by imitating the supposed divine fertility through ritual sexual activities.

It is not hard to perceive, then, why the whole fertility cultus, with its conceptions of a *hieros gamos* and the re-enaction of this by cult prostitutes, became obnoxious to the champions of Yahweh. To them, it seemed that the only way to purge the nation of the obsessive fertility cult was to remove all notions of a Goddess from Yahwistic religion, for in the ancient Near Eastern milieu any form of Goddess worship meant opening the door to the unequivocally sensual character of the vegetation deities. The female consort of Yahweh – although, at one time, she may have occupied a significant position in Israelite piety – increasingly became the object of invective from discerning Yahwists. Veneration of a Goddess alongside Yahweh involved ideas and actions which thoughtful Hebrews no longer found compatible with the nature of their faith in a unique and transcendent God. Since the service of the Goddess was irrevocably associated with the unhealthy sexual orientation of the fertility cultus, she must be abandoned.

There is no evidence in the Old Testament that the abandonment of the Goddess was due to anti-feminism. Rather, the rejection of the notion that Yahweh was a God who needed a wife was one consequence of a theological development which had deep and far-reaching effects upon all aspects of Hebrew religion. To suggest that antipathy to the Goddess was the result of some inherently male-chauvinist aspect of Hebrew thought simply trivializes the whole subject. The Old Testament rejection of Asherah was motivated not by suspicion of femininity but by a

growing awareness of the transcendence of Yahweh which preci-
pitated hostility towards the fertility cultus with its ascription of
male *and* female sexuality to its deities. Ideas about divine
maleness, *as well as* about divine femaleness, derive from the
fertility cult. Therefore, the objective of Old Testament writers
was not to acclaim the conquest of male Yahweh over a female
Asherah but to avoid, as far as possible, any projection of human
sexuality on to their God. *They believed Yahweh to be neither male
nor female but supra-sexual.*[27]

In sum, the essential dissonance is not between the Old
Testament and femininity but between the Old Testament and
nature religion. The conflict is between Old Testament theology,
which acknowledges God's radical transcendence of the world
which he has made, on the one hand, and, on the other hand,
fertility-cult notions which confuse the Creator with the creature
by implying that the deity partakes in human sexuality. Thus,
both the feminists who venerate a female deity and those who
react against this by stressing the maleness of God are revitalizing
the unhealthy emphases of the fertility cultus which the Old
Testament roundly condemns. They are departing from faith in a
transcendent Creator and Redeemer and re-mythologizing – even
re-magicalizing – religion.

NOTES

1. W. Oddie, article in the *Daily Telegraph*, 5 May 1982.
2. Oddie, *What Will Happen to God?* (London 1984).
3. R. R. Ruether, *Sexism and God-Talk* (London 1983), p. 53.
4. cf. N. Goldenberg, *Changing of the Gods* (Boston 1979), pp. 3f.
5. J. and G. Muddiman, *Women, the Bible and the Priesthood* (London 1984), p. 3.
6. On these issues see, for example, R. Hanson, *Christian Priesthood Examined* (Guildford and London 1979), *passim*; E. Schillebeeckx, *Ministry – A Case for Change* (London 1981) pp. 48f; 70; 87ff; M. Thurian, *Priesthood and Ministry* (London 1983) pp. 24f; 62f.
7. P. Trible, *God and the Rhetoric of Sexuality* (Philadelphia 1978), p. 23, n. 5.
8. R. Patai, *The Hebrew Goddess* (New York 1967), p. 22; cf. N. P. Bratsiotis, *'îsh 'ishshāh, TDOT*, I, p. 232.
9. Mascall, 'Women and the Priesthood of the Church', pp. 111–12.

10. C. S. Lewis, 'Priestesses in the Church?' (1948) *God in the Dock* (London 1979), p. 91.
11. For example, M. Bruce, 'Heresy, Equality and the Rights of Women', *Why Not?* pp. 40f.
12. G. Russell and M. Dewey, 'Psychological Aspects' in *Man, Woman, and Priesthood*, pp. 95, 98.
13. V. A. Demant, 'Why the Christian Priesthood is Male', *Women and Holy Orders* (London 1966) para. 10.
14. Goldenberg, op. cit., pp. 3–4.
15. Ruether, 'The Female Nature of God', *Concilium* (March 1981), see especially pp. 61–5.
16. There has also been much debate about the name by which Hebrews would have known the Goddess – was she Anath, Astarte, Asherah ...? See, for example, H. Ringgren, *Religions of the Ancient Near East* (London 1973), pp. 140ff.
17. The traditional view is that the monotheistic nature of Hebrew faith precludes any notion that Yahweh was envisaged as having a consort. (See, for example, Th. C. Vriezen, *The Religion of Ancient Israel* (London 1967), p. 12.) But this presupposes that Hebrew faith was monotheistic from very early times. Today, many scholars are less confident than their predecessors about the possibility of reconstructing an accurate picture of the incipience and development of Hebrew monotheism. For example, compare W. F. Albright, *From Stone Age to Christianity* (Baltimore 1940), pp. 86, 230ff and H. H. Rowley, *The Faith of Israel* (London 1956), pp. 71ff, with the contributions of H.-P. Müller and F. Stolz in *Monotheismus im Alten Israel und Seiner Umwelt*, ed. O. Keel (Freiburg 1980) and A. R. Johnson, *The One and the Many in the Israelite Conception of God* (Cardiff 1961), pp. 22, 37. Consequently, the impossibility of being certain that mainstream Hebrew piety consistently rejected the notion of Yahweh's consort must be admitted.
18. cf. W. L. Reed, *The Asherah in the Old Testament* (Texas 1949), p. 88.
19. One theory is that hostility to the Goddess developed because her cultus was borrowed from a foreign source; she emanated from Canaan and so could never be an integral part of the true faith of Israel (cf. Reed, op. cit., pp. 59ff, 68). This may have been a contributory factor – but the theory is too simplistic and does not provide an adequate explanation for the rejection of the Goddess. It draws too sharply the line of demarcation between 'foreign' and 'indigenous' and misses the point that, for many Hebrews, the female deity had come to be regarded as a Hebrew Goddess. On

Hebrew 'borrowing' from Canaanite religion see, for example: Rowley, op. cit., p. 15; J. Barr, *Old and New in Interpretation*, 2 (London 1982), pp.16–17; J. Gray, 'The Legacy of Canaan', *SVT*, 5 (Leiden 1957), p. 151; J. Pedersen, *Israel: Its Life and Culture* III–IV (Copenhagen 1940), pp. 466–76; G. W. Ahlström, *Aspects of Syncretism in Israelite Religion*, (Lund 1963), p. 51; Patai, op. cit., p. 26.

20. cf. Vriezen, *Religion*, pp. 52, 169f; M. Weber, *Ancient Judaism* (Illinois 1952), p. 189; Ahlström, op. cit., p. 54.

21. Y. Kaufmann, *The Religion of Israel* (London 1961), p. 23; cf. E. T. Culver, *Women in the World of Religion* (New York 1967), pp. 4f.

22. G. von Rad, *Theology*, I, p. 27.

23. For example, Num. 24.8. cf. Deut, 33.26. See A. S. Kapelrud, *The Ras Shamra Discoveries and the Old Testament* (Oxford 1965), p. 71. Note that exegetes see signs of redactional work censuring 'unsound' imagery and practices in some passages. See, for example, Pedersen, *Israel*, III–IV, p. 468, on the final form of the story of the golden calf, Exod. 32.3–6, 17f, 25.

24. cf. C. Westermann, *Isaiah 40–66* (London 1969), pp. 14, 16f.

25. For a discussion of the radical transcendence of Yahweh in the context of ancient Near Eastern religion see, for example, H. H. Schmid, *Altorientalische Welt in der alttestamentlichen Theologie* (Zurich 1974).

26. S. Sapp, *Sexuality, the Bible, and Science* (Philadelphia 1977), p. 3. Scholars like von Rad draw attention to the fact that in the Old Testament Creation narrative there is a radical purification and distillation of mythical elements. See *Genesis* (London 1972), pp. 63ff. The Genesis writers removed the sexual connotations common to the cosmogonies of other religions. Israel broke away from the ideas of neighbouring cultures and refused to see the world as the product of a sexual act between God and Goddess. cf. C. J. Vos, *Woman in Old Testament Worship* (Amsterdam 1968), p. 39.

27. Several authorities may be cited in support of this interpretation: for example, E. O. James, *The Cult of the Mother-Goddess* (London 1959), p. 258; Kaufmann, op. cit., p. 60; M. Buber, *The Prophetic Faith* (New York 1949), p. 75.

2
Feminine and Masculine Theological Vocabulary

In the preceding chapter it was maintained that the Old Testament effectively rules out – for those who accept as authoritative the scriptural revelation of God – any possibility of venerating a Godhead comprising a male and a female deity. Some feminists, however, adopt a different method of including notions of female divinity within their credo and of supporting their argument for women's ministry. They profess to believe in a God/ess, a deity who incorporates in a single entity what in human terms is manifested separately as man and woman. To substantiate their case they try to show that the Old Testament employs a considerable amount of feminine imagery in speaking of the Deity. By contrast, anti-feminists reiterate that Scripture uses exclusively masculine imagery, thereby indicating that the deity is male and (allegedly) endorsing the argument that God should be served by a male priesthood. It is necessary now, therefore, to examine some of the Old Testament theological vocabulary to ascertain what it might teach us about sexuality in God and what implications, if any, it holds for our understanding of the nature of priesthood.

This discussion must be prefaced with a general comment on the propriety of such an exercise. Some people dismiss as trivial and time-wasting any attempt to analyse masculine and feminine terms used of God in the Bible; others are offended by the idea of a 'probe into God's private life' which they think is involved in a discussion of divine sexuality. Clearly, there are aspects of the question about sexuality in God which can never be clarified by scholarship. Not a few theologians have fallen prey to the temptation of endeavouring to define exactly what is beyond definition. All theologians encounter some measure of semantic difficulty, but the semantic problem involved in this discussion is particularly acute. In this area, we become more aware than ever of the inadequacy of 'human language when applied to God, who by definition transcends human experience'.[1] Therefore, anyone

engaged in the task of elucidating what the Old Testament says
about sexuality in God must give heed to I. T. Ramsey's admonition: 'let us never talk as if we had privileged access to the diaries
of God's private life, or expert insight into his descriptive
psychology'.[2]

Language about God, especially about sexuality in God, is
necessarily inadequate; nevertheless, religious language need not
be totally erroneous. A proper awareness of the limitations
imposed on finite minds when they meditate upon the Infinite
should not deter deferential consideration of this subject. In view
of the contribution towards the formulation of doctrinal statements on the question of divine sexuality which may be drawn
from the Old Testament, and in the light of the way in which
such statements are employed in the debate about women's
ministry, it becomes evident that this is no inconsequential issue
but one that merits serious and sensitive treatment.

Feminine Imagery

A review of publications from various writers reveals that there
are different ways of approaching the Hebrew Scriptures to see
how far they employ feminine imagery when speaking of Yahweh. Some of these approaches seem so forced and unconvincing
that they do not merit attention here.[3] Other methods are worth
mentioning – if only to help us to construct a picture of how
different writers have used the Old Testament in this respect. But
I would state at the outset that, in referring to these methods, I
am not thereby commending them as helpful to discussions about
sexuality in God.

One method of tackling the material is to be found in the work
of P. Trible. She calls her method 'rhetorical criticism', and
describes it as 'a literary approach to hermeneutics' which
'concentrates primarily on the text rather than on extrinsic
factors' like historical background and archaeological data,
although these are not ignored.[4] Trible focuses on Genesis 1.27
and uses its 'metaphor' of God as male and female (as she sees it)
to interpret other verses containing diverse and partial expressions of the image of God male (for example, father, Ps. 103.13;
husband, Hos. 2.16; king, Ps. 98.6), and of the image of God
female (for example, pregnant woman, Isa. 42.14; mother, Isa.

66.13; midwife, Ps. 22.9). Furthermore, she believes that the use of the Hebrew noun *reḥem*, 'womb', is of great significance; she shows how in the plural form, *raḥªmîm*, the concrete meaning expands to give the abstractions 'love', 'compassion', 'mercy'. Trible argues that the biblical idea of Yahweh as merciful and compassionate draws its power from feminine symbolism and carries maternal overtones, although the usual translations are insensitive to this (cf. Deut. 4.31; Isa. 49.13, 15).[5]

The results achieved by this method meet with a mixed reception from other scholars. Some reach similar conclusions and agree that it is right to emphasize God's 'maternal' love and to balance male metaphors for deity with female images.[6] Their work provides a useful corrective to the negative attitude which is reluctant even to consider the feminine theological imagery. Yet some serious criticisms are levelled against Trible's methodology. Not all literary critics would agree with her application of the term 'metaphor'. Not all theologians would agree with her interpretation of Genesis 1.27 as a metaphor of God as male and female.[7] The majority of both literary critics and theologians would object that it is semantically inadmissible to say that the description of God's compassion in terms associated with the word *reḥem* necessarily reveals a 'maternal' aspect of the deity.

Another approach to the Old Testament material, represented by the work of L. Swidler, involves making a catalogue of those biblical references to God which appear to have feminine, or both masculine and feminine, connotations. For example, Swidler sees God described as a seamstress (Gen. 3.21); a midwife (Ps. 22.9); a loving mother (Isa. 49.13–15; 66.13; Ps. 131.2); in birth pangs (Isa. 42.14); as both master and mistress (Ps. 123.2).[8] It is interesting to list some of the verses catalogued by writers like Swidler, but I would agree with those who believe that there is little illumination on the subject of sexuality in God to be gained from this approach. It simply illustrates the folly of trying to attribute femininity – or, indeed, masculinity – to Yahweh on the basis of the gender of words and imagery used in the Bible.

Equally unsatisfactory is the approach which concentrates upon word gender. Several writers have professed to find great significance in the Old Testament usage of feminine nouns to describe 'aspects' of deity. For example, the 'righteousness' of God appears in both masculine (*ṣedeḳ*) and feminine (*ṣ³dāḳāh*) forms. Again, the Hebrew term for the 'spirit', 'wind', 'breath' of God is feminine (*rûaḥ*). Swidler lists many references in which he thinks that the feminine Spirit of God is hypostatized, or personified (for example, Gen. 1.1–2; Num. 24.2; Ps. 51.11; Isa. 63.10; Ezek. 3.24).[9] Or again, the Hebrew word for God's 'law' or 'instruction' is the feminine (*tôrāh*) – 'torah'. Particular attention is devoted to the 'wisdom' of God (Hebrew, *ḥokmāh*; Greek, *sophia*), which appears as feminine not only in the grammatical sense but also in the way that it is depicted as a woman (for example, Ecclus. 15.2; Prov. 7.4; Wisd. 8.2). Yet it is highly doubtful that feminine Wisdom, Torah, Spirit, Righteousness, or any other 'feminine figure', actually tell us anything about sexuality in God. The status of these forms in relation to God is so unclear that it is not legitimate to use them as information about divine sexuality.[10]

It would seem, then, that no coherent answers to our questions about sexuality in God may be gained from this sort of approach to the Old Testament material. It is true that the methods referred to above do demonstrate the inaccuracy of the assumption that the Hebrew Scriptures *never* theologize with feminine words. Furthermore, it is inconsistent to imply that the choice of masculine gender words is significant while the choice of the feminine is not. The fact that there are more masculine than feminine nouns in Hebrew theological vocabulary and that masculine pronouns are used of God is less likely to be due to a desire to attribute masculinity to God than to the patriarchal nature of Hebrew society, wherein the masculine could be used generically to include the feminine but the feminine did not stand inclusively for both genders.

Whilst it is difficult – if not impossible – to determine the significance of the choice of gender, it is clear that gender does not always correspond to sex. Moreover, as Tavard demonstrates convincingly, it is very doubtul whether language is an ideology and that 'sexist' language in particular is the ideology of male power.[11] All that may be said is that the Old Testament usage indicates that masculine terminology alone is insufficient for theological discourse. Even a complement of masculine and feminine vocabulary is stretched beyond its limits in the attempt to depict God's infinite Being and ineffable love.

Masculine Imagery

We come now to examine the argument which deduces from the theological vocabulary of the Old Testament that God is male. The central scriptural image taken up by those who insist upon the maleness of God and the concomitant maleness of his priests is that of the Fatherhood of God. It is assumed that the intention of biblical writers when calling God 'Father' was to emphasize his masculinity. Radical feminists like Goldenberg have reacted to this assumption by demanding that the image of Yahweh be overthrown because of its 'very basic quality of maleness'.[12]

I am convinced that all this reveals a total misunderstanding of Old Testament teaching about sexuality in God. Such a line of reasoning involves a serious misconception of the nature and function of biblical imagery. It has distorted many people's apprehension of divine reality, and it deserves to be abandoned.

Mascall's treatment of the scriptural imagery relevant to the subject of sexuality in God highlights the nature of the problem. While endorsing, with A. Farrer, the very special authority of the biblical images, he admits that human terms must be predicated of God analogically. 'Thus the application of masculine terms to God does not imply that he has male sex organs or indeed any physical organs at all.' Yet Mascall goes on to present an ultimatum: either we must reject the biblical revelation altogether or we must acknowledge, with him, that 'the notion of maleness is appropriate to God in a way that the notion of femaleness is not'.[13] Is this really a choice that a correct reading of the Old Testament asks us to make? Or has Mascall tended to rely upon pseudo-linguistic evidence which renders his argument untenable?

I agree with theologians like Mascall that biblical symbols and names for God may not be rashly dismissed. For instance, I have no intention of encouraging the rejection of the traditional address of God as 'heavenly Father'. Symbolism, however, is of little value unless we discern that it requires correct interpretation. The sign of a red circle transected by a thick white line, positioned at a road junction, means nothing unless the observer has some knowledge of the Highway Code. In similar fashion, biblical imagery must be understood in accordance with the guidelines of an accepted hermeneutical principle. The reader who simply jumps from page to page, taking one verse 'literally' and another 'metaphorically' according to whim, will not learn very much about the God of the Bible. This is no trivial matter of semantic hair-splitting, but a problem that is at the root of many of the theological controversies of the Christian era, since at its centre stands the vexed question of the interpretation of Scripture. It is not surprising, therefore, that it has great bearing upon the issue of the use and abuse of Scripture by those on both sides of the debate about women's ordination.

In order to ascertain whether or not Old Testament teaching about the Fatherhood of God was intended to emphasize divine maleness, it is necessary to return to the text and to try to see why the Hebrews referred to God as 'father'. How frequently, of whom, and in what sense, is God designated as 'father' in the Old Testament? Many people, their thinking conditioned by the regularity with which the title is used in the New Testament, are surprised to find how rarely the term is used of Yahweh in the Hebrew Scriptures. The king is sometimes referred to as a son of God (2 Sam. 7.14; Ps. 2.7, 89.26f); but most commentators agree that this is more likely to be a formula used to denote adoption rather than physical begetting.[14] In Old Testament times it is only collectively, as a nation, that Israelites may regard themselves as God's family; the individual Israelite (apart from the actual or messianic King) did not call himself God's son, although in post-canonical Jewish literature there are isolated examples of the use of 'Father' as a way of addressing God.[15] The notions of father and creator are, uncharacteristically, brought together in Deuteronomy 32.6 (cf. Exod. 4.22), but the thought is of God's freedom and authority as the Creator who claims his people's obedience rather than of any similarity to pagan notions of divine paternity.[16] Again, when, in Isaiah 63.16, the reserve is broken and Yahweh is confidently acclaimed as 'our Father', the context is not one of procreation and birth but of eschatological salvation and redemption.

The compassion of God is sometimes likened to that of a human father (for example, Ps. 103.13; Prov. 3.12). This is far from suggesting that Yahweh is the divine begetter of human children. Rather, the meaning is that God's compassion far surpasses, both in quality and quantity, that of an earthly father. The strongest expression of this comfort motif is, perhaps, to be found in Psalm 27.10: 'For my father and my mother have forsaken me, but the Lord will take me up.' The fact that Yahweh is accorded the ancient title 'father of the fatherless/orphans' (Ps. 68.6, Heb.; v.5, ET), also reveals the awareness that when God is called 'father' this means far more than the analogy of human experience can of itself suggest.

Old Testament references to the 'fatherly' love and care of Yahweh do not imply that God is a sentimental, over-indulgent figure. In ancient Israel, the father had authoritative and absolute rights to the obedience of his children, whatever their age; hopefully, he was wise and kind, but his power to discipline and direct his family was, in any case, unquestionable.[17] Thus, the reminder of the filial relation of Israel to God in Deuteronomy 14.1 introduces legal regulations which must be observed by those who regarded Yahweh as their 'father'. Later Judaism developed the synthesis between 'father' and 'lord (king)' prefigured in, for example, Malachi 1.6.[18] When Old Testament writers used the metaphor of fatherhood to expound aspects of God's relationship with his people, they were illustrating that God is One who must be honoured and respected to an eminent degree (cf. Exod. 20.12; Isa. 64.8). As de Boer puts it, '"Our Father" as title of God is no term of the nursery.'[19]

The designation of the deity as 'father' was 'current to the point of being commonplace in the ancient East', among 'both primitive and culturally elevated peoples'.[20] In pagan mythology those deities designated 'father' were regarded as 'begetters' – sometimes of other Gods, sometimes of human beings. It was probably the connotation surrounding the concept in other religions that made the Hebrews reticent about calling Yahweh 'Father'. The consensus of scholarly opinion stresses that the Old Testament 'wants to distance itself as far as possible from the pagan notion of the god as generative source who has a natural relationship with his people'. The Old Testament 'is at its most austere in speaking of God's fatherhood and almost never does so without careful qualification'.[21]

The Old Testament writers' sense of Yahweh's transcendence and of the distance between Creator and creature, between holy God and sinful man, made them hesitate to employ any concept that could be taken to imply a universal and natural relationship between divinity and humanity generally, or even between Yahweh and Israel specifically. This is evidenced, for example, by the fact that Creation, according to the Hebrew Scriptures, occurs by mere verbal command and not by sexual act (Gen. 1–2; cf. Ps. 148.5; 33.6). Man is created in the image of God, not begotten. It is also evidenced by the way in which prophets like Hosea remove from their usual setting fertility-cult motifs such as the marriage of the deity (Hos. 2.16f; cf. Jer. 2.2; Ezek. 16.8f; Isa. 54.5; Mal. 2.14), the offspring of the deity (Hos. 11.1ff; cf. Isa. 1.2f; Jer. 31.9) and the fecundation of earth from heaven (Isa. 45.8), and completely reshape the metaphor.[22] By illustrating Yahweh's relationship with his people in terms of the marital and parental bonds, the prophets, as adept apologists, refurbished familiar thought-forms and adapted them for the service of their own distinctive message.

When the term 'father' occurs in the Old Testament it is fundamentally applied to God only in a metaphorical sense, and if we are to understand it everything depends on finding the right point of comparison. I have argued that when Yahweh is likened to a father the point of comparison is not a sexual one; the intention was not to attribute male sexuality to God. Rather, scriptural imagery was quite naturally based upon the patriarchal realities of existing society and, furthermore, the limitations of the comparison are implicit in the symbolism. Like the paterfamilias, but far more so, God is to be revered and obeyed; like a father, but better than any human parent, God constantly protects and supports his children: the inadequacy of the comparison between God and the human model is part of the message of the image itself.

Hosea 11.1–11 is often heralded as one of the key pointers to the Old Testament belief in God's masculinity, with the poignant picture it presents of a father who aids, cherishes and heals his child. Yet the temptation to overwork the metaphor by saying that it teaches 'the maleness of the deity' is obviated for those who pay heed to the words in verse 9: 'I am God and not man, the Holy One in your midst.' Mays's comment is worth quoting at length:

> The salvation-history was portrayed by the most intimate and tender of human relationships (vv. 1, 3f) . . . But now the resolution of Yahweh is grounded on his utter difference from

man. The apparent inconsistency is a warning that Hosea's many anthropomorphisms are meant as interpretative analogies, not as essential definitions ... In the dramatic metaphor the personal reality of Yahweh's incursion into human life and history is present and comprehensible. But he transcends the metaphor, is different from that to which he is compared, and free of all its limitations.[23]

Certain scholars declare that, since the God of the Old Testament is a Creator-God, having life in himself, the only suitable term for him is 'father', never 'mother'. L. Bouyer asserts that 'from all eternity, in his inmost being, God is Father. That is to say, he is love, love that not only creates but is given, indeed that gives itself, and this self-giving is his life.'[24] Statements of this kind arise partly from the belief that a mother merely protects and hands on received life; among humankind, only the male reflects the God-like quality of handing on non-received life. This, it is said, is one of the reasons for the all-male priesthood of Yahwism and of Christianity. Quite apart from its poor psychology, this argument is, of course, biologically unsound; for both male and female are involved in the conception of new life.

Furthermore, Bouyer's use of the terms 'fatherhood', 'motherhood' and 'sexuality' seems very confused. He affirms that 'Scripture makes it absolutely clear that, in God, there is nothing that corresponds to sexuality. His transcendence rules out the dependence of one being on another that sexuality necessarily implies.' Yet, in his rationale, sexuality appears to be synonymous with femininity while the 'masculine' and the 'fatherly' are above creaturely sexuality. 'As Fatherhood belongs, properly, to God, so does Motherhood to the creature.' A close analysis of Bouyer's writing indicates that his usage of the terms 'fatherly' and 'motherly' does not follow after the manner of Old Testament imagery. Unlike Scripture, Bouyer tries to eradicate not so much sexuality as femininity from God's nature. While Trito-Isaiah boldly likens Yahweh's comfort of the people to a mother's comfort of her child (Isa. 66.13), Bouyer declares that motherhood 'can find no place, in however noble a form, in God'.[25] He utters such proclamations because he envisages motherhood only in a physically sexual sense, although he manages to divorce this aspect from fatherhood, describing God's fatherhood as 'virgi-

nal'. In the Old Testament, however, neither the fatherhood nor
the motherhood of God are associated in any way with physical
sexuality.

Again, the concept of God as Creator is inadequately expressed
by Bouyer. This becomes clear when his over-emphasis upon the
externality of God's creative acts is counterbalanced by the
insights of A. R. Peacocke. Bouyer seems to regard God's creati-
vity in terms of the male fertilizing the womb from outside,
creating something external to himself. By contrast, Peacocke
reminds us that:

> Mammalian females, at least, create within themselves and the
> growing embryo resides within the female body and this is a
> proper corrective to the masculine picture – it is an analogy of
> God creating the world within herself, we would have to say . . .
> God creates a world that is, in principle and in origin, other
> than him/herself but creates it, the world, within him/herself.[26]

This model embraces the poles of transcendence and immanence
essential to a balanced doctrine of God. Unlike Bouyer, Peacocke
discerns that 'feminine' images of God as Creator are necessary as
a corrective to purely 'masculine' images 'with their stress on
God as creating "externally" to himself a world from which he
might then be too readily deemed to be absent (the tendency of
deism)'.[27] Bouyer's writing does not aid understanding of theological vocabulary relevant to the subject of divine sexuality. On
the contrary, when he writes that 'there is no place for motherhood in God . . . maternity has its true place on the level of the
creature',[28] he betrays an unscriptural understanding of the
metaphors of fatherhood and motherhood, of the concept of God
as Creator, indeed of God's very nature.

It must be noted at this point that paternal imagery is not the
only Old Testament divine symbolism used by certain theologians to support their notion of the masculinity of God; *conjugal
imagery* – the Yahweh-bridegroom, Israel-bride symbolism – is
also said to establish the maleness of the deity. According to V.
Eller, for instance, God is masculine and the reason why Israel is
forbidden to venerate a Goddess alongside Yahweh is that
humanity, 'feminine' in relation to the 'masculinity' of God, is
Yahweh's consort. 'In Yahwism, the human race plays the role
that goddesses play in the religion of dual-gendered deity.' Eller

believes that 'God equals "masculinity" plus *"deity"'*. As masculine, he is *'Wooer-Husband* (to us as *beloved-bride)'.*[29]

The biblical principle, however, is that God stands quite
outside human sexual differentiation as masculine or feminine.
Statements which reduce God to a finite, relative category like
sexuality, including Eller's proposition that 'God equals "masculinity" plus *"deity"'*, are inconsistent with the infinite, absolute,
transcendent nature of God. Such statements reverse the Old
Testament teaching, 'I am God and not man' (Hos. 11.9). They
undermine God's transcendence by categorizing him as 'masculine', whereas 'the God of Israel is the reality that both links and
transcends the masculine and the feminine'.[30]

Biblical symbols modulate with amazing versatility, and we
abuse them if we try to insist that the grammatical gender of the
image is indicative of the essential maleness or femaleness of the
referent. The unsoundness of such an approach is soon exposed
when, for instance, it is noted that, in Jeremiah 2.23–4, the male
rulers of the nation (cf. 2.4, 5) are likened to a restive she-camel
and to a frenzied wild ass on heat. Similarly, although in Jeremiah
31.1–5 there is rejoicing over the marriage of the virgin Israel, the
movement of gender ensures that the passage may not be taken to
mean that God is masculine and Israel feminine: the nation is
spoken of first in the masculine gender, then in the feminine, then
in the masculine again. Not sexual differentiation but the joy of
faithful union, not maleness and femaleness but the intimacy of
God's relationship with Zion – this is the message of the prophecy.

Commenting directly upon the way in which this biblical
symbol has been used in the argument against women's ordination, Stuhlmueller concludes that the image of the divine Bridegroom does not dictate that priests in the Christian dispensation
must be of the male sex. The image is far too involved for such a
single-line application. Stuhlmueller believes that a priesthood of
men and women, celibate and married, would much more ade-
quately represent 'the rich biblical nuances of virginity and
marital union, simultaneously overlapping in the symbol of God
and Jesus as spouse'.[31]

Mascall and others often seem to be unwilling to concede that
biblical divine imagery is, in fact, imagery. This would appear to
be the reason for their proneness to deduce a dogma of God's

'maleness' from the Old Testament. Here may be detected the influence of the widespread fear that if something is labelled 'a metaphor', then aspersions are cast upon its truth-value: a metaphor is regarded as merely a piece of optional embroidery. It is not only with regard to the subject of sexuality in God that Mascall wants to take literally what most biblical scholars would define as metaphorical. We may compare, for example, a state-ment he makes about the Pauline doctrine of the Body of Christ: 'While it contains of course a certain element of metaphor, the description of the Church as the Body of Christ is to be taken ontologically and realistically . . . It is not a mere metaphor, but the literal truth, that the Church is the Body of Christ.'[32] Most grammarians agree, however, that words are used 'literally' when they are meant to be understood in their primary, matter-of-fact sense. This could hardly be said of the phrases 'the Church is the Body of Christ' or 'God is the father of his people'.

Caird's study of *The Language and Imagery of the Bible* furnishes a useful platform for a critique of Mascall's view. Although Caird rarely comments directly on biblical imagery relevant to the subject of sexuality in God, his insights may be extended to this issue. Caird shows that 'all, or almost all, of the language used by the Bible to refer to God is metaphor (the one possible exception is the word "holy")'.[33] This principle must, surely, form the basis of a healthy approach to religious language. It is essential not to confuse the 'real' with the 'literal'; any statement, literal or metaphorical, may be true or false, and its referent may be real or unreal. To say, therefore, that 'father-hood' is a symbol or metaphor of God's relationship with his people is in no way to undermine the truth-value of biblical teaching about God the Father. On the contrary, when the metaphor is correctly understood, it facilitates recognition of the truth that God transcends sexuality. As Lampe puts it, ' "Father" is an analogy which illuminates basic aspects of God's dealings with us; but it does not mean that God is literally a father, a masculine person.'[34]

Correct understanding of a metaphor depends upon the 'ability to detect and concentrate on the point or points of comparison, to the exclusion of all else'. When the psalmist pictures the sun coming out like a bridegroom from his wedding canopy (Ps. 19.5), we are not expected to enquire after the bride. When two things are compared, they are not to be considered alike in all respects; if we concentrate on irrelevant factors or wrongly identify the intended point of comparison, then 'communication breaks down, with ludicrous and even disastrous effect'.[35] In the useful classification of Ogden and Richards, the two constituent elements of a metaphor are called the 'vehicle' and the 'tenor'.[36] The vehicle is the thing to which the word normally applies; the tenor is that to which it is transferred. There are varying degrees of correspondence between vehicle and tenor; but even where there is a high degree of correspondence, it must still be recognized that the image *is* an image; it does not denote complete harmony between vehicle and tenor.

According to Lampe, the argument against women's ordination which draws upon scriptural language about God as 'father' involves 'a misuse of analogy which leads straight to the crudest anthropomorphic heresy'.[37] Old Testament writers did not take their anthropomorphisms literally, and neither should we.[38] God is not made in 'the likeness of male or female' in the Old Testament (cf. Deut. 4.16), either physically or on the level of intrinsic masculinity. Creative minds of prophets and Hebrew theologians who formed the metaphors of father and bridegroom were well aware of this. But many people seem to forget that vividness of expression is not the same as literality; they cease to discern the dual reference to vehicle and tenor, perhaps because they have grown over-familiar with the metaphor. When Mascall declares that 'the application of male predicates to God is neither arbitrary nor accidental but . . . its authentication by Scripture and tradition rests upon a real character of Godhead itself',[39] he is not only misrepresenting the biblical writers' motive for using masculine imagery, he is also confusing vehicle and tenor. Such an imbroglio is dangerous and contains the seeds of idolatry, for, as R. R. Marrett shows, 'even words are in some sense idols, and any use of symbols implies a possible misuse through the confusion of the spirit with the letter – of a meaning with its casual vehicle.'[40]

There is in Scripture, then, no attempt, corresponding to that in much pagan mythology, to assert masculinity at the expense of femininity. When the biblical images of God as father, bridegroom and other 'masculine' metaphors are rightly interpreted, it is clear that there is nothing 'sexist' about them. Just as the

Kingdom of God does not look like a mustard seed nor taste like yeast but acts like both, so the metaphor of God's Fatherhood does not teach a 'natural' relationship between a divine male progenitor and his offspring. When Israel is called God's son or his unfaithful wife, these parables do not imply that the character of God is predominantly masculine (and not feminine), paternal (not maternal). 'They are expressions of Yahweh's infinite love for his chosen people, expressed in terms of a patriarchal society.'[41]

It is true, of course, that for Christian theology, *God's Father-hood* must ultimately be defined *from a New Testament perspective*. Whilst my concern here is primarily with the Old Testament, it is important to ask at this point whether the New Testament assumes that because God is known to us as 'Father' he must be 'male'. Some people claim that the apparent maleness of God in the Old Testament would not necessarily render belief in the masculinity of God an essential constituent of Christian doctrine, were it not for the fact that Jesus himself and the New Testament writers after him also make this point. The 245 instances in which God is called 'Father' in the New Testament (compared with the meagre fifteen occurrences in the Old Testament) emphasize, it is said, the 'maleness' of the Judaeo-Christian deity.

I agree with those theologians who assert that, since Jesus addressed God as 'Abba Father' and gave his disciples the privilege of following this example through the empowering of the Holy Spirit (Mark 14.36; cf. Matt. 6.9f; Luke 11.2f; Rom. 8.15; Gal. 4.6) the Christian appellation of God as 'Father' is not a 'mere analogy' in principle replaceable by others.[42] But it is crucial to understand that the designation 'Father' in its biblical and theological contexts is not a univocal description implying that God was sexually responsible for our existence or, indeed, for Christ's existence. The Old Testament concept – which radically and deliberately dissociated divine fatherhood from the aspect of human paternity which is linked with male sexuality – provides a basic interpretative principle for New Testament teaching about God the Father.

This becomes clear, first, with regard to Jesus' own sonship. Christian theology, grounding itself in the New Testament, has always spoken of the relation between the first and second

Persons of the Trinity in terms of Fatherhood and Sonship; but the supposition that God the Father shares the biological characteristics of human males who procreate sons is a travesty of the doctrine. Jesus' characteristic designation of God as 'Abba Father' (Mark 14.36) takes on to a new and intimate level the double emphasis in the Old Testament concept of divine Fatherhood – namely, the trustworthiness and the authority of the deity – but this is in no way based upon a supposed masculinity of God.

The problem of word gender recurs here. Mascall claims that it is not a matter of chance that 'both the Father and the Son are denoted, both in Scripture and in Christian theology, by words of the masculine gender and never of the feminine'.[43] We have already seen the inaccuracy of the assumption that Scripture *never* theologizes with feminine words. But an even more serious flaw impairs Mascall's reasoning. One wonders why he does not heed his own remarks on the irrelevance of arguments based on the grammatical gender of words in various languages: 'The most traditional theologians, writing in a Romance language, will use, without any suggestion of femaleness, feminine nouns and pronouns for example "person" or "Trinity".' (*'La personne de Jésus-Christ . . . elle'*, *'la sainte Trinité . . . elle'*, etc.)[44]

It would seem that there is considerable inconsistency between the criterion which Mascall uses when assessing the significance of theological words of the masculine gender and that which he adopts to judge feminine theological vocabulary.

It is as false to assert that reference to God as the father of Jesus Christ implies maleness as it is to claim that feminine theological imagery predicates the femaleness of the Godhead (cf. Matt. 23.37; Luke 13.34; 15.8ff). The Council of Toledo (675 AD), for example, was not concerned with the gynaecology of God when stating that: *'Nec enim de nihilo, neque de aliqua alia substantia, sed de Patris utero, id est, de substantia eius idem Filius genitus vel natus esse credendus est.'*[45]

Again, Moltmann's comment that a father who 'begets' and 'gives birth' to his son is no mere male father, 'He is a motherly father', is helpful as a corrective to narrow ideas about God's 'masculinity'.[46] Yet it is wise to beware of the implication that God is bisexual and resembles an individual who possesses the biological characteristics of both sexes. Such a monstrous notion is alien to Christian belief in God as the 'Father' of Jesus Christ, which is based upon and is fully consistent with the Old Testament principle that the Deity transcends sexuality.

Secondly, an examination of some key points of New Testament teaching about God's Fatherhood shows that it is based, not upon notions of divine sexual reproduction nor of God as an abstract cosmic principle, but upon the Old Testament concept of a divine Fatherhood which is 'personal' but which transcends human sexuality. The message of Jesus and of the New Testament writers is distorted if it is said to ascribe masculinity to God.

In the Synoptic Gospels, God's Fatherhood is removed from the realm of earthly, physical paternity. For Matthew, the phrase 'your heavenly Father' is particularly significant (for example, 5.16, 45, 48; 6.32; cf. 6.9; 7.21; 12.50; 18.10, 14). It rules out confusion with the earthly father and describes the divine Father as exalted and as standing above all earthly fatherhood. God's Fatherhood is not to be defined by the projection of earthly originals on to the screen of the heavens and given infinite dimensions; rather it is unique and unparalleled on earth (Matt. 23.9).[47] Mark also records Jesus' employment of the expression 'your Father in heaven' (11.25). Again, Luke's concept of divine Fatherhood is dissociated from sexuality and focused upon God's 'Otherness', transcendence and kingly majesty (10.21; 11.13; 12.32; 22.29), alongside the emphasis on the mercy and compassion of the Father (15.11–32).

In John's Gospel, it is stressed that the Fatherhood of which Jesus speaks cannot be defined in terms of any human concept of fatherhood; rather, God's Fatherhood must be christologically defined (for example, John 1.18; 5.20; 6.46; cf. Matt. 11.25–7; Luke 10.21–2; cf. also Rom. 1.7; 2 Cor. 1.3). John is constantly concerned that God's Fatherhood and its implications for his people should be rightly understood (cf. John 2.16; 5.18f; 8.19f). Only the Son, who alone has seen the Father in heaven (1.18; 3.13), can make known the meaning of this Fatherhood. Through Christ, then, the caricatures which portray God either as a despotic, or a sentimental, progenitor are corrected.

Thus, the New Testament concept of the Fatherhood of God derives from and further develops the Old Testament concept, in that it precludes the belief that God is a father in the physical sexual sense in which a male human being is a father. In the New

Testament, as in the Old, God's Fatherhood has the twin connotations of protecting love and authority. 'Abba Father' designates the Father who cares – indeed, the Father who, through Christ, is shown to come even closer to his people in love and compassion than most Old Testament writers dared to think possible. It also designates the Father who has absolute authority and requires absolute obedience – indeed, the new intimacy of the *Abba* relationship, far from weakening God's transcendence, 'positively deepens the sense of awe' (cf. 1 Pet. 1.17).[48] The God with whom Jesus lives in closest communion is at the same time the Lord of heaven and earth (Luke 10.21f); there is no foundation for Marcionite separation of the Father-God of Jesus and the Creator-God of the Old Testament.[49]

It must be concluded, then, that in neither the Old nor the New Testament is the concept of divine fatherhood 'sexual' or 'sexist'. To use New Testament references to the Fatherhood of God in the attempt to 'prove' God's maleness is to wrench the New Testament material from its grounding in the Old Testament principle of God's sexual transcendence and to graft it on to pagan notions about the sexuality of the deity. For Scripture, the question of God's sexual differentiation can have no relevance whatsoever. As Hodgson puts it: 'When we are thinking of God in Himself, whether the unipersonal God of the Old Testament or the triune God of the Christian revelation, it is a theological mistake to think of Him as either male or female.'[50]

Mother–Father God?

At the beginning of this chapter, reference was made to feminist veneration of the God/ess – a deity who combines in a single being the characteristics of maleness and femaleness. This concept must now be viewed in the light of the foregoing discussions about feminine and masculine theological vocabulary. We can then draw some conclusions as to whether or not those feminists who claim to find the idea of a mother–father God in the Old Testament are justified in their argument.[51]

In one sense, the Old Testament outlook does seem to have something in common with modern feminist, and with ancient, notions of divine androgyny. Like these, the Old Testament seeks to express the truth that the Deity is not limited by a single set of

attributes, either male or female. Ancient religions often tried to
express this by envisaging the Deity as both mother and father.
P. A. H. de Boer is among those who believe that Yahweh, too,
was regarded as both mother and father to his people.[52]

Yet there is considerable ambiguity here. The passages that de
Boer cites as examples of Yahweh being 'mother and father' are
those that theologians like Swidler and Trible treat as feminine
divine imagery (for example, Isa. 46.3f; 63.9; Exod. 19.4; Deut.
32.18). In view of the difficulty of deciding whether certain of
Yahweh's activities are maternal, paternal or both, it seems
unwise to insist strongly upon the correctness of any one interpretation.

All we can say without misrepresenting the Old Testament is
that it would appear that certain 'motherly prerogatives' in
ancient Hebrew society – such as carrying and comforting small
children – became metaphors for Yahweh's activity *vis-à-vis* his
children Israel. Likewise, various 'fatherly prerogatives' – like
disciplining a son – became vehicles for divine imagery. Different
cultures and ages have different ideas about which roles are
proper to the mother and which to the father. The only paternal
and maternal functions that are never interchangeable are those
pertaining to the sexual reproductive process. But when motherly
and/or fatherly activities are predicated of Yahweh, the specifically sexual qualification is absent. In the world in which Israel
was set, the sexual activity of the deity was a basic feature of
religious thought. The Old Testament will have none of this; it
severs the Person of God from the web of myths and rites which
worshipped sexuality.

In the feminist notion of a mother–father God, as in its
antecedents in ancient religion, maleness and femaleness are
incorporated in the deity but are not transcended. The emphasis
remains upon sexuality. In the Old Testament, however, Yahweh
is supra-sexual. The key phrase in understanding the Hebrew
concept of sexuality in God is 'the transcending of all sexuality'.
According to the Old Testament, God transcends male–female
distinctions. Sexuality is part of God's creation; therefore it is
intrinsically good. Nevertheless, it remains part of the creation
and is not to be confused with the Creator, who far surpasses the
creaturely.

It is true that even after the Hebrews had perceived God to be transcendent, beyond such limitations as those of sexuality, Old Testament writers persisted in referring to Yahweh in terminology and imagery that included connotations of sexuality. This was unavoidable, however, because personhood on the human level involves sexuality. If God is not to be depersonalized, then terms which are characteristically applied to male or female persons must also be applied to 'him'. These terms, which carry inevitable undertones of sexuality, provide the only vocabulary with which to speak of the supremely personal yet sexually transcendent deity. But it must be recognized that it is the 'Personhood', not the 'sexuality', of God which is the central point of the figure.

Some people continue to draw attention to the abundance of masculine divine imagery in the Hebrew Scriptures, compared with the meagre feminine symbolism – none of which amounts to a direct address of God as 'Mother'. However, this has no significance as an insight into the subject of sexuality in God. The predominance of masculine over feminine imagery is a reflection of the thought-forms of a male-oriented society and not of a male God. If God appears more often in masculine guise than in feminine, this simply has to do with the conditioning of the verbal level of language by historical context. The God of Israel is more than any sexual appellation or images that may be used.

It was unavoidable that Old Testament writers should use more masculine than feminine symbolism and, particularly, that they should employ the image of fatherhood more frequently than that of motherhood, because 'in the whole pattern of Hebrew society the father was the central figure.'[53] A comparison is designed to illuminate the unknown or lesser-known by the known or better-known. If, therefore, an Old Testament writer wished to illustrate, for example, God's power and authority, it was inevitable that he should focus upon masculine imagery, for, whereas to the Israelite the name of father always spells authority, the same was not true of the name of mother. And since the aim of Old Testament divine imagery was not to teach about sexuality in God, it would not have entered the Hebrew mind that it might be necessary to 'redress the balance' by using an equal amount of feminine imagery when illustrating some other aspect of God's nature.

In my view, then, those people who wish to address God with a

combination of the two nouns 'Mother–Father' are following an
unwise course of action which may not be legitimated by an
appeal to Old Testament practice. The so-called inclusive term
'Mother–Father God', as an unqualified address, actually
encourages the misguided attribution of sexuality to God rather
than abolishing it. To add the term 'Mother' to the traditional
address of God as 'Father' implies that divine maleness must be
supplemented by divine femaleness or replaced by divine androgyny.

There is a distinction here, perceived by several theologians,
between the use of a blend of feminine and masculine theological
vocabulary in discourse *about* God on the one hand and on the
other hand the use of the name 'Mother–Father God' as a *mode of
address*, a direct appellation. Scripture, while employing both
feminine and masculine theological vocabulary, offers no precedent for addressing God as 'Mother–Father'. It seems preferable
for us, therefore, to use the term 'Father' in its scriptural, non-
sexist sense.

Divine Sexual Transcendence

In conclusion I would emphasize that the foregoing analyses of
theological vocabulary endorse the objection that when Scripture
is used to provide 'evidence' of God's masculinity, serious
misreading of texts is involved. Most theologians in theory admit
no sexual distinction, no physical sexuality, in the Godhead. 'Yet
they have hardly been consistent in applying this truth. While
they have assumed that God is not female, it has been less clear to
them that he is not male either.'[54] Moreover, as Caird explains: 'It
is precisely when theologians have claimed biblical authority for
their own beliefs and practices that they have been peculiarly
exposed to the universal temptation ... of jumping to the
conclusion that the biblical writer is referring to what they would
be referring to were they speaking the words themselves.'[55]

If such misuse of Scripture is to be avoided then the symbolic
nature of God-talk must be discerned. It must be acknowledged
that in both masculine and feminine imagery used of God the
sexual qualification does not enter the picture. When Yahweh
was called the bridegroom of his people, this was not to 'sexua-
lize' but to 'personalize' the image of God. And when due weight

has been given to the significance of the revelation of God as Father, it is erroneous to deduce from it the 'maleness' of God. Theology employs symbolic and anthropomorphic language to speak about God, and many of the features of these anthropomorphisms are mere accommodations to human speech. Maleness is one of the features of human fatherhood which cannot be attributed to God. To ignore this is to interpret the biblical imagery in a way that is inconsistent with the intention of the Hebrew writers.

Today a growing number of feminists teach that the God/ess combines male and female characteristics. They, like those who assume that God is exclusively male, should remember that *any* attribution of sexuality to God is a reversion to paganism. Many people harbour illusory views about the importance of recovering and appreciating feminine theological vocabulary in the Old Testament. Not only is the methodology adopted for such a task often semantically confusing and exegetically unsound, but most approaches to feminine imagery exaggerate the significance of their subject-matter.

Ultimately, whether theological vocabulary is masculine or feminine is of little consequence. The masculine terminology does not denote a male deity; the feminine terminology does not denote a female deity; nor does the mixture of masculine and feminine terminology denote an androgynous God/ess. Rather, the indications are that the God of the Bible uniquely incorporates and transcends all sexuality. As Sapp puts it: 'The distinction between the sexes is a creation by God since there is no such distinction on the divine level; the polarity of the sexes belongs to the created order and not to God.'[56]

Neither male nor female sexuality can be ascribed to Yahweh, for the limitations which characterize mankind do not affect the sovereign transcendence of God (cf. Isa. 40.25).

NOTES

1. cf. ed, A. E. Lewis, *The Motherhood of God* (Edinburgh 1984), p. 11.
2. I. T. Ramsey, *Religious Language* (London 1957), p. 91.
3. For example, I will waste no space in analysis of Patai's highly conjectural writing about the metamorphosis of the feminine divine element in Judaism, *The Hebrew Goddess* (New York 1967).

4. Trible, *God and the Rhetoric of Sexuality* (Philadelphia 1978), p. 8.

5. ibid., esp. pp. 22; 33ff; 69.

6. cf., for example, L. Swidler, *Biblical Affirmations of Woman* (Philadelphia 1979), especially p. 31; S. Terrien, 'Toward a Biblical Theology of Womanhood', *Male and Female*, ed. R. T. Barnhouse and U. T. Holmes (New York 1976), p. 21.

7. See below, Ch. 5.

8. Swidler, op. cit., especially pp. 30ff.

9. ibid., p. 50; cf. J. Otwell, *And Sarah Laughed* (Philadelphia 1977), p. 185.

10. On Wisdom, see especially Otwell, op. cit., p. 191; G. B. Caird, *The Language and Imagery of the Bible* (London 1980), p. 137.

11. G. H. Tavard, 'Sexist Language in Theology?', *TS*, 36 (1975), pp. 700–24.

12. Goldenberg, *Changing of the Gods*, p. 8.

13. Mascall, *Whatever Happened to the Human Mind?* (London 1980), pp. 144, 149; cf. A. Farrer, *The Glass of Vision* (London 1948).

14. cf. A. Weiser, *The Psalms* (London 1962), p. 113. On theophoric names, like Abi'jah (2 Chron. 13.20), which combine elements of 'father' and 'Yahweh' in Hebrew – possibly reflecting the idea of divine ancestry of a tribe – see, for example, H. Ringgren, *"ābh"*, *TDOT*, I, p. 16.

15. cf. Ecclus. 23; 51.10. See G. Schrenk, *'patēr'*, *TDNT*, V, p. 978; J. Jeremias, *New Testament Theology*, I (London 1971), p. 63.

16. cf. G. Quell, *'patēr'*, *TDNT*, V, p. 972.

17. cf. Ringgren, op. cit., p. 8; R. de Vaux, *Ancient Israel*, 2 (London 1965), p. 20.

18. cf. the link between 'lord' and 'father' in Ecclus. 23.1, 4; 51.10; Tob. 13.4; Wisd. 11.10.

19. P. A. H. de Boer, *Fatherhood and Motherhood in Israelite and Judean Piety* (Leiden 1974), p. 25.

20. C. Geffré, '"Father" as the Proper Name of God', *Concilium* (March 1981), p. 44; for source references, see Schrenk, op. cit., pp. 951ff; Quell, op. cit., p. 966; J. Jeremias, *The Prayers of Jesus* (London 1967), pp. 12ff.

21. T. A. Smail, *The Forgotten Father* (London 1980), p. 34.

22. cf. S. H. Hooke, 'Myth and Ritual: Past and Present', *Myth, Ritual and Kingship* (Oxford 1958), p. 20.

23. J. L. Mays, *Hosea* (London 1969), p. 157. cf. Isa. 31.3; Ezek 28.2; Num. 23.19.

24. L. Bouyer, *Woman and Man With God* (London 1960), p. 100.

25. ibid., pp. 100f, 148.

26. A. R. Peacocke, *Creation and the World of Science* (Oxford 1979), p. 142.

27. ibid., p. 207.
28. Bouyer, op. cit., p. 147.
29. V. Eller, *The Language of Canaan and the Grammar of Feminism* (Grand Rapids 1982), pp. x, 37, 40, 44.
30. J. G. Williams, *Women Recounted* (Sheffield 1982), p. 131.
31. C. Stuhlmueller, 'Bridegroom: A Biblical Symbol of Union, not Separation', *Women Priests*, ed. L. and A. Swidler (New York 1977), p. 283.
32. Mascall, *Christ, the Christian, and the Church* (London 1946), pp. 112; 161.
33. G. B. Caird, *The Language and Imagery of the Bible* (London 1980), p. 18.
34. G. W. H. Lampe, 'Women and the Ministry of Priesthood', *Explorations in Theology*, 8 (London 1981), p. 97.
35. Caird, op. cit., pp. 17, 145.
36. C. K. Ogden and I. A. Richards, *The Meaning of Meaning* (London 1923).
37. Lampe, 'Church Tradition and the Ordination of Women', *Exp. T*, 76 (1965), pp. 124–5.
38. Some scholars seem to have assumed that anthropomorphic imagery was taken literally in primitive society; see for example, E. Bevan, *Symbolism and Belief* (London 1938), pp. 44f. Caird, op. cit., pp. 188f, shows this to be an inaccurate account of Hebrew linguistic development.
39. Mascall, *Whatever Happened?*, p. 152.
40. R. R. Marrett, *Sacraments of Simple Folk* (Oxford 1933), p. 121
41. A. Dumas, 'Biblical Anthropology and the Participation of Women in the Ministry of the Church', *Concerning the Ordination of Women*, WCC Symposium (Geneva 1964), p. 23.
42. cf. R. W. Jenson, *The Triune Identity* (Philadelphia 1982), p. 107; ed. A. E. Lewis, op. cit., pp. 8; 17; 28.
43. Mascall, 'Women and the Priesthood of the Church', *Why Not?*, p. 111.
44. *Whatever Happened?*, p. 170, n. I.
45. 'We must believe that the Son was not made out of nothing, nor out of some substance or other, but from the womb of the Father, that is that he was begotten or born from the Father's own being.' cf. H. Denzinger, *Enchiridion Symbolorum* (34th edition, A. Schönmetzer), (Herder 1967), para. 276.
46. J. Moltmann, 'The Motherly Father', *Concilium* (March 1981), p. 53.
47. cf. Smail, op. cit., p. 55. There is some debate about whether 'heavenly' was a Matthean addition to Jesus' simple use of 'Father'. Compare, for example, T. W. Manson, *The Sayings of Jesus* (Lon-

don 1949), p. 168, and Schrenk, op. cit., p. 979, with Jeremias, *Prayers*, pp. 15–16, 31f. I see no substantial reason for doubting that Jesus himself, sometimes at least, used the phrase 'heavenly Father'.

48. C. F. D. Moule, 'God, NT', *IDB*, E–J, p. 433.

49. cf. W. Manson, *The Gospel of Luke* (London 1930), p. 127.

50. L. Hodgson, 'Theological Objections to the Ordination of Women', *Exp. T*, 77 (1965–6), p. 211.

51. On the significance for feminists of Mary Baker Eddy's term 'Mother–Father God', see R. R. Ruether, *Sexism and God-Talk*, p. 69.

52. De Boer, op. cit., pp. 40–53.

53. D. R. Mace, *Hebrew Marriage* (London 1953), p. 65.

54. Jewett, *Man as Male and Female*, p. 165.

55. Caird, op. cit., p. 80.

56. Sapp, op. cit., p. 3.

3

Monotheism, Patriarchy and Priesthood

In the two foregoing chapters I have maintained that the God of the Bible disclosed himself to the Hebrews as One who transcends human sexual distinctions. But some scholars, both feminists and their opponents, question this on the grounds that, if it was indeed the case that the Hebrews came to regard Yahweh as a supra-sexual, this belief about sexuality in God would have affected the sexual characterization of Israelite priesthood.

Given the basic datum that 'there were no legitimate priestesses in Israel',[1] the reason for the exclusion of women from Israelite priesthood must be sought. If this reason is found to derive from the very nature of God himself – in other words, if it can be demonstrated that the scriptural God is a masculine deity who must be served by male priests – there are serious implications for our discussions about women's ministry. Those who assume a close identity between Israelite and Christian priesthood regard the exclusion of women from Old Testament priesthood as an insurmountable objection to women's ordination in the Church. Even on those who do not believe that Christianity has 'priests' in the Old Testament sense, the argument that a male God must be served by male ministers still exerts a powerful (often subliminal) influence.

If an irrevocable link between sexuality in God and the sexual character of the ministry can be established, we must heed the warnings of those who fear that universal acceptance of women as priests and bishops would turn Christianity into a different, unbiblical religion. Women who have already been ordained, and their supporters, must be shown the grievous error of their ways. If, on the other hand, it can be demonstrated that the absence of priestesses in Yahwism had nothing to do with sexuality in God and that, consequently, the presence of women in Christian ministry does not contravene the biblical understanding of sexuality in God, then this objection to women's ordination must be abandoned once and for all.

In this chapter, therefore, examination will be made of the

conviction that only a male ministry is consistent with the
masculinity of the God of the Bible. Reduced to basic terms, the
argument is that a monotheistic religion gives rise to a patriarchal
society with a male priesthood, with the corollary that the
existence of priestesses necessarily implies that the deity whom
they serve must be female, or a member of a pantheon of Gods
and Goddesses, and that the society to which they belong must be
anti-patriarchal, if not matriarchal. With particular reference to
the Old Testament material, I wish to posit the following
objections:

   i) that the argument assumes too clear-cut a relationship
      between 'monotheism' and 'patriarchalism', and between
      'polytheism', or Goddess worship, and priestesses and
      'matriarchalism';
  ii) that the argument betrays an unyahwistic (and unchristian)
      attack upon the 'feminine' and the 'female';
 iii) that the argument reveals a misconception of the nature of
      Israelite (and Christian) priesthood.

Socio-Religious Interrelation

Initially, the relation between 'monotheistic' religion and
'patriarchal' society, and between Goddess worship, or poly-
theism, and 'matriarchy', must be considered.[2] Several scholars –
starting from the tenet that there is a fundamental link between
sexuality in God and the nature of priesthood – believe that the
most important argument brought forward to explain the non-
appearance of priestesses in authentic Yahwism is that only
polytheistic religions, in which Goddesses as well as Gods are
venerated, have female ministrants.[3] Doctrinal theologians draw
upon the 'evidence' of archaeologists and anthropologists to
endorse their views. For example, Demant believes that 'in the
history of the faiths, the monotheistic religions have male priesthoods only'. He does not try to argue that religions with male
deities have male priesthoods while those with female deities have
female priesthoods. But he does say that the one definite verdict
that may be drawn from the vast complex of data is that 'none but
male priesthoods belong to the monotheisms, in which the
Godhead transcends the created order and, as their Lord, stands
behind nature and history and society, as well as acting in them'.[4]

I believe that all this assumes too clear-cut a relation between monotheism and patriarchalism, and between Goddess worship and matriarchalism. There is too much confusion about these relations for dogmatic statements to be based upon them.[5] It is unproven that all patriarchal societies adhere to male-monotheist religions. The inaccuracy of the corollary of the argument – namely, that Goddess-centred and/or polytheistic religions give rise to female or mixed priesthoods and societies in which women enjoy equal status with men – further undermines the tenability of the first part of the argument.

For example, J. B. Segal maintains that 'the participation of females, as goddesses and priestesses, in pagan ritual assured them an honourable status in the community'.[6] Such simplistic assertions about the 'honourable status' of women in 'unmonotheistic' society may be refuted with reference to the Code of Hammurabi. This provides insight into a polytheistic religion with no shortage of priestesses – it was a society in which fathers and husbands wielded authority over daughters and wives.[7]

An inaccurate understanding of this issue is also displayed in Goldenberg's notion that to replace masculine religious images with feminine images transforms religion and prevents it from endorsing patriarchalism and the oppression of women. As P. D. Hanson argues, the dominance of a female metaphor is no guarantee of sexual equality. He draws attention to ancient religions (for instance, in Babylonia and Canaan) in which Goddesses and women took prominence, and he points out that these cults remained part of the male-dominated social structure.[8] By contrast, Hebrew religion, with its preponderance of masculine religious imagery and its patriarchal orientation, was concerned to safeguard woman's (albeit limited) rights to a much greater extent than most Goddess-worshipping societies.[9]

Moreover, it is by no means clear that Scripture upholds 'patriarchy' as instituted by divine ordinance to be the inviolable structure for godly society for all time. As Vos comments, 'one may hardly say that the Old Testament teaches that the patriarchate is the divinely instituted structure of society. It seems to assume it, rather than institute it.'[10] Conversely, the fact that Israel was ordered on patriarchal lines may not be interpreted as proof that the Israelites intended their God to be sexually determined as male.[11]

I believe that the conviction that a male-monotheist religion gives rise to a patriarchal society with a male priesthood, with the correlative linking of Goddess worship, priestesses and matriarchalism, is based upon mythological ideas about sexual rivalry between God and Goddess and between man and woman. Feminists often argue – from the human to the divine – that male-monotheist religion with its male priesthood is a product of patriarchal society.[12] Anti-feminists often argue – from the divine to the human – that God reveals himself as male because masculinity is supreme; worship of the *Magna Mater*, orders of priestesses and matriarchalism are all wrong.[13]

It is not always recognized that both parties are, in fact, theologizing on the basis of ideas about a 'battle of the sexes'. Their whole argument is far from the demythologization of religion and the transcendentalization of Yahweh which became the vital emphasis of the Old Testament. The Old Testament writers did not trivialize their theology by making confused, unfounded or inaccurate statements about the relation between monotheism and patriarchy, or between Goddess-worship and matriarchy. They did not diminish the dignity of Yahweh by fantasizing about his sexual rivalries. Rather, the God of Israel is transcendent; neither male nor female, God is utterly other than Israel and humankind.[14] Those who maintain that there exists an irrevocable link between sexuality in God and the sexual characterization of priesthood would do well to meditate afresh upon the denaturalization of religion and the transcendentalization of God which is at the heart of the Old Testament revelation.

The Feminine

The second objection to the argument that male-monotheism involves patriarchy and a male priesthood while priestesses are inevitably associated with Goddesses and matriarchy, is that the exposition of this theory entails an unyahwistic (and unchristian) attack upon the feminine and the female. Twentieth-century Western society has developed something of a fixation with 'the feminine'. The subject is approached from different standpoints: biological, psychological, cultural, sociological, historical and so on. Moreover, it is a subject which increasingly affects theology; it can have a positive or a negative influence upon discussion of such theological issues as sexuality in God and the sexual characterization of the priesthood.

We must recognize, however, that in Old Testament times the subject of 'the feminine' was not a primary concern in the way in which it is for many people today. It is confusing to say, either with condemnation or approval, that the Old Testament teaches that a male God must be served by a male priesthood, as if Hebrew theologians had made a systematic study of the issue and concluded that Yahweh was masculine and that female priests could not be permitted in Israel. Old Testament writers did not share the desire of the 'women's movement' to exalt the feminine. Yet neither did they make a deliberate policy of using masculine divine imagery and sanctioning a male priesthood in order to degrade females.

Why is it, then, that some contemporary theologians do read into the Old Testament a disapproving attitude towards the feminine and the female and, consequently, use Scripture to support their case against women's ordination? Here I believe, it may be shown that the increasing interest in the feminine has had a negative influence upon conventional theologians and ecclesiastics. It is now recognized that underneath many of the theological arguments against women priests lie deep fears and misapprehensions about sexuality, especially female sexuality: 'Historically, the Church has tended either to idealize women, or to see them as sources of temptation.'[15] The unrealistic attitude towards women and sexuality, which has tenaciously enthralled numerous minds through the ages, has been greatly inflamed this century by the growing emphasis upon the feminine. Many people undiscerningly regard *any* expression of the desire for sexual equality, *any* call for a realistic evaluation of femininity and the female, as part of the 'evil' of radical feminism. In their understandable rejection of the vagaries of extreme feminism they have, often unwittingly, abjured everything which sounds remotely 'feminist', including the case for women's ordination. Before women will be able to take a full and natural part in all forms of ministry in the Church, it is necessary to dissociate a right and proper attention to the feminine from radical feminism and to acknowledge and overcome the negative influence which misunderstandings of the feminine and fears about sexuality have had upon some Christian thought.

This negative attitude towards female sexuality is manifested by people like N. P. Williams and E. L. Mascall when they allege that leadership of worship by a woman would distract men in the congregation with 'carnal thoughts'.[16] Yet if one is going to argue that sexuality causes unwelcome diversions at public worship, then one must acknowledge that female worshippers are sometimes 'distracted' by a male officiant, as well as vice versa. Jewett believes that the insistence that the femininity of women ministers would cause insuperable problems in this area is 'simply a disarming nuance of the age-old assumption on man's part that woman is a sex object; that she differs from the man in that while he is *capable* of erotic love, she is *made* for it'.[17]

Much psychology and popular mythology contain inimical ideas about feminine sexuality which make it easy to see why the Church has frequently endeavoured to keep the female firmly under male control. The feminine symbolizes the enclosing and ensnaring, the unconscious and passive, the mysterious, the 'Other'; whereas the masculine represents the positive, creative force, light, intelligence, order.[18] The feminine is used to represent the 'darker' side of humanity and of the supernatural; it is more clearly associated with untamed nature than is the masculine, and it is said to pull mankind back towards 'paganism'. Thus Mascall warns that religions lacking a firmly masculine image of deity lapse into an immanentism in which the sense of a transcendent creator is absent and where there is a dissolution into fertility rites and all the sexual licence denounced by the Hebrew prophets.[19] Therefore he believes that maleness is intrinsic to God's being.

The influence of the Freudian school has encouraged fear of the 'bad mother', so that positive feminine symbolism in religion has become something of a theological lacuna. Images of the mother encompassing the child, absorbing and monopolizing it, depriving it of necessary autonomy, have encouraged several people in their insistence that, in order to avoid such unhealthy connotations, God must be thought of as masculine and be represented only by male priests.[20] Developing such thoughts, Russell and Dewey state that: 'One of the social and psychological functions of a masculine priesthood, Jewish and Christian, has been – as both cause and sign – to establish a balance: an institutionalized male equivalent, supernaturally sanctioned, to the

natural and numinous power of the mother-figure.' It is argued
that a 'bad father' does not have such harmful effects upon his
child as a 'bad mother'. This is said to have crucial significance
for the question of women's ministry from the psychologist's
viewpoint. 'A woman priest images the mother-archetype, and it
is widely accepted that this image is inimical to spiritual growth
and freedom in those exposed to it.'[21]

It is quite possible to meet the psychologists and pseudo-
psychologists on their own ground here. It can be argued that it is
wrong to concentrate upon negative feminine symbolism when
there are images of the feminine that are suitable for positive use
in religious language.[22] While it is true that negative feminine
symbolism is found in the Old Testament (for example, the harlot
and the foolish woman), on the whole, Scripture exhibits a
positive attitude towards femininity and masculinity.[23]

In much psychology and modern 'mythology', the feminine
has been poorly understood – whether under- or over-valued.
Christians should be aware of this and exert a timely corrective
influence. In their exposition of biblical teaching, theologians
may adduce, as secondary material, psychological insights which
are consistent with Scripture. The view that masculinity and
femininity are equally necessary to human wholeness is entirely
consistent with biblical ideas about sexuality. Thus, for example,
Jungian tenets about the complementarity of masculinity and
femininity might help some people to see that women priests
would not give rise to the terrible state of affairs envisaged by
writers like Russell and Dewey. Many others find common sense
telling them that there is nothing to choose between the 'bad
mother' and the 'bad father' figure.[24]

The Old Testament provides no legitimation for anti-feminine
psychological arguments against a dual-sex priesthood. It is most
unfortunate, therefore, if unbiblical, anti-feminist views are
allowed to distort the balanced scriptural attitude and to cloud
our thinking about sexuality in God and the nature of priesthood.
The Report of the Archbishops' Commission avoids this negative
influence and affirms that there are no biological or psychological
qualities of the female sex which preclude a woman from performing the duties of an ordained minister.[25]

We can, then, answer the anti-feminist psychological argument
on its own terms, but it must be emphasized that this does not

exactly represent the distinctive biblical approach. Many of the ideas examined in this section betray a derogatory attitude towards the feminine. In the effort to counter such an attitude, some people weight the scales the other way and put great stress upon the positive significance of femininity. Yet the Old Testament adopts neither course; it is not 'anti-feminist' or 'pro-feminist'. Hebrew theologians did not ask the same questions about sexuality in God and the nature of priesthood as are asked now; they were uninterested in the psychological problems about femininity which trouble some people today. Their belief that God transcends all human categories made them unconcerned even to stress the inclusion of what is good about masculinity and femininity within the deity. In sum, it must be said that if Old Testament writers did seek consciously to exclude women from the priesthood, it is extremely unlikely that their motivation was a desire to illustrate the un-Godlike quality of the feminine.

The Nature of Priesthood

The third objection to the argument which connects the maleness or femaleness of the priesthood with the supposed masculinity or femininity of the deity is that it reveals a misconception of the nature of priesthood. I have already stated my reasons for believing that Hebrew theologians did not conceive of their God as exclusively male; but even had they done so, this would not have necessitated an all-male priesthood since the Yahwistic priest was not regarded as an exact, iconic representation of God. Certainly there was a sense in which the priest 'represented' God to the people, as he also represented the people to God.[26] But this did not entail a representation of the sexuality of either party.

The argument is sometimes expressed in terms of the priest's role as a 'father-in-God' to the people. It is said that the Yahwistic priest had to be male in order to manifest the Father-hood of God on earth. In the preceding chapter, I emphasized the importance of acknowledging that when the Old Testament speaks of God's Fatherhood it does not do so in a literal, physical sense. It must now be stated that when the term 'father' is used of an Old Testament priest, this, again, is not in a sexual sense. When kings, royal stewards, wise men and priests are called 'father' in the Hebrew Scriptures, the idea is not that they represent Yahweh's masculinity, nor is the stress upon their own maleness. Rather, the term is used metaphorically to signify that the person so designated occupies a position of authority and responsibility. This claim may be substantiated with reference to the biblical phrase 'a father and a priest', Judges 17.10; 18.19. Clearly, the term 'father' in this narrative does not mean a substitute for a 'real' father; it has nothing to do with the sexual characteristics and functions of the man or his God. Rather, it denotes 'respected counsellor', an 'honoured guide'.[27]

Old Testament priesthood was not based upon a belief that priests must be male in order to represent the 'intrinsic maleness' of God. The origins of Israel's priesthood are obscure, the history of its development is complex, but we may discern that the biblical understanding of the concept expresses two central ideas. First, a person is set aside to be God's representative, to declare his law, to be a channel of his communication and counsel to the people. Second, that person functions as a representative agent for the community, leading its worship, making supplication and sacrifice.[28]

When the priest represents God, he does this as God's *representative*, not as a *representation*. Lampe elucidates the distinction:

> An ambassador represents the Queen. He acts in her name; he speaks for her . . . but he is not a representation of the Queen. He does not impersonate her. He need not be a woman; nor when a queen succeeds a king do all the sovereign's representatives have to be replaced, if they are men, by women. This notion that a priestly representative . . . must be male rests on a failure to understand the use of analogy and poetic symbolism in religious language.[29]

Although the language of priestly representation may illuminate the nature of ministry, it is essentially metaphorical; to take it literally is to destroy its usefulness.[30] As A. E. Harvey writes, 'the notion that he (the priest) "represents" God in a manner so literal that he has to be male to do so is an entirely illegitimate extension of the idea'.[31]

The comments of Lampe and Harvey are pertinent to both Israelite and Christian priesthood. It is beyond my brief to present a detailed discussion of every aspect of the priestly work of

Christ. Nevertheless, one crucial question must be considered now by way of an excursus on *the maleness of Christ and the sexual characterization of Christian priesthood*. It may well be objected that the foregoing observations about the priestly representation of Yahweh in Old Testament times are overshadowed by the function of the Christian priest as representative of the male Christ. As Mascall puts it, 'Christ exercises his priesthood in the Church through human beings who possess human nature in the same sexual mode in which he possesses it.'[32]

That maleness is essential to priesthood is also stated forcefully by J. Saward. The image of Christ as Bridegroom describes the redemptive work in sexual terms, and from this Saward deduces that maleness was essential to the priesthood of Jesus: 'the sexual-nuptial and sacrificial-priestly images are inter-dependent and inseparable . . . Christ's sacrificial death could be such only if it was the death of a God-*man*, one of the male gender who could be said to be Bridegroom'.[33] Thus, maleness is said to be essential to the Christian priest on two main counts. First, the priest must be male in order to act *in persona Christi*, especially at the Eucharist: 'For the "actor" who plays Christ in the sacred drama of the liturgy, more fundamental even than his spiritual qualities, is his gender: he has to have a man's body to play the part of Christ the God-*man*.'

Second, the priest must be male in order to be an icon and sacramental sign of Christ the High Priest: '*a priest is literally an icon of Christ*, created . . . by the Holy Spirit out of male flesh, an icon given colouring and form by the contours and dimensions of a male body'.[34]

Many scholars have pointed out that such argumentation betrays a flawed doctrine of priesthood. From incarnational, soteriological and sacramental perspectives it is distorted, since it appears to misunderstand the significance of Christ's life and work, the way in which he effects the salvation of men and women, and the nature of his relationship with his people through the sacraments. On the subject of Jesus' maleness, it must be stated that 'the fact that the Son of God took human nature in its masculine form is not based in the essence of God, for God stands beyond all sexual differences'.[35] The primary necessity of the incarnation was that Christ should be human, *homo*, *anthrōpos*, so that humanity might be taken up into the deity. The Nicene Creed, for example, does not stress that the Second Person of the Trinity became *vir*, *anēr*; rather, the emphasis is on *homo factus est*.

Moreover, to make the maleness of Christ a christological principle is to qualify or deny the universality of his redemption. It is the humanity, not the masculinity, of the Second Adam into which we are incorporated. If, from the incarnational and the soteriological standpoints, Christ's maleness is all-important, then, as Lampe shows, women would be excluded 'not only from the Ministry of Christ's Church but from its baptized membership'.[36] In theological reality, however, 'it is a secondary fact, a matter of divine economy, that Christ should be born of Jewish race, and of masculine sexuality'.[37] *In the circumstances of the time*, Christ's mission required him to be male. But neither the masculine imagery of Christ as Bridegroom nor the historical fact of his maleness, qualifies the theological meaning of his acts, still less of his nature – any more than the parables comparing Yahweh with a father or husband could 'masculinize' the nature of God.

Turning to the subject of the maleness of Christian priests, Lampe offers some definitive comments. Without explicit reference to the work of Mascall or Saward, he exposes the spurious notions about priesthood involved in the 'actor' and 'icon' argument. Principally, he states that the 'actor' idea is open to grave objections because, although the priest must resemble the male historical Jesus in so far as he needs to do what Christ did, such as to take bread and break it and say the words of thanksgiving, these are human actions, not specifically masculine actions. 'Since the priest is not playing the part of Christ in the sense in which this is done at Oberammergau, there is no reason at all why a woman cannot represent him.'[38]

The 'icon' theory of priesthood will not stand up to scrutiny. It has no place in ancient Christian tradition; as Norris maintains, the argument is virtually unprecedented. This is not only because the idea that a priest or bishop somehow 'images' Jesus in a special way is one which arrived rather late on the scene in Christian history. 'What is genuinely novel in it is the idea that Jesus' maleness is at least one of the crucial things about him which ecclesial priesthoods must image.'[39] Muddiman advises catholic Christians to treat the whole notion with 'extreme caution'. Those who believe that the greatest 'icon' of Christ in the Eucharist is the consecrated bread and wine should not be misled by inapplicable arguments about the maleness of his earthly humanity.[40] The argument falls down, also, on its doctrine of the Holy Spirit. It reflects a theology which gives too little place to the Spirit of God; for, as Lampe reminds us, 'it is the Spirit, not the priest, who makes Christ present to us and who initiates and carries through the transformation of ourselves into the likeness of Christ'.[41]

It must be concluded, then, that neither the Old Testament nor the New sets a precedent for the linkage of maleness of priesthood with maleness of God. Scriptural teaching about sexuality in God and the nature of priesthood is misinterpreted when it is taken to indicate that priests must be male in order to function as representations of a male deity. It is a total misuse of biblical analogy and symbolism to say, with reference to the Old Testament, that the Yahwistic priesthood had to be male so as to represent the Bridegroom, Father God. And the objection to women's ministry which appeals to the notion of the priest as representation and icon of Christ is based upon a false understanding of the Person and work of Jesus. This entire argument looks suspiciously like an *ad hoc* and alarmingly heterodox piece of theologizing, invented purely to rule out the ordination of women to priesthood and episcopate; as such, it deserves to be dismissed.

NOTES

1. Vos, *Woman*, p. 207
2. It might have been preferable to avoid the term 'monotheism' because most scholars now agree that Israelite religion may not legitimately be described as 'monotheistic' until late Old Testament times. (See above, Chapter 1, note 17.) However, Judaism is generally referred to as one of the great monotheistic religions, and the term 'male-monotheism' is commonly applied to biblical religion by feminist theologians like Ruether. It is convenient, therefore, to employ the term here, with the proviso that this is done to encapsulate the views of those who use it in a general sense rather than to give an accurate definition of Yahwism.
3. See, for example, R. S. Briffault, *The Mothers*, III (London 1927),

p. 114; E. O. James, 'An Anthropologist's Comments', *Women and the Priesthood of the Church*, Mascall (London 1960), p. 38.

4. Demant, 'Why the Christian Priesthood is Male', para. 9.
5. cf. F. W. Dillistone, 'Male–Female Symbolism', *Yes to Women Priests*, ed. H. Montefiore (Oxford 1978), pp. 30ff.
6. J. B. Segal, 'The Jewish Attitude Towards Women', *JJS*, 30 (1979), p. 131; cf. Ruether, *Sexism and God-Talk*, p. 53.
7. cf. D. R. Mace, *Hebrew Marriage*, pp. 77ff. On the legal subordination of Babylonian women and regulations for orders of priestesses, see G. R. Driver and J. C. Miles, *The Babylonian Laws* (Oxford 1955).
8. P. D. Hanson, 'Masculine Metaphors for God and Sex-discrimination in the Old Testament', *ER*, 27 (1975), pp. 317, 318. Hanson cites Herodotus' accounts of the Babylonian Mother–Goddess cult (I, 199).
9. For example, Exod. 21.17; Lev. 20.9; Deut. 27.16; 21.14; Prov. 19.26; 1 Sam. 1.22–3; Exod. 22.22; Deut. 10.18; 24.17–21; cf. Isa. 1.17; Jer. 22.3.
10. Vos, op. cit., p. 46; cf. R. T. Barnhouse, 'Is Patriarchy Obsolete?', *Male and Female*, especially p. 229.
11. cf. J. Moltmann, 'The Motherly Father', p. 52.
12. cf. S. de Beauvoir, *The Second Sex* (Middlesex 1972), p. 22; C. Halkes, 'The Themes of Protest in Feminist Theology against God the Father', *Concilium* (March 1981), p. 104.
13. cf. G. Russell and M. Dewey, 'Psychological Aspects', *Man, Woman, and Priesthood*, ed. P. Moore (London 1978), p. 95.
14. cf. J. G. Williams, *Women Recounted*, p. 131.
15. L. Brockett, *The Ordination of Women – A Roman Catholic Viewpoint* (London 1980), p. 15; cf. Jewett, *The Ordination of Women* (Grand Rapids 1980), pp. 4ff.
16. Mascall, 'Women and the Priesthood of the Church', pp. 98ff. He quotes from Williams' speech in *Convocation* (June 1938) reprinted in E. W. Kemp's memoir, *N. P. Williams* (London 1954). It is sometimes suggested that certain Old Testament passages (for example, Job 31.1f, Zech. 12.12–14) imply that the sexes should be separated for worship (cf. M. Friedmann, 'Mitwirkung von Frauen beim Gottesdienste', *HUCA*, 8–9 (1931–2), pp. 513–20). This is a dubious interpretation; verses such as Deut. 29.10f, Ps. 68.25, Ezra 10.1, Neh. 8.3, 2 Chron. 20.13 indicate that men, women and children worshipped together.
17. Jewett, *Man as Male and Female* (Grand Rapids 1975), p. 161.
18. See, for example, S. de Beauvoir, op. cit., pp. 112, 199, 285; E. Neumann, *The Great Mother* (London 1955), p. 292.

19. Mascall, *Whatever Happened?*, pp. 150–1; cf. C. S. Lewis, 'Priestesses in the Church?', pp. 195, 196.

20. cf. V. E. Watson and W. Brett, *Women Priests Impossible?* (London 1973), p. 8.

21. Russell and Dewey, op. cit., pp. 92ff.

22. For example, the female saint, the spiritual guide, wisdom, heroines of the Old Testament, the Virgin Mary. cf. A. B. Ulanov, *The Feminine in Jungian Psychology and in Christian Theology* (Evanston 1971), p. 37.

23. One indication of the positive light in which Yahwism viewed the right use of sexuality is found in the fact that priests were expected to marry.

24. It is interesting to note that psychologists like E. R. Moberly are drawing attention to the probable links between the causation of homosexuality and an ambivalent relationship between father and son. The 'mother fixation' of the male homosexual strikes Moberly as being an effect rather than a cause. *Homosexuality: A New Christian Ethic* (Cambridge 1983), especially pp. 2–3, 8.

25. *Women and Holy Orders*, p. 18.

26. See, for example, L. Sabourin, 'Priesthood', *SN*, 25 (Leiden 1973), p. 101; R. de Vaux, *Ancient Israel*, p. 357.

27. cf. A. C. J. Phillips, 'The Ecstatics' Father', *Words and Meanings*, eds. P. R. Ackroyd and B. Lindars (Cambridge 1968), pp. 189–94. See also Gen. 45.8, Joseph as 'a father to Pharaoh'; cf. P. A. H. de Boer, 'The Counsellor', *SVT*, 2 (1955), p. 57. 2 Kings 2.12; 13.14; 6.21, the prophet as 'father'; cf. J. Gray, *1 and 2 Kings*, 3 (London 1977), p. 598; on 1 Sam. 10.12, cf. J. G. Williams, 'The Prophetic Father', *JBL*, 85 (1966), pp. 344f. Note also the use of the term 'mother' in designating an authoritative counsellor, without any sense of sexuality; for example, Deborah, Judg. 5.7.

28. See, for example, Sabourin, op. cit., especially p. 150, on Deut. 33.8, 10; A. Cody, 'A History of Old Testament Priesthood, *AB*, 35 (1969), especially p. 191, on the post-exilic period; H. H. Rowley, *The Faith of Israel* (London 1956), especially p. 37; R. de Vaux, *Ancient Israel*, pp. 345ff.

29. Lampe, 'Women and the Ministry', p. 97.

30. In fact, as R. A. Norris, jun., points out, the language of priestly representation is susceptible to differing interpretations. The manner in which it is employed by those who appeal to divine maleness in their argument against the priesting of women, frequently conceals ambiguities of thought. 'The Ordination of Women and the "Maleness" of the Christ', *Feminine in the Church*, ed. M. Furlong (London 1984), pp. 71f, 84 n. 1.

31. A. E. Harvey, *Priest or President?* (London 1975), p. 69; cf. Caird, *Language and Imagery*, p. 131.
32. Mascall, 'Some Basic Considerations', *Man, Woman, and Priesthood*, p. 23; cf. *Whatever Happened?*, pp. 138ff.
33. J. Saward, *Christ and His Bride* (London 1977), p. 5.
34. ibid., pp. 9–10, 11.
35. H. van der Meer, *Women Priests in the Catholic Church?* (Philadelphia 1973), p. 143.
36. Lampe, 'Church Tradition', p. 124.
37. R. W. Howard, *Should Women be Priests?* (Oxford 1949), p. 24.
38. Lampe, 'Women and the Ministry', p. 97.
39. Norris, op. cit., p. 73.
40. Muddiman, *Women, the Bible and the Priesthood*, p. 8.
41. Lampe, 'Women and the Ministry', p. 97; cf. Hodgson, op. cit., pp. 211ff.

4

The Sexual Characterization of Priesthood in the Old Testament

If the absence of priestesses in Yahwism had nothing to do with sexuality in God, what is the true explanation behind Israel's all-male priesthood? It may well be the case that the definitive answer to this question is lost for ever in the mists of time. Nevertheless, various reasons have been put forward to explain the exclusion of women from the priestly service of Yahweh, and some of these theories can be shown to give a fairer interpretation than others of Old Testament teaching about the status and function of women. In this chapter, the plausibility of the different suggestions will be assessed in the hope that some of the most illusory notions can then be dispelled. The first step in this process is to elucidate as accurately as possible the position of women in the Yahwistic cult.

Women in the Yahwistic Cult

Is it strictly accurate to say that no female ever held cultic office in Yahwism? The traditional scholarly consensus gave an affirmative answer to this question. Indeed, most reputable authors who have discussed the subject of priesthood in the Old Testament have not thought it worth devoting more than a brief mention to 'women's ministry'. It has been assumed that, however 'fairly' women may have been treated in other respects, in what was for the Hebrew the most important sphere – namely, a person's place within the Yahwistic cult – women were virtually excluded. Judaism, it is said, has been a 'man's religion' from the early days when the injunction for 'all males' to attend the three annual festivals was promulgated (Exod. 23.17; 34.23; Deut. 16.16). Some theologians disagree profoundly with this interpretation. They argue that, far from being excluded from the worship of the God of Israel, women even held certain cultic offices. Clearly it is imperative to ascertain which of these opposing views comes nearer to the truth.

According to scholars like Peritz, the Semites in general and the Hebrews in particular (and the latter especially in the earlier periods of their history) exhibit no tendency to discriminate between man and woman regarding participation in religious practices. On the contrary, woman participates in all the essentials of the cult, both as worshipper and officiant. Only in later times does a tendency appear, not so much to exclude women from the cult as to make man prominent in it.[1] Peritz bases his tenet on such texts as 1 Samuel 1.4; Deuteronomy 12.12; 16.9–12, 13–15; Nehemiah 12.43; Judges 13.15–23; Leviticus 12; 15.19–38; texts which, he says, show that women were not mere idle spectators at religious gatherings but shared with men in central cultic acts like festal meals and sacrifices.

Again, Otwell draws attention to passages dating from different periods which attest to the presence of women on important cultic occasions (for example, Deut. 31.12; Neh. 8.2; Joel 2.16; 2 Chron. 20.13). In the effort to prove that women were 'full participants in the worship of the Lord', Otwell mentions references to women's prayers (for example, Hannah, 1 Sam. 1.10, 12–15; Rebekah, Gen. 25.32; Sarah, Gen. 30.6, 22)); to women singing in a religious context (for example, Exod. 15.20; Judg. 5.1, 12; 2 Sam. 19.35–36; 2 Chron, 35.27; Isa. 23.16); to women receiving theophanies (for example, Sarah, Gen. 18.1–5; the wife of Manoah, Judg. 13.2–25; Hagar, Gen. 16.7–13; 21.17f).[2]

It is also claimed that Exodus 38.8 and 1 Samuel 2.22 witness to the holding of cultic office by women in very early times. Exodus 38.8 speaks of the ministering/serving (Hebrew, *ṣābā'*) women who ministered at the door of the tent of meeting, and who gave their mirrors to make the bronze basin. The LXX version of 1 Samuel 2.22 does not mention those 'serving women' at all, and in Exodus 38.8 it understands their ministry to be that of fasting. What was involved in the *ṣābā'* of these women? Peritz believes that the Hebrew word has, in the Priestly Code, the very decided technical signification of 'to render service in connection with the tabernacle in a Levitical capacity' (cf. Num. 4.23; 8.24). According to Peritz, therefore, the attempt to translate the Hebrew with a word such as 'assemble' is inadmissible. Such mistranslation results from a hesitancy to allow the word to mean

the same thing when used in reference to women as when used
regarding men.[3] It must be admitted, however, that it is extremely difficult to interpret Exodus 38.8 and 1 Samuel 2.22
accurately in the absence of any illuminating cross-references.
There is certainly no proof here that woman's official position as a
cultic functionary was once on a par with that of man.

Some people make much of the Old Testament references to a
number of women who, apparently, exercised ministerial functions as 'prophetesses' and 'wise women'. The feminine form,
prophetess, $n^e b\bar{i}^{,}\bar{a}h$, is applied to five individuals in the Old
Testament: Miriam (Exod. 15.20), Deborah (Judg. 4.4); Huldah
(2 Kings 22.14); Noadiah (Neh. 6.14); and the unnamed 'wife' of
Isaiah (Isa. 8.3). There is also a reference to 'false' prophetesses,
(Ezek. 13.17 and contrast Joel 2.28–29). A 'wise woman' is
referred to in 2 Samuel 14.2–20 and 20.16–22.

How should we assess the significance of this? On the one hand,
it confirms that religion in Israel was not an exclusively male
concern. As Bird points out, 'none of the authors who introduce
these figures into their writings gives special attention to the fact
that these prophets are women – in contrast to Old Testament
commentators who repeatedly marvel at the fact'. On the other
hand, 'if female prophets were accepted in Israel, they were also
rare'.[4] Furthermore, there is little or no evidence that any of these
Old Testament prophetesses may be considered a *cultic* prophet
to the extent that she was connnected with the sanctuary and
officiated in the ritual there. Otwell's statement that 'it is clear
that Huldah was a major cultic official' is unfounded.[5] Huldah
may well have taken a favourable attitude to the cult; but the very
fact that her place of residence is mentioned (2 Kings 22.14)
suggests that she was not stationed in the Temple and was not
part of the Temple personnel.

The prophet of Yahweh was not so much a professional cultic
employee as a spokesman for the Lord; prophecy was a charisma-
tic gift and its authenticity was not subject to doubt on the basis
of sex. The wise-man or woman, the prophet or prophetess with a
message from God, would be sought out and heeded if his or her
word was felt to have validity. The Old Testament accounts of
female prophets indeed illustrate that God communicated with
and through women as well as men, but this does not indicate that
women were included among the Temple clergy.

It has become clear, therefore, that there is insufficient evidence to challenge the long-standing view that there were no legitimate priestesses in Israel.[6] The mere presence of women at cultic events is scarcely tantamount to a participation in the cult equal to that of men. The question must now be considered: why was it that, although other peoples in the ancient Near East worshipped in cults which used priestesses, such female ministrants were absent from Yahwism?

Practical and Maternal Considerations

Amongst the various reasons proffered to account for the absence of women priests in Israel, I shall examine, *first,* the type of theory which focuses upon *the practical and the maternal aspects of a woman's role.*

In line with the view that roles are determined according to physical capability, it is sometimes suggested that physical practicalities may account for the all-male priesthood of Yahwism. It has been supposed that some priestly duties required a male's strength: the slaughtering of sizeable animals could not be performed by a woman of average female stature.

No detailed analysis of priestly functions is necessary to show the fallacy of this hypothesis. A woman's physical strength was irrelevant to the sacrificial duties of a priest since, as de Vaux points out, the priest himself seldom performed the actual slaughter of the victim (cf. Lev. 1.5; 3.2ff; 4.24ff; Exod. 24.3ff). 'The priest in the Old Testament is not strictly a "sacrificer" in the sense of an "immolator"'; his role began when he had to use the blood.[7] Obviously, other priestly duties, such as teaching the Torah and mantic functions, could be performed with no more physical exertion than was within the capability of a woman.

Sometimes, the argument about woman's role is put another way. It is asserted that women, married young and soon preoccupied with maternal tasks, had no time left for other activities. Proponents of this theory concentrate not only upon practical but also upon theological aspects of the subject – namely, upon the idea that God has ordained different roles for men and women. For example, Rabbi J. Sacks highlights the Judaistic tenet that men and women have distinct and differentiated roles. He disclaims modern assumptions that a role has something to do with 'rights' or 'status', and argues that 'roles, in Judaism, mean obligations'; woman's role is to establish a creative marriage relationship.[8] Others have maintained that, in Old Testament times, woman's true 'priesthood' was to bear sons to perpetuate God's people till the coming of the Messiah.[9]

It is doubtful whether any good purpose is served by speaking of motherhood as a 'priesthood' (in the Old Testament understanding of the word). Maternal preoccupations embodied little that was analogous to Hebrew priesthood. The high value ascribed to motherhood probably resulted from the fact that in the ancient East – beset with disease, famine and warfare – survival was the overarching concern; the childbearer was regarded with an esteem less common in our world of over population and birth control. The responsibilities of motherhood may have placed a practical obstacle in the way of a woman's entering priestly office; but this cannot be said to account fully for her exclusion from priesthood, since these practicalities did not preclude the existence of priestesses in other religions. Neither the practical and theological aspects of woman's role as mother nor doubts about her physical ability to perform certain priestly roles satisfactorily explains the absence of priestesses of Yahweh.

Socio-Theological Considerations

A *second type* of explanation frequently put forward to account for the lack of women priests in the service of the God of Israel may be termed the *socio-theological hypothesis*. This suggests that *women's social status affected their theological standing* in the community: Hebrew women had such a despicably low status that it would have been impossible for them ever to rise out of their subjection to enter professional priesthood. In order to test the cogency of this hypothesis we must endeavour to ascertain whether or not women in Old Testament times were indeed the abject, obsequious tools and toys of men that many feminists would have us believe.

Unfortunately, there is no widespread scholarly agreement about the social status of Israelite women. Perhaps this is due to the ambivalent attitude towards women revealed in the Old Testament itself. For many people the image of women in the Old Testament is the image of Eve (sometimes in a positive light, as 'mother of all living', more often, negatively, as the cause of man's downfall), augmented by a sprinkling of bible-storybook 'heroines' or 'villainesses' – Sarah, Deborah, Ruth, Esther, Jezebel, Delilah. Like most 'popular' views, this one falls far short of an adequate impression of the Old Testament picture that only a careful reading of the text can give. When one has become familiar with the rich variety of Old Testament images of woman, one is aware of the dangers of trying to formulate an aphorism that would encapsulate the image of women in the Old Testament. As always, it is vital to be cognizant of the far-ranging historical period and cultural setting of the Old Testament documents, and great care must be taken in comparing different portions of the text.[10]

Some exegetes have maintained that more can be learnt about the place of women from Israel's laws than from the historical narratives. The assumption behind this is that the law reflects an attitude which was fairly constant throughout most of Israel's history. Such statements are misleading, since several scholars discern that the law reflects a *changing* attitude towards women. Phillips is among those commentators who point out that although the earlier legislation of the Book of the Covenant, reflected in a few Deuteronomic texts, was addressed solely to males (for example, Exod. 23.17, Deut. 16.16), this is contradicted by the new Deuteronomic legislation (Deut. 16.11, 14). The latter assumes that the law applies to all adults whether male or female, even though, true to the style of a patriarchal society, the wives are addressed through their husbands (cf. Deut. 29.10).[11]

Such changes are quite subtle, however. They do not alter the feminist belief that the Old Testament law code did not liberate women. Indeed, it has been said that the Hebrew woman was 'a legal non-person'.[12] The majority of laws, especially those of the apodictic type, are said to address the community through its male members and to focus upon the authority, honour, property of the male. Woman only becomes visible, as an inferior, in situations:

   (i) Where males are lacking in essential socio-economic roles (the female heir);

   (ii) Where she requires special protection (the widow);

   (iii) Where sexual offences involving women are treated;

(iv) Where sexually defined or sexually differentiated states
and/or occupations are dealt with (for example, the female
slave as wife, the woman as mother, the sorceress).

Moreover, the laws are said to reveal a double moral standard
weighted against women.[13] Again, the Decalogue lists a wife
among a man's possessions (Exod. 20.17). The husband is called
baal or 'master' of his wife, just as he is 'master' of a house or a
field (Exod. 21.3, 22; cf. 2. Sam. 11.26; Gen. 20.3; Deut. 22.22).

As in the Law, so in the Historical and Prophetic books, the
central images of woman are as wife and mother, with the harlot
as a kind of wife surrogate or anti-wife image. In ancient Israel,
the family was the crucial societal unit. The naming of children
has been taken by anthropologists to be an index of the division of
authority between husband and wife – the right to name a child
being an exercise of authority. Otwell shows that of the forty-
seven references to the naming of children in the Old Testament,
the mother exercised this right in twenty-four instances (for
example, Gen. 19.37; 30.6; Judg. 13.24; 1 Sam. 1.20).[14]

Within the family, the Old Testament does not describe
women as mere chattels; yet it remains true that women were
almost invariably subordinate to men – first to father and then to
husband. Furthermore, it is possible to detect both a growing
restriction upon woman's liberty and a 'lowering' of her status in
later biblical and intertestamental literature. The older books,
mirroring to a great extent the pre-exilic society, show woman
accorded the freedom proper to nomadic and rural societies,
where her toil was necessary to the subsistence of the group and
valued as such. By early New Testament times, though, woman's
position had altered: she could not move about freely in the
'man's world', nor even enter into discourse with a man in
public.[15]

Nowhere in the Old Testament are we given explicit answers to
our questions about the role and status of women. Deductions
can only be made from 'evidence' preserved for reasons having
nothing to do with this particular enquiry. It is possible, however, to ascertain enough information to be able to draw certain
conclusions. While, for the most part, Old Testament writers
were not 'out to repress women' and were not unconcerned with
the protection of women against the potential arbitrariness of
men, nevertheless the Old Testament does emanate from an

androcentric society in which women had very different status and functions from that which they occupy and fulfil in the Western world today. Most women, certainly, do not appear to have been accorded such a despicably low social status that they felt 'deprived of the opportunity to give meaning to themselves personally, physically and sexually'.[16] This is to interpret the Old Testament from the point of view of twentieth-century feminism and it is anachronistic to speak in such terms of the experience of a Hebrew woman living, say, in the milieu of Amos. A typical Hebrew wife and mother probably never considered herself to be starved of basic human rights; but it is clear that she did not share 'social equality' with the men of her society.

It would seem correct to deduce from this picture that, owing to the social status assigned to them by the patriarchal culture of the day, most Hebrew women were not suitably equipped to enter professional priesthood – an office which carried with it no small degree of authority and prestige. It is unlikely that, on its own, this modified form of the sociotheological hypothesis accounts for the exclusion of women from Old Testament priesthood, but it does highlight a contributory factor. The priesthood was a profession – one lived by it and supported a family by it (Lev. 7.8ff; Deut. 18.3–8) – and such professions were not open to Hebrew women.

The Theological Status of Woman

Is it enough to say that male 'professionalism' succeeded in preventing the appearance of a single woman priest throughout the history of Old Testament priesthood? And is it strictly accurate to identify the direction of influence as being from woman's social status to her theological position? Doubts about the adequacy and accuracy of the sociotheological hypothesis prompt a consideration of a *third type* of explanation: namely, one which focuses upon *the theological aspect of woman's status*.

M. E. Thrall pursues an interesting line of argument with regard to the theological status of women in the Yahwistic community. She believes that women were disqualified from performing priestly functions in Israel because services of professional priesthood were a symbol and representative token of the priestly community of Israel (cf. Exod. 19.6), and women were not full citizens of Israel. They had the status of sojourners and aliens and therefore could not possibly carry out the representative service of cultic priesthood: 'The most striking fact which confronts us is that women were not, theologically speaking, members of Israel at all . . .'. Thrall thinks that the Law, so vital a part of the Old Testament relationship between God and man, had only an indirect claim upon women – through obedience to their husbands: 'For this reason women can have no direct and independent part in God's covenant with Israel.'[17]

This type of explanation for the non-priesting of women has both weaknesses and strengths. Perhaps its main weakness is that its description of woman's low theological status is too uniform and too extreme to serve as a theological appraisal of womanhood as it is portrayed in each and every instance in the Old Testament. Phillips, for example, believes that it was the Deuteronomic law 'which apparently for the first time brought women within the scope of the covenant community' (cf. Deut. 12.12, 18; 16.11, 14; 29.11, 18). This radically altered their status. 'They thereby became equally liable with men under the law' (cf. 7.3; 13.6; 15.12–17; 17.2–5; 22.22).[18]

Again, in the prophetic strictures against apostasy and fertility-cult practices, both men and women are condemned (for example, Hos. 4.13f; Jer. 7.17f; 44.7–10, 15–27; Amos 4.1f; Isa. 3.16–4.1). It was not the case that the prophets regarded women as more inherently sinful than men; the imagery depicting Israel as either harlot or bride shows a realism about the duplicity of all human beings (for example, Jer. 3–4; Ezek. 16; 23; Isa. 62; 66). This does not entirely accord with Thrall's assertions that because women were not directly subject to the law they could have no direct awareness of sin and 'could not have performed the priestly acts for the expiation of sin which the law required'.[19]

In later Judaism, Thrall's tenet that women did not have the same theological status as men is more clearly exemplified. The second- (or even, third-) class citizenship of women in religious legislation is expressed in the constantly repeated formula: 'women, (Gentile) slaves, and children (minors)'.[20] As Jeremias comments: 'Like a non-Jewish slave and a child under age, a woman has over her a man who is her master; and this likewise limits her participation in divine service, which is why from a religious point of view she is inferior to a man.'[21]

In ancient Israel, 'priestly functions' fell naturally into the hands of the paterfamilias as the oldest and most experienced male member of the family. Gradually, however, it became 'not customary' and finally 'not permitted' for women to lay hands on the heads of the sacrificial victims or to wave the portions of the sacrifice. This indication of the 'inferior' religious status of women has been perpetuated in Judaism by the synagogue pattern of worship. Jewett reminds us that women do not count as members of the congregation; at least ten men must be present to constitute a congregation: 'Nine men plus all the women in Israel would not be sufficient.'[22]

Other scholars have expressed the belief that there was something about the theological status of women – as this was perceived before the coming of Christ – which made it impossible for them to become Yahwistic priests. J. and G. Muddiman have developed a line of argument which seems to interpret the Old Testament material more accurately than does Thrall's theory. They begin by reminding us that it was not only women who were barred from the priesthood. According to the legislation in Leviticus 21, many Hebrew men were unable to become priests because in order to be a priest a man must fulfil several conditions. For example, he must be descended from Aaron; he may not marry a widow or a divorcee. The crucial qualification for being a priest is that a man must have no physical deformity or skin blemish. The priest must be 'not just a man, but a perfect specimen of manhood'. In the following chapter of Leviticus, we see that, like the priest, the animal chosen for sacrifice must be without blemish. 'Only those men and animals which are perfect examples of their class may approach God or be offered to him.'[23]

The reason for the injunctions in both cases is explained by the command of God: 'you shall by holy; for I the Lord your God am holy' (Lev. 19.2; cf. 21.7, 8; Num. 8.14; Deut. 10.8; 1 Chron. 23.13). In the Old Testament, the root meaning of the concept of holiness is separateness, wholeness, completion. The main function of the priesthood was, by sacrifice and worship, to assure, maintain and constantly re-establish the holiness of the elect people (cf. Exod. 28.38; Lev. 10.17; Num. 18.1). One of the major sacerdotal duties was to determine what was 'clean and unclean'. 'Set apart' for divine service, the priest could move on sacred ground without sacrilege, so long as he remained detached from profanities and was subject to special purity regulations (cf. 2 Chron. 23.6; 35.5; Ezra 8.28, 30). Clearly, the ritual holiness of the priest was the *sine qua non* of Old Testament priesthood.

J. and G. Muddiman identify in this passionate concern for 'holiness', the basic motivation behind the barring of women from the priesthood. 'The Old Testament writers feel that women are not perfect specimens of humankind.'[24] Any bodily emission, particularly involving blood, was regarded as defiling; therefore a woman was frequently 'impure'. She had to contend with periodic uncleanness which involved a seven-day-per-month time of separation from 'holy' things. Consequently, she could not come into contact with sacred implements or places (cf. Lev. 12.4; 15.19) for one quarter of that duration of her life in which she might have served as a priest (cf. Num. 4.3f; 8.24–6).

As well as woman's bodily emissions, childbirth brought further 'uncleanness'. The cultic inferiority of the female sex is expressed in such verses as Leviticus 12.1–8. This passage gives the female birth a double uncleanness effect, shown also in the double period required in this case before the mother is once more clean. The biblical interdicts about menstruation, sexual intercourse and parturition preserve some very archaic customs, associated with fertility religion and superstitious magic. As researchers like Briffault and de Beauvoir reveal, anything concerning a woman's reproductive functions was surrounded by the most severe taboos.[25]

Female 'impurity' must not be envisaged as a moral defilement, nor priestly 'purity' as an ethical holiness, as a Christian would understand these terms. Yet, since 'physical wholeness' and ritual purity were the essential conditions for sacred service (Lev. 21.1ff; Ezek. 44.15ff), woman's periodic uncleanness as menstruant and mother must have played no small part in excluding her from priestly office. Characteristic of the Priestly Code, embodied in Leviticus, is the concept of varying degrees of holiness; the priest has a higher measure of ritual holiness than the layman but is not as 'holy' as the high priest. The woman, however, remains inferior to high priest, priest and layman on Israel's sanctification scale.[26]

Yahwism and Priestessess

There would, then, appear to be considerable evidence which

may be used to support the theory that woman's theological status prevented her from assuming priestly office; however, a further aspect of the subject remains to be examined before we draw our conclusions. The question about the absence of women priests in Yahwism is somethimes phrased in this way: other Semitic peoples had priestesses, so why was Israel different? This question introduces the *fourth type* of explanation for the non-priesting of women in the Old Testament – an explanation which has its point of departure in *a comparison between Yahwism and other religions*, and which concludes that Israel had no priestesses because of the *intention to be different* from other Semitic peoples.

This type of explanation requires elaboration. 'Priesthood is found very early, among all peoples, even where other class distinction is wanting.' In general, though, 'little distinction seems to be made between the sexes as regards their qualification for priesthood'.[27] If Yahwism was content to share the basic concept of priesthood with other religions, why should it, unlike many religions, permit only men to serve as priests? What was it about the nature and function of priestesses in other religions that led Old Testament writers to accord them no place in Yahwism?

Reference must be made to the role of women ministrants in religions contemporary with the Old Testament period. In the Arabic world, women shared cultic duties with men; 'in matters of religion there is no sign of any discrimination' against women on account of their sex.[28] Sources like the Gilgamesh epic reveal that Babylonian women formed part of the regular staff of the great temples. Among the Phoenicians, too, priestesses served alongside priests in the cults. It was considered a privilege to belong to the order of priestesses; kings dedicated their daughters to the priestly calling. As Jastrow points out, in the historical texts of Babylonia from the days of Hammurabi onward, references to women attached to temples, fulfilling various 'priestly' functions, are not infrequent. Examples of women as exorcizers and as furnishing oracles may be instanced in Babylonia as well as Assyria: 'A specially significant role was played by the priestesses in Ishtar's temple at Erech.'[29]

This 'specially significant role' was probably sacred prostitution. Many scholars believe that cultic prostitution was rife in the ancient Near East. In Babylonia, for example, as the Gilgamesh epic shows, there were three classes of what scholars have variously termed 'harlots' or 'priestesses'.[30] They were attendants

of the fertility Goddess Ishtar, and their chief function was the
part they played in the *hieros gamos* ritual.[31] Their task appears to
have been to symbolize the activities of the fertility divinities and
to stimulate in the worshippers the psychology of productivity.
Sacrifice accompanied by ritual intercourse was meant to work an
imitative magic which would induce the God and Goddess to
assure fertility in crops, animals and man.[32]

It is clear from the frequent references to cult prostitutes in the
Old Testament that the practice, under Canaanite influence, had
permeated the very fabric of Israelite life. Some commentators
believe that later narrators glossed over the cultic terms to
represent them as common harlots rather than sacred prostitutes.[33] But, in any case, plenty of evidence remains to suggest
that male and female cult prostitutes were attached to shrines
throughout Palestine, and even to the Temple of Jerusalem (2
Kings 23.7). Strenuous – and often futile – efforts were made by
prophets and lawgivers to suppress these *hieroduloi*.

It is highly probable, then, that Israel deliberately avoided a
female priesthood in order to distinguish the worship of Yahweh
from that of fertility cult deities. We have already seen that, while
Hebrew theologians were not 'anti-sex', they were radically
opposed to fertility cult notions about divine and human sexuality.[34] When so many of the 'priestesses' have a sexual function as
seems to be the case in Babylon, then it was not at all surprising
that women were excluded from Yahwistic priesthood.[35]

When the existence of male and female priesthoods in other
religions encroached upon Israel, Yahwism had to follow one of
four paths. One was overt syncretism: a legitimization of cultic
prostitution and all that it represented. This would have resulted
in the disappearance of the faith which the Old Testament now
proclaims. Second, Hebrew theologians might have attempted to
'demythologize' a dual-sex priesthood – to allow women and men
to function on equal terms within the cult, but with all the
invidious elements of sacred prostitution and fertility-cult sympathetic magic removed. Such a task would, however, have been
well nigh impossible in the atmosphere of the ancient Near East,
where fertility religion had so tenacious a hold. Third, in order to
eradicate as far as possible all ideas about the sexual role of the
priesthood, Israel could have confined the priesthood to women.
Or, fourth, with the same aim in view, Israel could have confined
the priesthood to men.

Why was the fourth path chosen and not the third? Some people have suggested that it was because women were more prone to fertility-cult practices than men. This is an unsatisfactory postulation. In the other religions whose ways Israel was commanded not to imitate, there were male priests as well as priestesses, there were as many male cult prostitutes as female, and both men and women availed themselves of their service. Moreover, as Otwell points out, 'the frequency with which the technical term for cult prostitute (*q^edeshah*) appears in the Old Testament is almost equally divided between male and female functionaries'.[36] Since both men and women participated in cultic promiscuity, we must be wary of the inference that fertility worship was primarily a female fad. We must also be suspicious of the deduction that a simple ban upon female cult personnel would safeguard against the transference of fertility-cult notions into Yahwism.

There is much more cogency and credibility in the proposition that if Israel had to choose *either* a male *or* a female priesthood, then, from both a sociological and a theological standpoint, men were the only suitable candidates. Most of the functions required of Israelite priests had to do with leadership, teaching and corporate representation – roles which, in a patriarchal society, sat unnaturally upon female shoulders. This factor, combined with woman's low theological status and her frequent times of 'impurity', disqualified her from priesthood. Vos summarizes the situation well:

> One effective way to keep cultic acts free from the sexual motif would be to bar one of the sexes from the priesthood. If it had to be decided as to which sex should be barred – *it is very doubtful that this question was ever asked in Israel's history* – there is little question which sex that would be. One need only to think of the practical considerations ... plus the intensely androcentric nature of that society ... to see how natural it was for Yahwism to have a male priesthood.[37] [Italics mine]

Résumé of Part One

A brief résumé must now be given of the results of my study which have been enunciated up to this point. Throughout the foregoing chapters it has been demonstrated from various angles

that the Old Testament does not link the sexual characterization
of Yahwistic priesthood with beliefs about sexuality in God. The
assumption shared by most radical feminists and their opponents – that the God of the Bible is male – has been countered
with the tenet that God transcends the human categories of
masculine and feminine. Their second assumption, that the
maleness or otherwise of the deity has a practical effect upon the
maleness or otherwise of the priesthood, has been shown to be
highly unsatisfactory on several grounds. Intelligent Christian
thinkers would do well, therefore, to abandon once and for all the
argument that the ultimate reason for the maleness of Judaistic
and Christian priesthoods is the maleness of the God whom they
represent, with its corollary that the acceptance of women priests
would turn Christianity into a different, non-biblical religion.

If the nature of priesthood was not determined by a desire to
represent God's sexuality, what does account for the absence of
women priests in Israel? Several of the suggestions offered to
answer this question are patently fallacious – such as the idea that
the duties of priesthood demanded more physical strength than a
woman possessed, or the notion that motherhood was an order of
priesthood in its own right. I found some truth in the hypothesis
that the social status of the Hebrew woman did not equip her for
the priestly profession, although it must be reiterated that feminists have frequently misstated and exaggerated this type of
explanation.

Explanations of Israel's all-male priesthood which are based
upon the theological status of women are on much firmer ground.
A major barrier between women and priesthood was created by
the fact that woman was subordinated to man and was treated as
his religious inferior. There seems, also, to be considerable
substance in the theory that woman's periodic uncleanness
debarred her from priestly office. Again, it does appear to have
been the case that the function of priestesses in the fertility cultus
established a pattern which Israel refused to follow. In the nature
cults of the ancient world, priestesses were often synonymous
with prostitutes. If Israel was to dissociate cultic acts from the
pervasive sexual motif, the priesthood must be single-sex; and
since women's low theological status and religious 'impurity'
disqualified them *ipso facto*, the only candidates for this priesthood were men.

Thus, the available evidence suggests that the rope which barred the admittance of women to Old Testament priesthood was composed of several strong, intertwining strands. Frequently, some of these strands are brought into modern arguments against the admission of women to holy orders in the Church. Yet, even from the perspective of people who maintain that the catholic view of priesthood has its basis in the Old Testament, most of the reasons posited to explain the exclusion of women from Yahwistic priestly office are actually irrelevant to the current practice of the Christian Church.

However low woman's social and legal position may have been in ancient Israel, the cultural framework of pre-Christian patriarchal society is far removed from the twentieth-century Western world in which we are discussing female participation in the Church's ministry. Woman's emancipation in secular spheres cannot be of decisive significance for the theological issue. But it is still important to note that several of the 'practical' objections to the priesting of women in Yahwism – objections which continue to be advanced against women's ordination – are the same as those which were passionately espoused by people who were hostile to the admission of women to the medical, diplomatic, political and legal professions. Experience has shown these objections to be groundless. The availability of contraceptives, for instance, has facilitated the emergence of the 'working wife'; most professions call for no greater physical energy than women can offer; the 'burdens' of maternity have been lightened sufficiently to allow women to pursue careers outside the home. Whilst motherhood is undoubtedly a God-given vocation for a vast number of Christian women, it is as inappropriate to speak of an order of priestly motherhood today as it was in ancient Israel.

Even less appropriate, under the new covenant, is the argument against the priesting of women which bases itself upon woman's alleged ritual uncleanness. I would agree with J. and G. Muddiman that this is a clear example of the kind of culturally conditioned regulation which is not binding for the modern Church.

We no longer examine male candidates for the priesthood for spots and pimples or disqualify them if they are short-sighted. Much of the motivation behind the barring of women is of that

order, connected with primitive ideas of holiness and purity
which are no longer relevant. A woman's menstruation no
longer seems the mysterious, uncontrollable, defiling occur-
rence that it was to the Israelites . . .[38]

What of the argument that in Christendom as in Israel women
priests must be shunned as part of the avoidance of the perversions of fertility religion? It seems to be the opinion of observers
like Oddie that the ulterior motive behind the campaign for
women's ordination involves apostasy from the traditional faith
and a return to fertility-cult notions, sympathetic magic, ritual
prostitution and incantations to the Great Mother. This outlook
does not reckon with the fact that the overwhelming majority of
men and women who support women's incorporation into
ordained ministry are *not* ardent feminists demanding priesthood
as a woman's 'right'. They recognize the primacy of a God-given
vocation to priestly ministry; they realize that such a vocation is a
gift from the God who alone can equip the saints for the work of
ministry (Eph. 4.11ff). It is not something to be seized upon for
self-aggrandizement by frustrated women, or by ambitious men.
And they contend that feminists who, like Goldenberg, want to
'bring about the end of God' by improving the position of women
and by 'making the world less and less like the one described in
the Bible',[39] are misreading Scripture even more grossly than
people who base their rejection of women's ordination upon so-
called biblical teaching about a male God and divine sanction for
a male-dominated Church and society.

Yet these advocates of women's ordination do dare to suggest
that, in the bestowal of his charism in ordination, as in all
charisms, God would show no partiality, neither between Jew
and Greek, slave and free, nor between male and female – so long
as Christ is in all. Those who genuinely desire to encourage
ecclesiastical acknowledgement of the belief that God can use
women as well as men in the priestly task of building up the Body
of Christ have no intention of distorting Christianity with magic
and fertility-cult remnants. They know, as not every one in Israel
knew, that God will not be worshipped by 'sacred intercourse'
and sorcery. Therefore, the situation pertaining in the Old
Testament milieu, which rendered the institution of a dual-sex
priesthood a real threat to the true faith, no longer applies in a

serious, objective and non-reactionary discussion of women's ministry today.

Thus, most of the factors which combined to prevent women from entering priestly office in Old Testament times no longer preclude the acceptance of women into the Christian ordained ministry – even for those with a catholic view of priesthood. One crucial factor remains, however. It has been demonstrated that perhaps the chief theological barrier to women priests in the days of the old covenant was woman's low theological status and her subordination to man; does this still pertain in the new covenant era? This question is as pertinent to those who see no link between Old Testament priesthood and Christian ministry as it is to those who maintain that such a link exists. It concerns all Christians, because its axis is not so much in notions of priesthood as in the doctrines of Creation, Fall and Redemption.

On the one hand, many Christians have discerned in Scripture a 'timeless' principle of appointive male leadership in both familial and ecclesial structures.[40] Upon this they base a doctrine of woman's situational subordination which constitutes a serious obstacle to non-discrimination between male and female in Christian ministry. On the other hand, an increasing number of people are coming to believe that in and through Christ woman is given a new theological status – one which renders her no less fitted for priestly ministry than man.[41] The questions to which detailed consideration must be devoted in the second part of this book, therefore, concern the precise nature of Old Testament teaching on woman's position in the created order and the way in which this teaching is interpreted in the New Testament in the light of the effect upon fallen humanity of Christ's redemptive work.

NOTES

1. I. J. Peritz, 'Woman in the Ancient Hebrew Cult', *JBL*, 17 (1898), p. 114.
2. Otwell, *And Sarah Laughed*, pp. 153–4; 174; 163–4.
3. Peritz, op. cit., pp. 145–6. Note the explanation of the demotion of the ministering women in terms of their association with cultic prostitution: Vos, *Woman*, p. 204; Ahlström, *Aspects of Syncretism*, p. 32.

4. P. Bird, 'Images of Women in the Old Testament', *Religion and Sexism*, p. 69.

5. Otwell, op. cit., p. 158.

6. Some scholars see additional corroboration of this conclusion in the fact that the feminine form of the word 'priest' does not appear in the Old Testament. cf. de Vaux, op. cit., pp. 383–4.

7. De Vaux, op. cit., p. 356; cf. Vos, op. cit., p. 193.

8. J. Sacks, 'The Role of Women in Judaism', *Man, Woman, and Priesthood*, pp. 29, 30, 35.

9. cf. A. Dumas, 'Biblical Anthropology and the Participation of Women in the Ministry of the Church', *Concerning the Ordination of Women* (Geneva 1964), p. 32.

10. As a short selection, the following verses might be compared: Judg. 5.24, 26; Mic. 6.4; 1 Kings 10.1–2; 2.19; Lev. 20.9; Judg. 5.7; 1 Kings 1.1–4; Judg. 19.22–4; Deut. 21.10–14; Gen. 30.1–2, 22–3; Lev. 12.45; Judg. 9.53–4; Isa. 3.12; 2 Kings 11.1, 3; Jer. 31.22; Prov. 31.10, 16–18; Prov. 5.10–19; Isa. 3.16; Prov. 27.15; Song. 7.6–9; Lev. 21.9; Hos. 4.14; Gen. 1.27.

11. A. C. J. Phillips, *Deuteronomy* (Cambridge 1973), p. 114.

12. Bird, op. cit., p. 56.

13. For instance, on the adultery laws see E. B. Cross, *The Hebrew Family* (Chicago 1927), p. 154. Note also the debate about whether a Hebrew girl was 'bought' by her prospective husband. cf. Cross, op. cit., p. 115; M. Burrows, *The Basis of Israelite Marriage* (New Haven, 1938), *passim*; R. de Vaux, op. cit., p. 27.

14. Otwell, op. cit., p. 112.

15. cf. J. Jeremias, *Jerusalem in the Time of Jesus* (London 1969), pp. 359ff. See also Mishnah Aboth 1.5; Genesis Rabbah 45.5.

16. cf. Halkes, 'The Themes of Protest', p. 104.

17. M. E. Thrall, *The Ordination of Women to the Priesthood* (London 1958), pp. 44, 47. cf. L. Köhler, *Old Testament Theology* (London 1957), p. 69.

18. Phillips, *Deuteronomy*, p. 50.

19. Thrall, op. cit., p. 49.

20. cf. Talmud b Menakhoth 43 b; Tosephta Berakoth 7.18.

21. Jeremias, *Jerusalem*, p. 375.

22. Jewett, *Male and Female*, p. 91.

23. J. and G. Muddiman, *Women, the Bible and the Priesthood*, pp. 3, 4.

24. Muddiman, op. cit., p. 4.

25. De Beauvoir, *The Second Sex*, pp. 181f; Briffault, *The Mothers*, I I, pp. 365ff. cf. de Vaux, op. cit., p. 460.

26. cf. J. R. Porter, *Leviticus* (Cambridge 1976), p. 167; Cody, op. cit., pp. 191f.

27. Sabourin, 'Priesthood', pp. 5, 10.
28. Peritz, op. cit., p. 117.
29. M. Jastrow, *The Religion of Babylonia and Assyria* (Boston 1898), p. 660.
30. Sixth tablet, 11.184, 185. See also the Code of Hammurabi, sections 178–182, *ANET*, pp. 174; 427; C. H. Gordon, *Ugaritic Manual* (Rome 1955); W. F. Albright, *Archaeology and the Religion of Israel*, 3 (Baltimore 1953), pp. 75ff, 158ff.
31. On the *hieros gamos*, see, for example, Ahlström, *Aspects of Syncretism*, pp. 79ff, 34; Oesterley, 'Early Hebrew Festival Rituals', *Myth and Ritual*, ed. S. H. Hooke (Oxford 1933), pp. 139ff; S. Smith, 'The Practice of Kingship in Early Semitic Kingdoms', *Myth, Ritual and Kingship*, ed. Hooke (Oxford 1958), pp. 42ff.
32. cf. W. C. Graham and H. G. May, *Culture and Conscience* (Chicago 1936), pp. 94–6, 229; B. A. Brooks, '*Fertility Cult Functionaries in the Old Testament*', *JBL*, 60 (1941) pp. 227–53; Ringgren, *Religions of the Ancient Near East* (London 1973), p. 167.
33. For example, Gen. 34.31; 38.15, 21; Jos. 2.1ff; cf. James *Mother-Goddess*, p. 82
34. See above, Chapter 1, pp. 14ff.
35. Vos, *Woman*, p. 194; cf. Vriezen, *Religion*, p. 189.
36. Otwell, op. cit., p. 159.
37. Vos, op. cit., pp. 194–5.
38. Muddiman, op. cit., p. 5.
39. Goldenberg, *Changing of the Gods*, p. 10.
40. For example, J. B. Hurley, *Man and Woman in Biblical Perspective* (Leicester 1981), pp. 56–7.
41. For example, Thrall, *Ordination, passim*.

Part Two

Woman's Status and Function in
Ministry

5
Male and Female in the Image of God

The concluding statements of the preceding chapter drew attention to the debate about whether the Bible embodies a timeless dogma of male leadership and female subordination. Does such a scriptural principle exist to govern men and women in the Church today? If it can be shown that it does not, then this argument should no longer be used to forbid women's ordination to priesthood and episcopate or to limit in any way their participation in ministry. In the following two chapters, then, I shall examine the relevant verses from Genesis 1–3, for it is this section of the Old Testament which is alleged to teach woman's inferiority and subordination to man.

A word must be said here about the relation between the two Creation accounts – known as 'P' and 'J', for 'Priestly' and 'Yahwist' respectively – as this affects the use made of Genesis in the debate about the status of man and woman. Some scholars assume that the two accounts are consistent in stressing female subordination. Others believe that, while the accounts are indeed consistent, both show that woman's subordination was not part of the original divine plan. Others again make much of the difference between the two accounts, highlighting various 'contradictions' between Genesis 1 and 2.4b–3. Clearly, it is vital to beware of assuming that questions raised in one account may simply be answered with information drawn from the other. Therefore, in this study, whilst the complementarity and interrelation between the two accounts will not be ignored, we will approach the P and J narratives individually.

Genesis 1–3 and Women's Ministry

First, it is necessary to outline the case against women's ministry which is drawn from the first three chapters of Genesis. The argument is propounded with varying degrees of intensity. At one end of the scale are those who believe that although male and female are created in God's image and are 'equal' in his sight, none the less Scripture teaches that they must have different roles. In Genesis, then, a perpetual order is revealed wherein, without denying 'equality', man has a certain 'headship'.

For example, S. B. Clark writes that the account of the creation of man and woman in Genesis 2 portrays a subordination in their relationship: 'To be sure, there is no explicit statement that the woman has to obey the man . . . But there is an overall sense of her being subordinate to him in God's creation of the human race.'[1] This revealed order must be respected now as ever by the Church; since the exercise of ministry within the Christian community involves the exercise of authority (2 Cor. 10.8, 1 Tim. 5.17; 3.4–5), a woman can never be a suitable candidate for ministry.

Others, however, particularly in past centuries in an explicit form but still implicitly today, have inclined towards encratism; they have used scriptural texts to condemn sex and, by the same token, womanhood. They have followed Gratian in seeing Adam as God's 'vicar' while 'woman is not made in God's image', and Aquinas in viewing woman as a 'misbegotten male'.[2] If woman is, at best, only secondarily in God's image, she is *ipso facto* incapable of receiving holy orders.

We are confronted, then, with a complex problem about the relation of the sexes in the order of creation, redemption, and the Church's life. K. Ware declares:

> Unlike the differentiation between Jew and Greek or between slave and free – which reflect man's fallen state and are due to social convention, not to nature – the differentiation between male and female is an aspect of humanity's natural state before the Fall . . . the distinction between male and female is not abolished in the Church.[3]

Mascall echoes this: 'Sexual differentiation is of an entirely different type from all the other differentiations of which human nature is capable'.[4] J. I. Packer develops the point when he laments the world's 'disregard of God's order for the sexes, and the violence done by some women to their womanhood by claiming leadership roles among men'. He pleads that 'in God's church, at any rate, God's order for the sexes should be observed, and ministry structured in the light of it'.[5]

All this raises important questions about the way in which the

Bible is used by those who employ the Creation and Fall narratives to support their own understanding of male and female status and function. A growing number of scholars are becoming highly suspicious of the interpretation of, for example, Genesis 2, which says that because God created man first and woman last, man is superior and superordinate and that, because woman was taken out of man she has a derivative, not autonomous, existence. Trible is convinced that, of the interpretations of specific verses used to support traditional views of female inferiority, 'not one of them is altogether accurate and most of them are simply not present in the story itself'. But she alerts us to the fact that persuading people of the correctness of any re-interpretation of Genesis 1–3 is a daunting task, since 'over the centuries [the] misogynous reading has acquired a status of canonicity so that those who deplore and those who applaud the story both agree upon its meaning'.[6]

The Priestly Narrative and the *Imago Dei*

> Then God said, 'Let us make man in our image, after our likeness . . .' So God created man in his own image, in the image of God he created him; male and female he created them. – Gen. 1.26–7.

Over the centuries, a great deal of exegetical energy has been expended in the effort to elucidate the biblical teaching about 'the image of God'. Considerable use has been made of the concept in modern doctrine. Much of this material does not touch upon our subject, but certain background details must be clarified here.

The phrase 'image of God' occurs three times in Genesis: 1.26–7, 5.1–3, 9.6 (cf. Wisd. 2.23, Ecclus. 17.3). Although no other Old Testament verse employs this particular phrase, the notion does recur elsewhere. For example, Psalm 8.6ff, customarily associated with Genesis 1, in the phrasing has close similarities.[7] Few scholars would want to argue that sparseness of direct reference undermines the significance of the concept. Many believe that the idea depicted in the Creation hymn in terms of 'image and likeness' is expressed in the J account, in 2.7, in the reference to the insufflation of the *nišmat ḥayyīm*. God imparts his own breath to man, thereby marking the special relation between the human and the divine and the dignity of man above the animals.[8] Many complexities and misunderstandings surround any employment of the *Imago Dei* concept in doctrinal discussion. Three dangerous tendencies, in particular, will be noted in order that they may then be avoided.

First, the temptation to read our own questions and answers into the text must be resisted. Many theologians have asked the wrong questions of the Genesis narrative. We are at fault if we try to divorce the biblical concept from its literary and spiritual context. Clearly, the Priestly writer intended to say that man is in some way like God. And even if the similarity between man and God could not be defined more precisely, the significance of this statement could not be over-emphasized. 'Man is the one God-like creature in all the created order.'[9] At the same time, however, the writer shared the Israelite delicacy about the idea of representations of God (cf. Deut. 4.16). It must continually be kept in mind, then, that the Priestly terminology was 'moulded by questions and concerns different in character from the problems which have generally been in the minds of those who have sought to identify the content and location of the image of God in man'.[10]

Second, the view that 'image' (*ṣelem*) and 'likeness', *dᵉmūt*, refer to different elements in man must be resisted. Most Old Testament exegetes agree that the latter phrase is but a further definition of the former. Barr believes that the term *dᵉmūt* was added to define and limit the meaning of the primary term, *ṣelem*, by indicating that the sense intended for *ṣelem* must lie within that part of its range which overlaps the range of *dᵉmūt*.[11] The full expression underlines the fact that an image is not itself the thing it represents, so that the very use of this phrase delineates mankind's status. As Clines points out, the statement that man is 'made' in the image of God, that man is a creature, 'imposes limitations upon the range and degree of his similarities to God'.[12] This defining purpose having been accomplished when both words were used together (1.26), it then became possible to use one of the two alone without risk of confusion (for example, 1.27, 9.6). Thus, those dogmatists who have speculated on the distinction between the *imago* and the *similitudo* are on the wrong track.

Third, it must be recalled that the Old Testament says nothing about the divine image being lost. The Priestly writer emphasizes that the 'image' was transmitted from generation to generation, from Adam to Seth, even after sin has entered the world (Gen. 5.3); its existence is still mentioned in Noah's time (9.6). Certainly, 'the story of the Fall tells of grave disturbances in the creaturely nature of man'.[13] Nevertheless, the Old Testament implies that in the *Imago Dei* concept 'something is meant which distinguishes man, always and forever, which is not affected by the contrast between sin and faith'.[14]

In sum, then, the *Imago Dei* concept teaches that God has created the whole man, a physico-spiritual creature who, though by no means on the same plane as the Creator, yet bears some resemblance to him and may communicate with him.[15] The Priestly writer believed that it was man's vocation to be God's vicegerent on earth and to reflect in his nature something of the image of God, just as the child is the image of the parent (cf. Gen. 5.3). This God given capacity for reflection of the divine by the human and for relationship between man and woman and their Creator can be 'violated, desecrated, and ignored by people; but it cannot be destroyed by them . . . as long as men exist, they are as God has created them in relation to Him'.[16] 'To be human and to be the image of God are not separable.'[17]

Man and Woman in God's Image

We are now in a position to examine specific issues regarding the relation of male and female in God's image. In the past, several deductions have been made from the Genesis passages which seem to me to be based upon misinterpretations of the text. There is need, therefore, for a reappraisal of the biblical material if it is to be used correctly by modern doctrinal scholars in the debate about the role of women in the Church.

First, there has been a persistent tradition which declares that while the 'whole man' as male is in God's image, *woman does not participate* in the *Imago Dei*, or that woman is only in the divine image in a *secondary sense*. Diodore of Tarsus, for instance, in his commentary on Genesis, states that woman is not in God's image but is under man's dominion. Again, by 'the image of God' in man, John Chrysostom understands Adam's sovereignty over the rest of creation, including woman. Tavard comments: 'Diodoros or Chrysostom do not include woman in the natural image of

God, since this image is one of power and dominion, of which woman has been deprived by God and society.'[18]

An unbiased exegesis of Genesis 1.26f and 5.1f provides no grounds for holding that woman participates in the image of God in a different way from man. It is as false to say that only the male is created in the divine image as it would be to make the same claim for the female. The implications of this for the debate about women's ministry are succinctly put by Lampe:

> Genesis 1, . . . with its reminder that male and female together constitute that humanity which has been created in the image of God, is a standing witness against the belief that an inferiority of the woman to the man belongs to the intention of the Creator; and it is on the basis of a supposed inferiority that the refusal of ordination to women has historically rested.[19]

Second, it has been suggested that *originally humanity was sexless or androgynous* and that *the fact of the two sexes was a result of the Fall*. Sexuality in general, and femininity in particular, came to be regarded with fear and suspicion by many Christians. This tallied with some of the motives behind ascetic and monastic movements and the effort to bring man to the level of an angelic, sexless life. Through subversive influences from Gnosticism and Platonic Hellenistic mysticism large sections of the early Church were permeated with the idea that the sex element is something low and unworthy of intelligent man – an idea which, as Brunner points out, has 'more or less unconsciously and secretly . . . determined the thought of Christendom down to the present day'.[20]

A notable twentieth-century spokesman for the view that man's sexual duality is an expression of fallen nature is N. Berdyaev, who refers with approval to the androgynous ideal which he finds in Plato's *Symposium*. As with most supporters of the androgynous ideal, in the end it is not sexuality as such that Berdyaev despises, but femininity. For example, more than a hint of misogyny characterizes the remark that 'Man's slavery to sex is slavery to the feminine element, going back to the image of Eve'.[21]

I believe that Genesis 1.26–8 provides no evidence to support such views. The subject of this passage, 'man', *'ādām*, is referred to by the collective Hebrew noun for 'mankind'. Genesis 5.2 confirms that male and female together were named Adam, man,

when they were created. In Genesis 5.3, 'Adam' is used as a
proper name; but this is not the case in Chapter 1, nor in 5.1–2.[22]
Therefore, efforts to harmonize the first Creation narrative with
the ancient Greek myth of the androgyne or hermaphrodite
cannot be sustained. Vawter states correctly that 'the man formed
from the ground and destined to return to it is all Mankind, men
and women together, as is the man who is driven from the garden
of Eden'.[23]

This has important implications for our thinking about the role
of women, and their relative position to men in the created order,
since it stresses both the unity and the differentiation of the sexes.
First, the singular word *'ādām* with its singular pronoun, 'him',
'ōtô (Gen. 1.27), indicates God's intention for the harmony and
community of males and females in their shared humanity and
joint participation in the image and likeness of God. Second,
sexuality is presented as fundamental to what it means to be
human and procreation is the subject of a positive command
(Gen. 1.28); the differentiation between the sexes and the means
of procreation were not retrograde steps away from an ideal
androgyny. This accords with the positive value ascribed to
marriage and sexual love in other parts of the Old Testament. For
the Hebrews, reproduction, and so sexual life, too, are a special
gift to all living creatures. Third, since man and woman were
created together, with no hint of temporal or ontological superiority, the difference between the sexes cannot be said to affect
their equal standing – before God and before one another. 'Sexual differentiation does not mean hierarchy.'[24] There is no sexual
stereotyping of roles regarding procreation and dominion here;
male and female are blessed together and together are commanded to 'fill the earth and subdue it' (Gen. 1.28); neither sex is
given dominion over the other. If there is any relationship
between the image of God and dominion it must be noted that the
record ascribes the image of God to man and woman indiscrimi-
nately.[25]

Thus, Genesis 1.26–8 does away with any justification for the
view that sexuality resulted from sinfulness. Furthermore, by
stating that men and women were together created after God's
image, the passage forbids us to hold the female half of the human
race in contempt as inferior, or in some way 'closer to the
animals', or as needing redemption in the form of a transforma-

tion of feminine nature into the 'more noble' spirituality of the
masculine or the asexual.

Partly in reaction against the low view of sexuality and theories
of divine androgyny, and partly as a result of a distinctive
exegesis of the Genesis material, a *third* approach to the relation
of male and female in God's image has been to say that human
sexuality is part of what it means to be like God. It must now be
asked, therefore, whether or not the fact of the two sexes in
humankind tells us anything about the deity. The earlier discussion of the question of sexuality in God must be recalled as
material from Genesis 1.26f, 5.1f (cf. 3.22; 11.7) is considered.

Some people have asserted that the use of divine plurals in
Genesis I (*'elōhîm*, 'God', 'let us create . . .', 'our image') and the
subsequent creation of mankind as male and female indicate the
presence of sexuality in the Godhead. It has been maintained
that, in common with the Canaanite divinization of sex, the
Hebrew believed that the human capacity for reproduction was a
means by which man could become aware of kinship with God
and gain access to divine power. The employment of divine
plurals by Old Testament writers poses a problem with which
exegetes have frequently wrestled. It is beyond the scope of this
study to evaluate each of the possible interpretations, but the one
which bears directly upon the subject of divine and human
sexuality must be taken into account here.[26] It is possible that the
divine plural expresses a Hebrew belief in the sexual duality of
the Godhead? And is it true to say that the *Imago Dei* resides in
human sexual polarity?

According to K. Barth, the basis of the *Imago Dei* doctrine is to
be found in the relationship between man and woman, particularly in the marriage relationship: 'By the divine likeness of man
in Genesis 1.27f there is understood the fact that God created
them male and female, corresponding to the fact that God himself
exists in relationship and not in isolation.'[27] This definition has
been much criticized by other scholars. For example, G. Tavard
writes:

> I cannot see the image as residing specifically in a man–woman
> relationship, whether this takes place at the level of sex through
> the sacrament of marriage, or at a spiritual level through the
> co-operation and complementation of man and woman in
> church and society. This would seem much too narrow.[28]

To such scholars it is preferable to see the *Imago* as in some sense finding its existential expression in the interrelatedness of man with others, regardless of whether the 'other' is male or female. The seat of the image is then the 'person' as distinguished from the solipsist individual.

Again, it may be said that Barth's stress upon the importance of marriage as the 'crucial expression' of human I–Thou relationships is more the result of a reading into the text of his own ideas than of objective Old Testament exegesis. Although it was probably against Barth's intentions, his hypothesis can lead to the view that *only* in marriage or at least through sexual experience does a person become fully human. Vital as marriage might be in Barthian doctrinal schemata, Genesis 1 itself treats of sexuality in general and is not concerned first and foremost with the institution of marriage.

It may be justifiable to say that the use of divine plurals for God, such as the term *'elōhîm*, shows that the fullness of deity is comprehended in Yahweh. Whatever the origin of this practice, the Old Testament usage may be interpreted in an inclusive sense: Yahweh, as *'elōhîm*, embraces the whole range of divinity, including any facets of masculinity or femininity which may legitimately be predicated of deity. Above and beyond the feminist term God/Goddess, the term *'elōhîm* as applied to Yahweh can denote that the God of Israel incorporates and transcends masculinity and femininity. Thus, Macquarrie believes that if the image of God is represented by male and female, then:

> This implies that already in the divine Being there must be, though in an eminent way beyond what we can conceive, whatever is affirmative in sexuality and sociality, in masculinity and femininity ... God transcends the distinction of sex, but he does this not by sheer exclusion, but by prefiguring whatever is of value in sexuality on an altogether higher level.[29]

Such a sensitive and carefully worded statement marks the limit to which we may go in making deductions about sexuality in God from Genesis 1.26f and 5.1f. By contrast, when Frazer declares that we gather from Genesis 1 'that the distinction of the sexes, which is characteristic of humanity, is shared also by the divinity', he seems to be reading back human male- and femaleness on to God.[30] As Barr reminds us, the question behind

Genesis 1.26–8 is not so much 'What is God like?' but 'What is man like?' The Priestly theologian 'is saying not primarily that God's likeness is man, but that man is in a relation of likeness to God'.[31] It is incorrect therefore, to state bluntly that the *Imago* concept and the divine plurals in Genesis are illustrative of a sexual distinction in God.

Sexuality and the *Imago Dei* – Conclusions

What deductions and conclusions may legitimately be drawn from the Priestly Creation narrative to contribute to our under-standing of divine and human sexuality and the status of woman? First, Genesis 1.26f and 5.1f confirm emphatically the view that woman as well as man participates in the *Imago Dei*. Whatever it is correct to say about the creation of the male in the image and likeness of God applies also to the female. Anything and every-thing that may be deduced from the text about 'man', 'mankind', 'humanity', is relevant not simply to one half of the human race but to all men and women. Women's role and status is no mere addendum to the doctrine of man but an integral and essential part of it. Brunner declares that the primal truth is that God created man in his own image; 'male and female he created them'. 'This truth cuts away the ground from all belief in the inferior value of woman.'[32]

Second, it must be concluded that there is no place in biblical doctrine for theories which advocate ideal androgyny, or sexless humanity, or which equate woman with earth-bound sexuality and man with ascetic transcendence and freedom from sensuality. Genesis affirms that sexuality, maleness and femaleness, was part of God's original intention for human beings, part of the creation which was 'very good' (Gen. 1.31), and not a secondary and corrupt development consequent upon the Fall. Sexuality is a fundamental part of the creation and there is no suggestion that one of the two sexes is somehow evil or inferior.

Third, it must be concluded that, in Genesis 1, there is no deification of sex. As Trible writes, 'the metaphorical language of Genesis 1.27 preserves with exceeding care the otherness of God ... God is neither male nor female, nor a combination of the two'.[33] It must be reiterated that the Priestly theologian ascribed neither maleness nor femaleness to God. Sex is firmly rooted in the good creative purposes of God, and the essential need of male and female for each other is underlined. Yet precisely because sexual differentiation is a God-given gift to the created order, it cannot serve as an adequate description of the deity, since God, transcending the limitations of created beings, has no need or use for sexuality *qua* sexuality. God's blessing hallows human reproductivity and sexual love, so that there is no room for an ascetic denigration of these faculties. But the assertion that man's procreative ability is an emanation or manifestation of his creation in God's image must be discarded. Sexuality is not, *per se*, a sign of God-likeness.

In all, then, the Priestly creation narrative encapsulates several crucial points which may be taken up and learnt from by modern theologians who seek to present a biblically based doctrine of sexuality and the status of woman. Genesis does not adulate sexual polarity as being itself the *Imago Dei*; but it reveals a balanced attitude towards sexuality and a sane egalitarianism regarding the man–woman relationship. As Brunner writes: 'That is the immense double statement, of a lapidary simplicity, so simple indeed that we hardly realize that with it a vast world of myth and Gnostic speculation, of cynicism and asceticism, of the deification of sexuality and fear of sex completely disappears.'[34]

NOTES

1. S. B. Clark, *Man and Woman in Christ* (Michigan 1980), p. 24.
2. cf. G. H. Tavard, *Woman in Christian Tradition* (Notre Dame 1973), pp. 48ff; eds J. H. Boehmer and E. L. Richter, *Decretum Gratiani, Patrologiae Cursus Completus series Latina*, Vol. 187 (Paris 1855), II, c. 23, q. 5, ch. 13; T. Aquinas, *Summa Theologica*, pt. 1, 4, Q.xcii, art. 1, 2; Q.xciii, art. 4.
3. K. Ware, 'Man, Woman, and the Priesthood of Christ', *Man, Woman, and Priesthood*, p. 82.
4. Mascall, 'Some Basic Considerations', p. 21.
5. J. I. Packer, 'I Believe in Woman's Ministry', *Why Not?*, p. 170.
6. Trible, *God and the Rhetoric of Sexuality*, p. 73.
7. cf. also Ezek. 1.26. Von Rad, *Theology*, I, pp. 145–6.
8. For example, J. Skinner, *Genesis* (2) (Edinburgh 1930), p. 57; R. Davidson, *Genesis I–XI* (Cambridge 1973), p. 31.
9. D. J. A. Clines, 'The Image of God in Man', *TB*, 19 (1968), p. 53.

10. Barr, 'The Image of God in the Book of Genesis', *BJRL*, 51 (1968), p. 26.
11. ibid., p. 24.
12. Clines, op. cit., pp. 53–4.
13. Von Rad, *Theology* I, p. 147.
14. H. E. Brunner, *The Christian Doctrine of Creation and Redemption: Dogmatics* II (London 1952), p. 76.
15. cf. D. Cairns, *The Image of God in Man* (London 1973), p. 26; C. Westermann, *The Genesis Accounts of Creation* (Philadelphia 1964), p. 21.
16. Westermann, *What Does the Old Testament say about God?* (London 1979), p. 40.
17. Clines, op. cit., p. 101.
18. Tavard, *Woman*, p. 86. Diodore, 'Commentary on Genesis', *PG* 33, 1564 d; Chrysostom, 'In Gen. hom.', 3, 2; 9, 4; Homily VIII, on Gen. I, No. 4, *PG* 53, 54.
19. Lampe, 'Church Tradition', p. 124.
20. Brunner, *The Divine Imperative* (London 1937), p. 364.
21. N. Berdyaev, *The Destiny of Man* (London 1937), pp. 80, 300f.
22. cf. Von Rad, *Genesis* (London 1972), p. 70.
23. B. Vawter, *On Genesis* (New York 1977), p. 90.
24. Trible, *God and the Rhetoric of Sexuality*, p. 18.
25. Commentators are divided about the relation between the *Imago Dei* and dominion. Compare, for example, Vawter, op. cit., p. 57 with Skinner, op. cit., p. 32.
26. For further reading, see Clines, op. cit., pp. 62ff; P. D. Miller, 'Genesis 1–11, Studies in Structure and Theme', *JSOT*, Supplement Series 8 (1978), pp. 9ff.
27. Barth, *Church Dogmatics*, III.4.117. cf. III.1.185ff.
28. Tavard, *Woman*, pp. 190–1. cf. Brunner, *Dogmatics* II, p. 65; Eichrodt, *Theology*, II, p. 129, n. 5.
29. J. Macquarrie, *Principles of Christian Theology*, 2 (London 1977), pp. 329–30.
30. J. G. Frazer, *Folk-lore in the Old Testament*, I (London 1919), p. 3.
31. Barr, 'The Image of God', p. 24.
32. Brunner, *Man in Revolt*, p. 358.
33. Trible, op. cit., p. 21; cf. Davidson, op. cit., pp. 25f.
34. Brunner, op. cit., p. 346.

6

Man and Woman in Creation and Fall

Those who posit a scripturally based theory of female subordination which precludes the ordination of women rely not only upon the Priestly Creation narrative but even more upon material drawn from the Yahwistic account. For example, E. F. Brown states that: 'The story of the Fall reveals the distinction between the sexes, which in spite of occasional exceptions, is permanent and fundamental; a man's judgement is clearer and sounder than a woman's. The readiness of women to be deceived unfits them for the office of teachers in the Church.'[1] Amongst feminists, Genesis 2–3 has acquired the reputation of being the primary Old Testament foundation for the depreciation of women and their debarment from positions of leadership in the Church. One feminist study declares that the second Genesis Creation account 'makes clear at the outset the subservience in the created order of female to male. The Genesis account of paradise lost also makes clear that Eve bears prime responsibility for yielding to the temptation of the beguiling serpent.'[2] It must now be asked, therefore, whether or not Genesis 2–3 deserves such a reputation.

Almost more than any other Old Testament text, these chapters have undergone a vast range of different interpretations. Scientists and sophists, poets and patristic scholars, rabbis and radical feminists have turned to the text and all too often have made it say only what they want to prove. In fact, the history of interpretation shows how easy it is to press these verses into the service of contemporary philosophical and religious, scientific or romantic thought. Nor is this a problem which may be ignored by serious biblical and doctrinal theologians. Much of the supposedly Christian discussion, on both sides, is sadly lacking in Christian and scholarly perspective, and it requires critical comment.

It is right to be suspicious of both the feminist and the anti-feminist arguments; for dictums born out of the heat of controversy are frequently deficient or deformed. On the one hand it is said, for example, that Eve, being created after Adam, is second-

ary and inferior; on the other, that Adam was a rough draft while
it was in Eve that God produced the perfect human being. Each
argument at once suggests its opposite, and both are fallacious.
The fact that interpreters have been too much inclined to read
concepts from the anthropological and religious standpoints of
their own milieu into the biblical text should prompt modern
theologians to seek the meaning of the text in its own context and
to ascertain whether there is an abiding theological principle to be
deduced from it.

Genesis 2 – Woman in the Creation

In the *first* place, the deduction that *woman is secondary to man
and therefore subordinate* is often drawn from the *temporal priority*
which the J account appears to give the creation of man over that
of woman: '*Unde convenienter ex viro formata est femina, sicut ex
suo principio*', wrote Aquinas.[3] This theme, that man has precedence by birth, is taken up by modern writers like Clark. He
makes the highly dubious observations that 'it is the man who is
called "Man" or "Human" and not the woman', and that the text
speaks of 'Human and his wife' (Gen. 2.25; 4.25), indicating that
it is the male partner who is 'the embodiment of the race'. He
concludes that 'the most normal reading of the account would
indicate that the woman is subordinate to the man throughout
chapters two and three'.[4]

Is it true to say that in the J narrative the apparent temporal
priority assigned to the male's creation implies an ontological
superiority also? Or is it, rather, the case that the entrance of
woman marks the climax and crown of creation? I believe that the
view of man as privileged first-born and woman as a divine
afterthought rests upon faulty exegesis. Two alternative interpretations may be suggested – neither of which permits the inference
of female subordination.

On the one hand, there is the interpretation that the Yahwist
in Genesis 2 – like the Priestly author in Genesis 1 – does not in
fact write of the prior creation of male humanity. This line of
interpretation, advocated by scholars such as Trible, takes its
point of departure from the shifting meanings of the term *'ādām*,
'man'. Trible argues that in Genesis 2 the term is at first
undifferentiated: 'Grammatical gender (*'ādām* is a masculine

word) is not sexual identification ... The earth creature is not male; it is not "the first man".'[5] This hypothesis helps to explain the problem of how the woman was expected to know the details of God's instructions about the garden trees (3.1f) if these instructions had been imparted to the man alone (cf. 2.16f). The plural prohibition in 3.3 makes sense if it is understood to have been given to undifferentiated humanity and not to the male alone.

It must be noted that this line of interpretation does not presume that *'ādām* was at one time androgynous. Trible, in 'Depatriarchalizing in Biblical Interpretation', proposed an original androgyny. In her later book, however, she censures her earlier view as incorrect, because androgyny assumes sexuality whereas the earth creature is sexually undifferentiated, a kind of 'proto-humanity'.[6] There is no ideal androgyny in Genesis, and humanity as singular is 'not good' (2.18). This is the only place in the Creation narrative where such a judgement is pronounced. It indicates that the creation of man is incomplete. Therefore, references before Genesis 2.22 – such as that to cultivating the earth (2.15; cf. vv.16–17) – embrace in advance, by a kind of literary device, the whole man, male and female. The story then proceeds to state who and what is the whole man. Only after 2.22 is the earth creature first designated by the term for man as male, *'īš*; and, with the advent of sexuality, the word *'ādām* acquires a second meaning in the Yahwist narrative.

It has been necessary to present this interpretative method in some detail since it is not covered by the standard commentaries on Genesis; however, the other alternative to the view that the Yahwist depicted the woman's creation after that of the man in order to demonstrate that she is secondary and subordinate to him is rather more familiar and straightforward. It is simply that in neither the Priestly nor the Yahwistic Creation narratives does the statement that A was created before B denote A's superiority to B or B's subordination to A. In Genesis 1 the creation of man and woman is recorded as God's last act in the creative sequence – but there is no implication that this renders mankind secondary and subordinate to all the other living creatures. In Genesis 2, woman is said to have been created after the animals – but there is no hint that she is thereby inferior to them.

In fact, it seems more in keeping with the movement of thought in Genesis 2 to regard the creation of woman as the climax of the narrative. Even if *'ādām* in 2.18 is still taken to refer to the male and not to undifferentiated humanity, the narrator is quite clear that it is not good for *'ādām* to be alone. Whether as male or as sexless humanity, *'ādām*, the earth creature, did not represent full humanity but a provisional, inadequate form of life. E. Jacob believes that: 'The Old Testament insists on the subordination of the woman to the man. Man by himself is a complete being, the woman who is given to him adds nothing to his nature, whilst the woman drawn forth from the man owes all her existence to him.'[7] By contrast, the Yahwist was not so unwise as to base a theory of female subordination upon such an argument. He knew that 'man' by himself could only have been a lonely, inferior being. According to the author of Genesis 2, then, the creation of man was unfinished until the fellowship of male and female was made possible through sexual differentiation. Thus, even if Trible's theory does not convince everyone and *'ādām* in Genesis 2.18 is still interpreted as referring to the male rather than to undifferentiated humanity, there remains no ground for the argument that temporal priority of creation in itself signifies superiority of either being or function.

Second, it is sometimes said that the Hebrew word *'iššā*, 'woman' implies a *supernumerary addition* to *'īš*, 'man', *or* (as medieval authors thought) *a subtraction* from man. Barth comments on the word *'iššā*:

> The fact that the relationship is not one of reciprocity and equality, that man was not taken out of woman but woman out of man, that primarily he does not belong to her but she to him, and that he thus belongs to her only secondarily, must not be misunderstood. The supremacy of man is . . . a question . . . of order.[8]

This supposition is so weak that it may be dismissed with a brief reference to the shifting meanings of the term *'ādām* and to the semantics of the words *'iššā* and *'īš*. Germanic languages can express the sense of the Hebrew terminology better than English or French; as Vogels points out, in Genesis 2.7 'the man is not created first, but *Mensch*'.[9] Man as male only has identity where there is also woman as female, and vice versa. It should be noted how *'ādām*, *Mensch*, reappears in the divine judgement, Genesis

3.22–4. These verses, too, were once interpreted as referring solely to the male; but common sense demands that they apply to man and woman together.

No indication of female subordination is contained in the use of the word *'iššā*; it is simply a Hebraic figure of speech. *'Iššā* is 'taken out of' *'īš*, but so is *'ādām* 'taken out of' *'ªdāmāh*, 'earth', and *'ādām* is not portrayed as a supernumerary addition to the earth nor as subordinate to it. In man's poetic outburst at the sight of woman, the Yahwist 'resorts to a pun, for the word for woman, *ishshah*, is interpreted as a play on *ish*, man, though in fact these words have no etymological connection'.[10] Through this employment of *'iššā* and *'īš*, then, the Yahwist indicates the deep relationship between the two and their mutual power over each other.

Third, the description of *Adam's rib* has been used to demonstrate a supposedly *divine ordinance of male superiority*. Not only has Genesis 2.21–23a been interpreted as meaning that woman, 'taken from' man, has a *derivative*, not autonomous, existence; it has also been alleged that the manner of woman's creation underlines her *ignominious* status. For example, Frazer thought that according to Genesis 2 woman 'apparently marks the nadir of the divine workmanship'; man was not content with the animals as 'playmates', so 'at last, as if in despair, God created woman out of an insignificant portion of the masculine frame'.[11]

The motivation behind the Yahwist's description of the creation of woman from a rib has been a moot point amongst commentators. It is probable that an aetiological concern about the constitution of the human body underlies the narrative, but Von Rad believes that this question 'no longer raised lively interest at the time of the Yahwist'.[12] What point, then, did the narrator of Genesis 2 wish to make?

It is highly unlikely that the Yahwist thought that his portrayal of woman's creation was humiliating or degrading. What, after all, could be more humbling than to be told that one was made out of the dust? (cf. 3.19; Ps. 103.14.) It is also unlikely that the purpose of the narrative was to stress that woman was derived from man, in order to deny her autonomy. Strictly speaking, only on a very superficial level is it permissible to talk either about woman's derivation from man or about the autonomy of man or woman. According to the theological perspective of both Creation narratives and the Fall narrative, mankind is not autonomous; rather, both male and female are responsible to the Creator for their actions (cf. 3.9, 13) because both male and female ultimately derive their existence from God. Dust of the earth and rib of the earth creature are but raw materials for the Creator's activity; for man and woman, the essence of life originates with God.

It would seem that what the Yahwist intended to emphasize here was not the difference between man and woman or the subordination of one to the other, but their relatedness (cf. 2.23). Woman alone amongst all living creatures is *homoousious* with man; man and woman are of the same nature and substance. The reason for depicting woman as being formed from man's rib to become bone of his bones was to establish the unity of the male and the female halves of humanity; *'īš* and *'iššā* are ontologically identical; man and woman share the same human existence, their essential being is exactly alike. The description of Adam's rib, then, far from indicating that the formation of woman was an anticlimax or a secondary and inferior stage of creation, shows it to be the apex of the total process of the creation of humanity, the development and completion of what was begun in the first fashioning of the earth creature.

A *fourth* point at which some people have found the Yahwistic Creation narrative to endorse female subordination is man's alleged *naming of woman*, Genesis 2.23b. It is claimed that the man's naming of the animals as a sign of his authority over them (2.19–20) is paralleled in cause and effect by his naming of the woman.[13] This is a tenuous inference. There is no justification for seeing an exercise of authority in every act of naming. According to Trible's exegesis, the Hebrew verb 'to call' only connotes an establishment of power over something when it is linked wth the noun 'name' (*šēm*). The standard formula was used, for example, in the naming of a child, which was an exercise of parental authority (cf. Gen. 4.25; 19.37; 30.6; Judg. 13.24; 1 Sam. 1.20). In Genesis 2.23b, 'she shall be called woman', the noun *šēm* is absent. *'Iššā*, 'woman', is not a proper name but a common noun designating gender. It illustrates that the issue is not so much the naming of woman as the recognition of sexuality. There is, then, no hint of hierarchy in Genesis 2.23b. 'In calling the woman, the man is not establishing power over her but rejoicing in their mutuality.'[14] This verse should be contrasted with 3.20 where Adam does give the woman a name, 'Eve', and does assume authority over her at that point.

Fifth, examination must be made of the phrase 'I will make a helper fit for him' (*'ēzer kᵉnegdō*), Genesis 2.18. This phrase, even more than any of the four preceding points, has been used to construct the case that woman was created solely for the sake of man, to serve him, more or less as a bondslave serves a master. The spoken or implied corollary of this is that on her own woman has little worth or value; she is fit *solely for assisting man in the establishment of a home and family*.

Augustine conceded that 'the woman together with her husband is the image of God, so that that whole substance is one image'. But he continued,

> When she is assigned as a helpmate, a function that pertains to her alone, then she is not the image of God; but as far as the man is concerned, he is by himself the image of God, just as fully and completely as when he and the woman are joined together into one.[15]

Thomas Aquinas finds woman inferior to man at the level of her soul, as well as in the physical imperfection of her body. Aquinas believes, therefore, that woman was made *only* to assist in procreation.[16]

Similar views are expressed, with varying nuance, by many modern writers. For instance, Packer declares: 'Ideally, the man will always be felt to be initiator and leader, and the woman to be helper, encourager and supporter, and to the extent that this fails to happen the relationship will fall short of being a fulfilling one on either side.'[17] Clark states that 'Genesis describes her part in the marriage as being a helper to the man in the work of establishing a household and a family.'[18] Clearly, if the man's role is to be initiator and leader and the woman has no divine mandate to function in authoritative roles outside her own home, then any position involving responsibility and authority over men in the Church is automatically closed to her.

The thesis against women's ministry which is generally advanced on the basis of this interpretation of Genesis 2.18 is questionable on two important grounds. First, while it is true to say that in Israelite society woman's indispensable role was within the family, this was a sociological factor, not an unalterable creation ordinance. Genesis 2.18 is not primarily and explicitly concerned with marital relations, as Clark himself admits in the footnote.[19] Second, it is misleading to leave the impression that '*ēzer* denotes a 'subordinate assistant'; the Hebrew word carries no such connotation. It should also be noted here that it is inaccurate to speak of woman as 'helpmate' or 'helpmeet' absolutely, as though she were some special genus of domestic servant.[20] Of twenty-one appearances of '*ēzer* in the Old Testament, fifteen refer to God as 'helper' to humanity, God as the one who assists the desperate and helpless (for example, Exod. 18.4; Deut. 33.7; Pss. 33.20. 115.9, 124.8). As the human needs the divine, so the male cannot exist without the female. This precludes an interpretation of '*ēzer* in Genesis 2.18 as an assistant of inferior status.

Since '*ēzer* more often than not in the Old Testament refers to a superior, some feminists have argued that Genesis 2.18 provides biblical support for the view that woman is superior to man. This supposition is illegitimate, however, since '*ēzer* is here modified by 'fit for him', *kᵉnegdō*, with its connotations of 'counterpart', 'corresponding to', 'alongside of'. *kᵉnegdō* tempers the hint of superiority with ideas of mutuality and equality. The word *kᵉnegdō* contains the notion of similarity as well as supplementation.[21] In Genesis 2.18, therefore, the point behind the use of the phrase '*ēzer kᵉnegdō* is the emphasis of a need which can be met by an equal and complementary figure, not by a superior or an inferior.

Thus, it may be concluded that those who contend that a divine ordinance lies behind man's domination over woman may only draw support for their case from Genesis 2 by misusing the text. In reality, the value which the Yahwist set on the relation of the sexes in his Creation narrative is markedly different from the evaluation of woman generally obtaining in the ancient world, which regarded her simply as an instrument of pleasure and procreation.[22]

Genesis 3 – Woman in the Fall

It has become clear that the Yahwist in Genesis 2, like the Priestly writer in Genesis 1, taught that God's intention in the creation of mankind was not female subordination but an equality of nature and status for man and woman. Yet as the Yahwistic narrative moves into Chapter 3 and the description of human disobedience, we encounter several verses which have been taken to illustrate the inferiority of woman. These verses and the arguments based upon them must now be discussed.

First, it has been said that the whole female sex was shown to be 'weak and fickle', 'the whole female race transgressed' (Chrysostom).[23] This is because woman 'nagged' her husband to follow her into sin when she should have listened to and obeyed him (Gen. 3.17). This interpretation is highly unlikely. The lesson imparted by the narrator in 3.17 is not that men should dominate and control their wives and never listen to them. Rather man and woman are both pronounced unfaithful to God; they should refuse to listen to the tempter and should hear and obey the voice of God. As Jewett discerns, the fathers' opprobrious comments about woman were really an emulation of fallen Adam, who blamed the woman rather than confess his own guilt (3.11–12).[24]

Second, what are we to make of the negative image of Eve as beguiling temptress? According to Tertullian's interpretation of Genesis, the daughters of Eve should wear penitential garb to remind themselves that it was through Eve that sin entered the world.[25] More recently, Bouyer has stated that Eve drew Adam into sin 'through warping their relations into a seeking after pleasure as a primary end'.[26] This, however, is not the Yahwist's portrayal. The 'fall', as J depicts it, is not the fault of a female; it is a collective, social act.

Third, it has frequently been alleged that because Genesis shows woman as the first to fall into temptation, this provides biblical authentication for the belief that the female is by nature weaker than the male, indeed that woman is generally simple-minded, gullible and untrustworthy. Thus, Tertullian blamed woman for the sufferings of mankind and of Christ himself:

> You are the one who opened the door to the Devil, you are the one who first plucked the fruit of the forbidden tree, you are the one who first deserted the divine law; you are the one who persuaded him whom the Devil was not strong enough to attack. All too easily you destroyed the image of God, man. Because of your desert, that is, death, even the Son of God had to die.[27]

Again, Luther perceived Satan's cleverness in that he attacked the weak component of the human race, woman, and not man.[28] Not only is the tenet about the serpent's knowledge that woman's nature was weaker than man's based upon mere conjecture; it is also self-destructive. If the man was so strong that he was unsusceptible to temptation, he would have obeyed God in spite of the woman's perfidy, and then Tertullian might have had more grounds for his claim that Christ died because of woman's sin.

To begin to understand why Genesis 3 depicts woman as the victim of the serpent's deceit, it is necessary to know something about the background ideas which were likely to have influenced the narrator. As Phillips reminds us, 'the snake plays a prominent role in the literature and cults of the ancient world, echoes of which are found in Israel's religion (Num. 21.9; 2 Kings 18.4)'.[29] A serpent features in the epic of Gilgamesh and robs Enkidu of immortality. The creature's ability to shed its old skin led to the widespread belief that it had learnt the secret of renewing its youth. Furthermore, the serpent was associated with the fertility cult – with the worship of Astarte and with Baal, who was often iconographically represented in serpent form.[30]

Such mythological elements have faded into the background when the serpent appears in Genesis 3; but there is little doubt that they influenced the Yahwist in his choice of a serpent for the role of tempter. The point which I wish to draw from this is that the close association of the serpent with the fertility cultus provides the clue as to why the Yahwist pictured the woman in conversation with this creature. The connection between women and snakes was not a new idea of the biblical writer; it was firmly established in contemporary thought by the Goddess-cult, her prostitutes and the serpents of her licentious rites. Writing in a milieu where fertility-cult worship was a constant threat to the purity of Yahwism, the Yahwist need have had no anti-feminist axe to grind when he depicted a woman as the first victim of the serpent's wiles. If anything, it was antipathy to the fertility cult which influenced this feature of the Yahwist's story. The role in which the serpent is cast might well have been intended to emphasize that enthralment to the fertility cult, far from generating life, led to death. To heed the serpent's voice, to follow the deceptive enticements of nature religion, was to disobey Yahweh, the Creator and life-giver.[31]

Thus, it must be concluded that if there is any significance in the fact that woman was portrayed as mediator of the serpent's temptation, it is that this detail of the Yahwist's narrative was influenced by hostility to everything associated with the fertility cultus. It was not a theory of female weakness and untrustworthiness which moved the narrator of Genesis 3 to write as he did, but simply his observation of the particular vulnerability of women to a temptation associated with the allurements of the fertility cult in a society where woman's overriding concern was fecundity and childbearing. But no greater condemnation was heaped upon the woman than the man on this account; nor does the Yahwist suggest that woman was any weaker than man, for Adam, like the husbands of Jeremiah 44.19, was a willing accomplice. The description of woman's temptation by the serpent, then, provides no firm evidence upon which to construct a dissertation on the weakness of the female sex.

The Yahwistic Narrative and Female Subordination

It has been ascertained that Genesis 3 is misread when a theory of female subordination is based upon allegations that Eve 'nagged' Adam, or upon the image of Eve as beguiling temptress, or on the supposition that woman was depicted as first to fall into sin because the female is by nature weak and gullible. The problem to which further attention must now be given is this: does the Yahwistic narrative imply that God's original plan for relations between male and female involved the subordination of woman to man from the very first? Or does Genesis 2–3 suggest that female subordination is a consequence of that human sinfulness which may be referred to as the 'Fall'?

In order to understand the dogma of female subordination to which many Christians subscribe, reference must be made to the work of some of those who have done much to develop and maintain it. The teaching of Thomas Aquinas must be mentioned first. Aquinas developed a theory of two kinds of subjection: slavery, *subjectio servilis*, which is *post peccatum*, the result of sin; and domestic or civil subjection, *subjectio oeconomica vel civilis*, which is *ante peccatum*, obtaining even before sin. This latter type of subjection was necessary from the beginning because human groups need the order which pertains when weaker members are governed by the wiser. 'Such is the subjection in which woman is by nature subordinate to man, because the power of rational discernment is by nature stronger in man.'[32]

There are echoes of this Thomistic argument in Clark's account of his belief that female subordination represents a divinely given ideal for mankind. He denies that subordination, being 'ordered under', has connotations of inferior value. ' "Subordination" simply refers to the order of a relationship in which one person, the subordinate, depends upon another person for direction.' He believes that in Genesis 2 we encounter the timeless principle that man is to be 'head' over his wife and family unit. Primarily, Clark says, the scriptural teaching focuses upon marriage, but female subordination extends to all areas of society because the marriage relationship is the foundation of all man–woman relationships and 'the pattern in the broader community is an extension and reflection of the pattern in marriage'. Subordination, therefore, is not a curse but something desirable, a blessing for the woman.[33]

The subordination of one party to another, however, cannot be arbitrary if it is to be fair. Unless it is to fall into Aquinas' first category – subjection as slavery – there must be good reasons behind the submission of some members of society to the governance of others. In this respect, the Thomistic argument is logical: Aquinas believed that women were the weaker members of society and so it was quite consistent for him to argue that they should be subject to the authority of the stronger, wiser persons, that is, to the men. If one accepts that a system of subordination of the weak to the strong is necessary for the smooth functioning of a community, then the only questionable facet of Aquinas' case is whether women really are inferior to men in *discretio rationis*. Clark's variation of the argument does not have the same inner consistency. When he endeavours to maintain, in the face of some of his other conclusions, that women are not inferior to men, he removes the rationale of the case for female subordination.

In order to steer a way through these muddied waters, some comment must be made upon Genesis 3.14–19 and the Yahwist's view of the consequences of human sinfulness. Tertullian writes as though all women are cursed by God for being 'the devil's gateway': 'Do you not believe that you are an Eve? The sentence of God on this sex of yours lives on even in our times and so it is necessary that the guilt should live on, also.'[34] The text of Genesis 3, however, contains no direct curse upon male and female; only the serpent (v.14) and the ground (v.17) are described as cursed. Childbearing itself is not a punishment for sin (cf. 1.28), nor is the need to work on the land (cf. 2.15). Rather, the consequence of transgression is the increase of pain and hard labour which mars the satisfaction of bringing forth the fruits of the body and the soil. Since disobedience has disrupted the creative processes and the creation, the body and the earth themselves (not the deity) will now produce pain and pang, thorn and thistle. Furthermore, the punishments of man and woman are essentially the same; both childbirth and work become 'hard labour'.[35]

'Yet your desire shall be for your husband and he shall rule over you' (Gen. 3.16.). Man and woman have disrupted their relationship with God. This sin leads to a disruption in their relationships with all creation, including with one another. Woman becomes subservient, man becomes domineering; neither is a healthy position to occupy, neither represents God's original intention for male/female relations. This is, in outline, the thesis which I would derive from Genesis 3. As Sapp says, 'it is crucial to note that only in Genesis 3, *after* the sin of disobedience – when the state of existence God had intended for his creatures has been disrupted – is woman seen as subordinate'.[36] 'Sexuality,' says Trible, 'has splintered into strife.'[37] In 3.12, after both man and woman have flagrantly broken God's command, oppositions already begin to split the one flesh, shattering its unity and harmony, as the man declines to take his own share of responsibility and passes the blame to the woman.

Genesis 3 embodies further examples of disarrayed human sexuality. For example, in 3.7, 10f, there is the experience of shame, encountered only after man and woman have tasted the forbidden fruit. 'Shame in the form of embarrassment and inhibition only penetrates the duality of man and woman as the result of their mistrust towards God and their disobedience towards his world.'[38] (Cf. 2.25 and 3.21.) Or again, the usage of *'ādām* also bears witness to the changed relation between male and female. No longer denoting undifferentiated humanity, it becomes, in 3.22–4, a generic term that keeps man visible but pushes woman into obscurity. Some scholars have asserted that it actually refers to the male alone; but this is highly unlikely, since if *'ādām* is not generic in these verses then woman was not expelled from the garden. More plausible is the view that here, as in much subsequent biblical usage, only the male is referred to explicitly while the context implies that both male and female are involved. Generic *'ādām* has subsumed *'iššā* ('woman') in the androcentric, 'fallen' world. Thus Trible remarks: 'What God described to the woman as a consequence of transgression, the story not only reports but actually embodies.'[39]

The biblically based verdict on the distortion of sexuality finds support from the psychological perspective of Ulanov. She believes that Genesis 3 provides a parable of the way in which both sexes over- or under-value each other (for example, 3.16, 12). 'Instead of each person living his own distinct sexuality and blend of male and female psychic factors, each sex now clashes with the other and each exacerbates the negative expression of the other.' Ulanov speaks in terms of a fall from sexual polarity, which was good and proper, to polarization:

> In polarity, the opposites are related to each other by mutual attraction; they are drawn to unite with each other without destroying the distinct individuality of each pole; on the contrary, the individuality of each is heightened and realized. In polarization, the opposites pull away from each other and conflict with each other. The two poles split apart and destroy the individuality of each other.[40]

Sexual polarization, then, is a facet of sin. At one end of the scale it produces female subordination and male chauvinism; at the other end, radical feminism and effeminacy.

At this juncture it is instructive to return to the theological views of male–female relations which Barth and Brunner have derived from Genesis 2–3. Barth's argument contains valuable insights but is clouded in inconsistencies. On a superficial reading he seems to align himself firmly with those who believe in the super- and sub-subordination of male and female respectively and who hold that man precedes woman in the order of creation and should, therefore, always take the lead as inspirer and initiator.[41] He repeats what I have found to be the confusing and misguided allegory that 'man is primarily and properly Yahweh, and woman primarily and properly Israel'.[42] Many of those who

disapprove of women's ordination support their case by citing
Barth's dictum that 'both physiologically and biblically a certain
strength and corresponding precedence' characterize man whilst
'a weakness and corresponding subsequence' distinguish
woman.[43]

On closer examination, Barth's position is not so clearly
defined. As it was noted earlier, the cornerstone of his doctrine of
the *Imago Dei* and of sexual relationships is not that man
represents deity and woman humanity, but that it is in the
interrelation of male and female that the image of God resides. He
criticizes Brunner for enunciating a phenomenology of the sexes,
which 'cannot be stated in such a way that probably every third
man and certainly every second woman does not become agitated
and protest sharply against the very idea of seeing themselves in
these sketches'.[44] Since God nowhere commands man to be
objective and woman subjective, men and women should not be
enslaved to preconceived ideas but allow the divine command to
tell them in the 'here and now' what is specific to their masculine
and feminine nature.[45] Moreover, Barth concurs with the tenet
that it was when the human–divine relationship was distorted
that human sexuality floundered and the 'battle of the sexes'
commenced.[46]

When these statements are compared with those endorsing
man's role as 'head' and 'initiator', the outgoing, dominant
partner, it is hard to avoid the conclusion that Barth accepts in
one place what he denounces in another. He would have stayed
closer to the scriptural approach had he better heeded his own
advice that sexual typologies 'may sometimes be ventured as
hypotheses, but cannot be represented as knowledge or dogma
because real man and real woman are far too complex and
contradictory to be summed up in portrayals of this nature'.[47] As
it is, his proviso that since we cannot define what it means to say
that 'man is the head of woman' the issue is 'better left unre-
solved' simply opens the way for the false dogmatism that he
attacks and makes him vulnerable to being misquoted by parti-
sans on both sides of the debate.

Similar discrepancies mar the writing of Brunner on this
subject. Like Barth, he appears at times as a staunch advocate of
the sexual stereotyping in which the male is dominant and
primary, the female submissive and passive. 'Woman is not only

physically different from man, she is also different in soul and spirit.'[48] The sex difference is said to penetrate and determine the whole of human existence. This renders woman more suited to persevering, adapting and adorning, since her nature is receptive rather than productive, directed inwards, quietly retentive rather than enquiring.[49] Man is better suited to leadership, headship, and roles which exhibit his objectivity and superordination. Moreover, although both man and woman are sinners, 'they are sinners in different ways'.[50]

At other times, however, Brunner cautions reserve in the acceptance of such theories of sex types.[51] He admits that many of these theories are due to 'conditioning'. Undermining his own statement that 'the woman's mind is less creative than that of man', he concedes that man has hindered the free development of the female mind, shaping woman according to his desire of what she should be.[52] Undermining his own assertion that man is the head of woman, he announces that 'a true marriage is only possible where the wife is in every way equal to the husband in independence and responsibility'. Undermining his elucidations of the differences between the sexes which affect even our sinfulness and our spirituality, he writes: 'We find no trace – not the faintest – in the Scriptures of the idea that in our relation to God there is any difference at all between the two sexes.'[53] In the light of all this, Tavard's assessment seems all too apt: 'Emil Brunner's approach to the question of womanhood is disconcerting, beset with paradoxes or contradictions.'[54]

Genesis 2–3 – Conclusions

How, then, may Genesis 2–3 be used correctly in the formulation of Christian doctrine regarding human sexuality and male/female roles? This chapter has highlighted several of the misconceptions and misreadings of the text which have exerted considerable influence in the Church for hundreds of years. The weight of patristic and medieval theological opinion regarded women as inferior beings. Contemporary Christians with a personal predilection for a view of woman as inherently inferior or subordinate to man claim the support of Scripture and tradition for their beliefs, ignoring the fact that fathers and reformers frequently projected their own suppositions on to Genesis.

In most other areas where conclusions of earlier scholars appear to have been culturally conditioned or determined by private presuppositions, these conclusions are now treated with a necessary degree of reserve. Generally, discerning scholars scrutinize patristic and medieval remarks carefully before endorsing them. Yet with regard to the question of scriptural teaching on woman's position, there is a disconcerting degree of uncritical acceptance of dubious conclusions. Women's ordination is ruled 'out of court' on the basis of scriptural interpretations that have been formulated in strange disregard of otherwise highly regarded principles of biblical criticism.

Clearly, the problem of the use of Scripture in the debate about women's ministry is an integral part of the wider issue of biblical interpretation. In theory, it is agreed that there should be applied to the subject of 'woman and the Bible' the same level of impartiality and open-mindedness, of scholarly care and critical attention which should be devoted to any other exegetical or hermeneutical problem. In practice, faulty exegesis is often perpetuated by modern scholars who employ scriptural texts to support partisan views of woman's status before God and in the Church.

The analysis of Genesis 2–3 made by Frazer summarizes the ideas of many people – feminist and anti-feminist alike – about Old Testament teaching on women. The author of the J narrative, writes Frazer,

> hardly attempts to hide his deep contempt for women. The lateness of her creation, and the irregular and undignified manner of it – made out of a piece of her lord and master, after all the lower animals had been created in a regular and decent manner – sufficiently mark the low opinion he held of her nature; and in the sequel his misogynism, as we may fairly call it, takes a still darker tinge, when he ascribes all the misfortunes and sorrows of the human race to the credulous folly and unbridled appetite of its first mother.[55]

I have endeavoured to show that, at each point, such an analysis fails to appreciate the nature and purpose of the J account. In its place, I would offer the following conclusions.

First, the Yahwistic Creation narrative, like the Priestly account, maintains throughout *a positive attitude towards sexuality*

and sexual polarity. Genesis 1 and 2 stress that sexual distinctiveness was not itself a result of sin, as some of the fathers suggested,
but was laid down by God in the creation of the world.

Second, Genesis 2–3 maintains throughout a thoroughly *positive attitude towards female* (as well as male) *sexuality*. Neither the
timing nor the manner of the male's creation renders him
superior to the female. There is no note of authoritarianism in the
man's words of 2.23, only a joyful cry of recognition that it is
from the one flesh of humanity that male and female take their
meaning and personhood. There is no hint of subordinationism
in the *ʿēzer kᵉnegdō* and the 'Adam's rib' concepts, only a striking
expression of woman's standing as an indispensable counterpart
of the same nature and substance as man, so that they can provide
one another with the companionship for which no animal substitute would suffice. There is no notion that woman's sin is greater
than man's, her nature weaker or less valuable to God.

Third, Genesis maintains *a negative attitude towards sexual
polarization*, and *the creation ideal contains no blueprint for sex
stereotyping*. Those who discuss the biological and psychological
differentiation of masculine and feminine, or who believe that
'masculine psychology is completely different from the feminine',
cannot legitimately claim the support of Genesis for their
hypotheses. Nor, again, is D. Davies justified in drawing his
anthropological argument against women's ordination to the
priesthood from Genesis and other biblical texts. He declares
that:

> The Church, as the Christian community, should demonstrate
> maleness in authority and femaleness in loving care and ser-
> vice, and these phenomena must be seen to exist in the father
> and minister, as symbolising one pole of the personality conti-
> nuum, and in the mother and woman, who visits the sick, cares
> for the needy and teaches the children, as the other.[56]

This 'job description', however, not only distorts the scriptural
ideal of Christian service by over-identifying the minister with
the remote, bureaucratic authority figure; it also forces 'maleness'
and 'femaleness' into false categories. It is unscriptural and
erroneous to depreciate motherhood, as many feminists have
done; but it is equally unscriptural and erroneous to restrict
woman's contribution to Church and society to the realm of

childbearing and homemaking. Why should a woman not exercise the ministerial authority of word and sacrament as well as loving care, and a man combine tender concern for the sick and the young with other, more 'typically masculine', qualities of leadership?

There is no general agreement among psychologists and anthropologists about what is transtemporally, typically 'male' and 'female', and Genesis provides no such definitive comment here. Chapters 2–3 acknowledge the societal conventions of the ancient world regarding male and female, and the judgement in 3.16 contains a notable aetiological element, an attempt to explain what had caused things to be as they were. The Yahwist sees Israelite society as sin has warped it, a social order which accorded woman an inferior status and often rendered her the chattel of her husband. There is no tirade against this state of affairs here, but neither is it portrayed as adhering to a divine prototype for the right relations of the sexes.

Fourth, in Genesis 3 *female subordination is shown to be a consequence of sexual polarization and a result of sin*. It is Genesis 2, not 3.16, which represents the Creator's intention. God designed male and female to be suitable partners, peers, for each other; that woman was often the object of man's arbitrary dominance is here ascribed to human interference with a higher design (cf. Matt. 19.8). The Yahwist 'was sensitive enough to regard this order ... as a dis-order that derived from human mismanagement rather than from a divinely decreed ideal'.[57]

It is quite unnecessary to adhere to a dogma of 'the Fall' as a once-and-for-all historical event which occurred hundreds of years ago in order to share the Yahwist's belief that it was human disobedience to the divine will which initiated the struggle for power between the sexes. God is eternally Creator; he is eternally making man and woman and holding them in being. And, just as 'Creation' is an eternal activity, so 'Fall' is an ingredient of every moment of this world's existence. Outside Christ, man and woman fall into the perennial failure to become what God desires them to be.[58]

It is this 'fallenness' which distorts, and perpetuates the distortion, of the relation between men and women – a disequilibrium which manifests itself even in the efforts of feminists and anti-feminists to manipulate scriptural texts to prove a point.

Humanity brings the disaster of distorted relationships upon itself, as part of the nemesis of sin. Thus, God's words in 3.16 are descriptive, not causative or prescriptive (compare Isa. 6.9ff). As Trible explains fallen relationships between man and woman: 'His supremacy is neither a divine right nor a male prerogative. Her subordination is neither a divine decree nor the female destiny. Both their positions result from shared disobedience. God describes this consequence but does not prescribe it as punishment.'[59]

Genesis 3, then, shows in a nutshell the turning bad of what God made good: *corruptio optimi pessima*. Sexuality, created good in principle, has become corrupted through self-seeking. Genesis 2.18, 21–5 manifests the grace of sexuality; Genesis 3.12–21, the sin of sexism. Man and woman no longer co-ordinate because the anchor of true order – obedience to and right relationship with God – has been jettisoned.

Fifth, contrary to much popular opinion, *Genesis does not declare that female subordination is a necessary concomitant of sexual distinctiveness*. A 'divine plan of creation' in which man would be the head of the woman is not apparent. Genesis shows that the ideal expression of sexual distinctiveness is not the hierarchical model of the man–woman relationship but mutual submission and dependence, partnership and respect. According to the creation ordinance, writes Jewett, 'man and woman are properly related when they accept each other as equals whose difference is mutually complementary in all spheres of life and human endeavour'.[60]

The Yahwist and the Priestly writer both reveal man and woman to share identical humanness, an equal dignity and a common task. In view of the many important variations between Genesis 1 and 2, this agreement regarding the male–female relationship is all the more significant. In the beginning, man and woman are created alike in the image of God; they owe an equal and independent obedience to their Creator, have an equal claim upon one another, and are possessed of an equal authority over the rest of creation. In the light of the Fall, male and female are still equal in nature and value before God: he provides garments for both partners in the sinful couple, for neither is spiritually, mentally or physically superior to the other in his sight (3.21). But man and woman are no longer equal in each other's eyes, and woman becomes vulnerable to abuse by man as he rules over her instead of sharing with her mankind's authority as God's viceregent in the world.

In summary, then, the Genesis Creation and Fall passages are misused if they are called upon as biblical examples of the depreciation of sexuality or of womanhood. According to these texts, it is human sinfulness which initiates and maintains prejudice and inequality between the sexes. By contrast, Genesis bears witness that in no way was woman's status and function intended by the Creator to be subordinate or secondary or inferior to that of man. Moreover, Genesis certainly does not outline a creation ordinance according to which sexual differences signify something about woman's unsuitability for ordained ministry. It must be concluded, therefore, that the Creation and Fall texts may not be used as scriptural 'evidence' against the ordination of women in the Christian Church.

NOTES

1. E. F. Brown, *The Pastoral Epistles* (London 1917), p. 20.
2. S. Dowell and L. Hurcombe, *Dispossessed Daughters of Eve* (London 1981), p. 25; cf. M. Daly, *The Church and the Second Sex* (London 1968), pp. 34ff.
3. Aquinas, *S. Th.*, Ia.92.2. 'The woman was rightly formed from the man, as her origin and chief.'
4. Clark, *Man and Woman in Christ*, pp. 25, 26.
5. Trible, *God and the Rhetoric of Sexuality*, p. 80
6. Trible, 'Depatriarchalizing in Biblical Interpretation', *JAAR*, 41 (1973), pp. 37f; *God and the Rhetoric of Sexuality*, p. 141 n. 17.
7. E. Jacob, *Theology of the Old Testament* (London 1958), pp. 172–3.
8. Barth, *CD*, III.1.301.
9. W. Vogels, 'It is not good that the *Mensch* should be alone', *E et I*, 9 (1978), pp. 26–8.
10. A. C. J. Phillips, *Lower than the Angels* (Oxford 1983), pp. 23f.
11. Frazer, *Folk-lore*, p. 4; cf. Aquinas, *S. Th.*, Ia.92.2.
12. Von Rad, *Genesis*, p. 84.
13. For example, A. Richardson, *Genesis I–XI*, pp. 68–9.
14. Trible, *God and the Rhetoric of Sexuality*, p. 99; cf. Otwell, *And Sarah Laughed*, p. 18.
15. Augustine, *De Trin.*, 12.7.
16. Aquinas, *S. Th.*, Ia.92.1.

17. Packer, 'I Believe in Women's Ministry', p. 170.
18. Clark, op. cit., p. 22.
19. ibid.
20. cf. G. Carey, *I Believe in Man* (London 1977), p. 136. Note Driver's comment, *The Book of Genesis*, p. 41 n. 2.
21. Von Rad, *Genesis*, p. 82.
22. cf. Eichrodt, *Theology*, II, pp. 121–2.
23. 'Homilies on Timothy', IX, *Works of Chrysostom*, XIII, ed. P. Schaff, pp. 436ff.
24. Jewett, *Ordination*, p. 5.
25. Tertullian, '*De cultu fem.*', 1.1.1. *The Fathers of the Church*, 40, p. 117. cf. Ecclus. 25.24.
26. Bouyer, *Woman and Man with God*, p. 55.
27. Tertullian, op. cit., 1.1.1., p. 118.
28. Luther, 'Lectures on Genesis', *Luther's Works*, I, XLII, 113, 114, p. 151.
29. Phillips, op. cit., p. 25.
30. cf. S. G. F. Brandon, *Creation Legends of the Ancient Near East* (London 1963), pp. 129f; J. A. MacCulloch, 'Serpent-Worship', *ERE*, 11, pp. 403ff.
31. See, for example, F. Hvidberg, 'The Canaanitic Background of Genesis I–III', *VT*, 10 (1960), pp. 289ff.
32. Aquinas, *S. Th.*, Ia.91.1.
33. Clark, op. cit., pp. 23, 27, 32.
34. Tertullian, op. cit., I.I.1–2 (pp. 117–18).
35. P. D. Miller, 'Genesis I–XI', p. 48, n. 49.
36. Sapp, op. cit., p. 13.
37. Trible, op. cit., p. 132.
38. H. H. Wolff, *Anthropology of the Old Testament*, p. 172.
39. Trible, op. cit., p. 135.
40. A. B. Ulanov, *The Feminine*, pp. 296–7; cf. 301–3.
41. Barth, *CD*, III.4.169–70.
42. *CD*, III.2.297.
43. *CD*, III.2.287.
44. *CD*, III.4.152–3; cf. Brunner, *Man in Revolt*, p. 358.
45. *CD*, III.2.287.
46. *CD*, III.1.310f.
47. *CD*, III.2.287.
48. Brunner, *The Divine Imperative*, p. 374.
49. *Man in Revolt*, pp. 352, 358ff.
50. ibid., pp. 353, 359.
51. ibid., p. 354.
52. *The Divine Imperative*, p. 375; *Man in Revolt*, pp. 356, 355.

53. *The Divine Imperative*, pp. 379, 374.
54. Tavard, *Woman*, p. 181.
55. Frazer, op. cit., p. 5.
56. D. Davies, 'An Anthropological Perspective', *Why Not?*, p. 147.
57. Vawter, *On Genesis*, p. 85.
58. cf. Westermann, *What Does the Old Testament Say About God?*, pp. 41, 54; A. S. Peacocke, *Creation and the World of Science*, pp. 191–2.
59. Trible, op. cit., p. 128.
60. Jewett, *Male and Female*, p. 14.

7
New Testament Woman and the Old Testament

In the foregoing chapters the attempt has been made to show that the Old Testament may not legitimately be used as ammunition in the argument against the ordination of women to Christian priesthood and episcopate. The Old Testament, however, is only part of the whole regarded by the Church as 'Holy Scripture' and reckoned as authoritative in matters of faith and doctrine. Serious problems arise when, having decided that the Old Testament does not enunciate female subordination as God's original intention, we are confronted by an apparent appeal from a New Testament writer to the Old Testament creation ordinance in support of female subordination. In this chapter, therefore, we must turn our attention to the use of the Old Testament in the New with reference to the role of women.

According to the traditional view, God's will for the relation between male and female is described in the Bible in terms of a sexual hierarchy: the man *qua* man is the 'head' of the woman, and the woman *qua* woman is subordinate to the man. This hierarchy is certainly manifested in Old Testament society; and even if modern exegesis finds this to be characteristic of fallen society (cf. Gen. 3.16) and not of God's original plan for partnership (cf. Gen. 1.26; 2.18), it is objected that 'neither Jewish nor Christian tradition' has 'read the creation story to say that women will one day be equal to men'.[1] Advocates of the continuance of female subordination in the redeemed community declare that Paul and other New Testament writers believed the sexual hierarchy to be an integral and abiding part of the order of creation. It is said, therefore, that the Church should read the Creation narratives from the New Testament perspective and not from that of so-called 'liberationist' interpreters of Genesis. To ordain women is to disobey both the New Testament and the New Testament's understanding of the Old Testament on the subject of woman's 'rightful' place. According to this view, the New Testament 'impresses upon woman her duty of being under

obedience and withholds from her the office of word and proclamation in the assemblies of the congregation'.[2]

In recent years this position has come under heavy attack. It is
questioned not just by 'extremists' but also by scholars who sense
that ideas about the inferiority of woman within the created order
may have come less from Paul himself than from misinterpretations of Genesis by Jewish, patristic and medieval theologians,
which were then read back into Paul's writing. Thus, a probe
must be made beneath the superficial readings to look closely at
Paul's use of the Old Testament, particularly in such passages as
1 Corinthians 11. An attempt must be made to discover what the
Apostle did believe about the place of women in the order of
creation and whether his views were derived from the Old
Testament directly or via Jewish exegesis. Accredited Pauline
passages must be compared with the statements of other New
Testament writers and it must be asked why their use of the Old
Testament differs from Paul's. Only when we have reached some
conclusions to these complex questions can we begin to consider
how far New Testament use of the Old Testament should
continue to influence and be incorporated into twentieth-century
Christian exegesis of Scripture.

1 Corinthians 11.2–16

Controversy rages over the correct exegesis of 1 Corinthians
11.2–16. The traditional view is that Paul intended to express his
belief, derived from the Old Testament and reinforced by Christian insights, that man is 'head' over woman – a state of affairs
which woman must acknowledge by veiling herself at public
worship. Moreover, it is presupposed that this 'headship' automatically entails woman's subordination to man and his God-
given prerogative to exercise authority, to be 'supreme', over
her. Increasingly and on several counts modern scholars are
questioning this interpretation. It is necessary, therefore, to re-
examine significant verses from the passage, to discuss the
premises upon which the traditional view has been based and,
where appropriate, to offer alternative interpretations.

In the first place, attention must be given to the idea of
hierarchical headship which many people have professed to find in
verse 3: 'But I want you to know that the head of every man is

Christ, the head of a woman is the man, and the head of Christ is
God.' On a superficial reading, this does seem to set forth the
hierarchical order: God, Christ, man, woman. This is said to
indicate that male priority over female in the created order is the
theological basis upon which Paul constructs his argument that
women should be veiled at worship so as to manifest their proper
place in the divine scheme of things. Many commentators have
taken the verse in this sense, presupposing that the term *kephalē*,
'head', denotes one who has authority over another.

One of the major problems surrounding the elucidation of 1
Corinthians 11 is uncertainty about the meaning and application
of some of the vocabulary. S. Bedale initiated a reappraisal of
verse 3, based upon an examination of the term *kephalē*. Bedale
has shown that the idea of a descending hierarchical order is
weakened once it is acknowledged that *kephalē* used to signify
'source' and not 'superior rank' in pre-biblical Greek.[3] C. K.
Barrett takes up Bedale's point; he thinks that the idea that verse
3 refers to man as origin of woman's being, and not to man as
authoritative head over woman, is also suggested by the fact that
Paul does not pronounce man as 'lord' (*kurios*) of woman.[4] The
correctness of interpreting *kephalē* as 'source' or origin is also
indicated when verse 3 is compared with verse 8 – 'for man was
not made from woman, but woman from man' – which reiterates
the idea that woman was derived from man.

Thus, even if (as seems probable) Paul is taking Genesis 2.21–
23 in a literal sense, and is assigning temporal priority to the
male's creation, this does not mean that he was thereby assigning
the female to an inferior and subordinate position. As it was
stated in Chapter 6 the Yahwist himself is most unlikely to have
intended a theory of woman's subordination to be built upon the
relative priority of man's creation. 'Derivedness' does not necessarily imply subordination.[5]

Second, while the notion that 1 Corinthians 11 teaches the
hierarchical headship of man over woman can be countered, what
assessment is to be made of the claim that the passage embodies
Paul's belief that woman must be subordinate to man since *she
does not directly represent the Image of God*? In 1 Corinthians 11.7
there are overtones of Genesis 1.26f: 'man' (*anēr*) is 'the image
and glory of God'. But Genesis 1.26f appears to have been taken
in the light of an androcentric interpretation of Genesis 2.18f to

suggest that it was the male (*anēr*, *'īš*), not Mankind, male and female (*anthrōpos*, *'ādām*), who was made in the *Imago Dei*. Again, in verse 9, Paul draws upon the *'ēzer k^enegdo* idea from Genesis 2.18 in a way which apparently disregards (what I have maintained to be) the real sense of the verse, namely that man and woman are created for a relationship of mutuality and equality. Instead, the Apostle seems to favour the interpretation (which quickly became prevalent) that woman was created solely for the sake of man to serve him in obedience and submission.

These verses prompt several people to quote Paul as declaring that it is the male prerogative to exercise dominion over the rest of creation including woman, and to represent the deity. Goudge commented on verse 7, that 'here may be the special thought, that man represents God, even in His sovereignty, while woman does not'.[6] Beckwith is among more recent writers who also find this 'special thought' conveyed through Paul's use of the Genesis material. Disagreeing with the belief that woman's subjugation is part of fallen existence (cf. Gen. 3.16) and is therefore abrogated in Christ, Beckwith sees 1 Corinthians 11 as confirming that female subordination is part of the divine order for society, because woman receives the image of God indirectly. 'The subordination of the woman is not argued from her sentence at the Fall, but from the manner of her very creation'.[7]

There is no doubt that in verse 7 Paul makes a distinction between man and woman which is not found in Genesis 1.26f but which is part of the Jewish interpretation of that passage. Like the rabbis, Paul contrasts the sexes as to *doxa* (glory) – the glory of God being confined to man and integral to his authority over the rest of creation. Writers like Tavard believe that Paul was influenced in his handling of the Genesis material by a common Jewish exegetical tradition.[8] Furthermore, it was a tradition which was based upon faulty exegesis of Genesis. Caird shows that the whole argument depends on a misquotation of Scripture which is without excuse in Greek. In Genesis 1.27, 'it is not man the male but man the human being who was made in the image of God, so that the whole scriptural argument for the subjection of women falls to the ground'.[9] Powerful criticisms, then, have been levelled against the treatment of Genesis and the attitude towards women manifested here. It is necessary, therefore, to relate these verses to the whole theme of the passage in order to ascertain whether or not they form a coherent part of Paul's teaching on woman.

Popular opinion, supported by (or derived from) certain commentators, assumes that *the theme* of 1 Corinthians 11.2–16 is Paul's indignation at 'the scandal of unveiled women'. The assumption is also that the Apostle's purpose in writing is to command the strident female to resume her veil – the symbol of her subordinate position in the created order. Verse 10 is regarded as the apex of Paul's case: 'That is why a woman ought to have a veil on her head, because of the angels.' This verse, however is elliptical, and many scholars are now unconvinced that it – and, indeed, the whole passage – means what popular opinion has taken it to mean. It is beyond the scope of this study to probe into every aspect of the problem; the question to be considered here is this: to what extent was Paul's teaching governed by contemporary attitudes towards women and Jewish exegesis of Genesis?[10]

It is my view that while Jewish presuppositions certainly form the background of Paul's thinking about the place of women, Paul has not simply adopted and 'Christianized' them. In 1 Corinthians 11.2–16 Paul does not write about woman's status and function at worship in the same way as a rabbi would have done. He could not merely ignore the ideas which formed part of his contemporary world-view. But instead of endorsing them and making them the fundamental positive axioms of his own argument, he used them as a foil against which woman's new status in Christ could be contrasted.

This becomes clear, I believe, when detailed discussions about the meaning of particular words and the correct exposition of minutiae are set on one side for a moment, and an overview is taken of the import of the passage as a whole. Paul's main point is *not* to subordinate Christian women. Many of those who have extracted verses from this text and employed them in support of the argument against women's ordination, have obscured the crucial factor that, on the evidence of 1 Corinthians 11.2–16 itself, women were able to pray and prophesy in the Christian assembly. If 'Paul had thought it wrong for them to do this he would certainly not have wasted time in discussing what, in these circumstances, they should do with their heads; he would simply have forbidden the practice'.[11] On the contrary, however, the

Apostle permits something which constituted an 'astounding' contrast to woman's position in the synagogue. Praying aloud and prophesying in public were totally incompatible with female status in the orthodox Judaism of Paul's day. Thus, Paul may well have penned these verses in response to the need felt by thoughtful Christians for women to convey their new status to the angels who watched for breaches of law. 'The guardians of an outmoded tradition had to be shown that things had changed.'[12]

So greatly does this line of interpretation deviate from the traditional one that the evidence in its favour must be given in more detail. M. Hooker was the first significant advocate of the ambitious revision of the traditional interpretation of 1 Corinthians 11. Her thesis centres upon the meaning of *exousia* in 1 Corinthians 11.10. Traditionally, translators have rendered *exousia* as 'veil' taking the veil as the sign that women were submitting to the authority of man and God, according to Jewish custom. Hooker, however, insists that *exousia* means what it says: 'authority'; nor does it refer to the man's authority over the woman, symbolized in her headcovering, but to her own authority to pray and prophesy in the new order of the Christian community. 'Although the differences of creation remain, and are reflected in the differences of dress, it is nevertheless true that in relation to God "There is neither male nor female; for you are all one in Christ Jesus."' Far from subjugating the Christian female to male domination, Paul shows her that in Christ she has a new status and authority.[13]

After reviewing the evidence, it seems to me that Hooker has resolved the hitherto unexplained puzzle surrounding the use of *exousia* in 1 Corinthians 11. Why would Paul have written *exousia* if he meant *hupotagē*, 'subjection'? Other occurrences of the word *exousia* in the Pauline correspondence illustrate that the Apostle normally used it to convey the idea of 'control' (RSV; RV: 'power' – 1 Cor. 7.37), 'liberty' (1 Cor. 8.9), 'right' (1 Cor. 9.4, 5, 6, 12, 18; cf. Rom. 9.21; 2 Thes, 3.9), 'authority' (1 Cor. 15.24; 1 Cor. 10.8; 13.10; cf. Rom. 13.1, 2, 3; cf. Col. 1.16; 2.10; Eph. 1.21). There is no plausible reason why it should be presupposed that in 1 Corinthians 11.10 Paul used the word in an abnormal sense.

Some commentators insist that the context makes clear that Paul intended to endorse woman's subordination. What, then, is to be made of verses 11–12 – themselves part of the context – which stress the interdependence of man and woman 'in the Lord'? Was Paul himself unconvinced by the arguments for women's subordination which, supposedly, he had enunciated in verses 8–10, so that in verses 11–12 he made a volte-face, breaking the thread of the logical development of the argument? Or do verses 11–12 suggest that the previous statements are misread if they are taken as the full expression of the Christian understanding of woman's status and functions?

I believe that both contextual and thematic considerations confirm that verses 11–12 are not a parenthesis but express Paul's own view of the relationship between man and woman in Christ. They show that Paul did not simply reiterate contemporary notions. Although pre-Christian Jewish ideas affected the way in which Paul presented his beliefs, their influence did not induce the Apostle to make a blatant denial of the freedom of a Christian woman.

Thus Hooker's exegesis of 1 Corinthians 11.10 leads naturally into verses 11–12: 'Nevertheless, neither is woman without man nor man without woman in the Lord; for as the woman is of the man, so also is the man through the woman; and all things are of God'. This is the theological climax of Paul's argument. 'Nevertheless' (*plēn*), introduces the Christian corrective to the rabbinic understanding of Genesis 2.18–22 (vv.8–9). The Greek of the strophe is terse, but scholars like Scroggs have no doubt that Paul is affirming the equality and mutual dependence of men and women in the Church, with God as the ultimate *kephalē* of all: 'The climax of the midrash shows man and woman reunited in mutual dependence on each other and in mutual subjection to God ... In the eschatological community, where liberation reigns, woman no longer stands chained to the subordinate roles of the old creation.'[14]

One further point must be discussed here to clarify the exposition of Paul's understanding of the place of woman in the old and the new order as he expresses this in 1 Corinthians 11.2–16. If woman has new freedom in the eschatological community to be equal to man, why is it her headcovering that represents her new authority under the new dispensation to do the things which formerly had not been permitted her? The Jewish custom regarding the veiling of women has already been mentioned. Yet there is much debate amongst New Testament exegetes as to whether Paul was actually writing about veiling or about the arrangement of hair during worship. The Greek word *kalumma*, 'covering', 'veil' nowhere occurs, and since v.15 clearly refers to 'long hair', *komē*, it seems most likely that Paul is speaking about hair.

According to E. S. Fiorenza, closer attention to this detail reveals the key to the problem. She demonstrates that dishevelled hair was characteristic of the ecstatic worship of oriental divinities. In the Isis cult, for instance women wore their hair unbound, while the male initiates had their hair shaven. Naturally, Paul would have wanted to keep Christian worship free from such similarities with orgiastic, frenzied rituals. Furthermore, Fiorenza draws attention to a 'more sinister' association with long hair in a Jewish Christian context: loose hair continued to be a sign of uncleanness even to Paul's day (cf. Num. 5.18 LXX; Lev. 13.45 LXX; contrast Jdt. 10.3, 16.8). 'As Paul argues, since the angels are present in the pneumatic worship service ... women should not worship as cultically unclean persons by letting their hair down but should pin it up as a sign both of their spiritual power and of control over their heads.'[15]

A further highly plausible suggestion is offered by Scroggs. He argues that Paul did not wish any value-judgements to be drawn on the basis of sexual distinctions. What concerned the Apostle was that Christians should adhere to accepted customs for distinguishing between the sexes in order to dissociate Christian worship from spurious cults which encouraged sexual perversions. Scroggs thinks that Paul's 'hidden agenda' for this passage was 'his fear of homosexuality'.[16] Murphy-O'Connor's researches also lead him to believe that long, styled hair on men was associated with homosexuality, whilst short hair could mark a woman out as a lesbian.[17]

The theme of 1 Corinthians 11.2–16, then, concerns not just 'disorderly women', but the appearance of both men and women at worship. Paul directs his multi-pronged argument against hair arrangements which tended to blur the distinction between the sexes. Women's new power and equality under Christ is related to her being fully woman (vv.10–12). She did not have to abandon her femininity and become 'masculine' (as in later Gnostic schema) to be acceptable in God's sight. As Murphy-O'Connor puts it, 'new status is accorded to woman, not to an ambiguous being whose "unfeminine" hair-do was an affront to generally accepted conventions. Hence, in so far as her way of doing her hair clearly defines her sex, it becomes a symbol of the authority she enjoys (v.10).'[18] Thus, since headdress and hair provided traditional Jewish means of distinguishing between women and men, discussion of the topic would have come as no surprise to Paul's first-century readers.[19]

The subject-matter of 1 Corinthians 11.2–16 covers such perennially sensitive issues as homosexuality, which also involves what was, at the time, the highly emotive topic of hair-arrangements. Entering this potentially explosive area, it is understandable that Paul's logic should become rather strained in places, and that he should occasionally rely upon traditionally accepted dictums and conventional Jewish wisdom. Throughout the passage, the complex combination of Old Testament, Jewish and early Christian ideas makes Paul's argument hard to decipher. In vv.7–9 especially, Genesis is used in Jewish fashion. Superficially, this creates the impression that Paul is simply reiterating the popular notion that woman is not the *Imago Dei*, or at least not to the same degree as man. I have maintained that when these verses are taken in the context of the whole passage and balanced against the statements of vv.11–12, it becomes clear that Paul is not intending to affirm the old view that women are (spiritually) inferior to men and therefore unfit to lead worship. In fact, Paul's insistence that male and female adhere to contemporary custom regarding what is 'proper' for delineating the sexes was designed to protect woman's new status in Christ. If this custom was not followed, then, given the sexual mores of the day, the Church would be threatened with disgrace and Church leaders might react (and, I shall argue later, did react) by withdrawing much of woman's new-found freedom.

1 Corinthians 11.2–16, then, undoubtedly presents exegetes with an opaque passage, and it is a section of Scripture which has raised more problems than it has solved for theologians who endeavour to use it in formulating modern doctrine. The fact that divergent interpretations are still forthcoming prevents us from declaring that all is now clear. Yet Caird is confident that it may safely be asserted that the passage has been 'evacuated for ever of any suggestion of the subordination of women'. Nothing must be allowed to detract from Paul's 'unambiguous statement that "in

Christ's fellowship woman is as essential to man as man to woman" (v.11)'.[20] It must now be asked how far this assessment of Paul's use of the Old Testament in his teaching about woman's nature and place is substantiated elsewhere in the New Testament.

1 Corinthians 14.33–6

The tenet that Paul did not appeal to the Old Testament to enforce the subordination of Christian women seems to be shattered in 1 Corinthians 14.33–6, 'The women' are not permitted to speak *(lalein)* 'in the churches', but should be subordinate *(hypotassesthōsan)* 'as indeed the law says'. 'As the law says' – which law? 'The law' *(nomos)*, can mean so much that exegetes are divided about whether the reference is to Holy Scripture in general or to a particular Old Testament injunction, and if so, to which injunction. The common assumption is that 1 Corinthians 14.34 refers to Genesis 3.16, although female subordination was taken for granted throughout much of the Old Testament and the Jewish oral law.

If the author of 1 Corinthians 14.33–6 was drawing upon Genesis 3.16 then he was reapplying in a Christian context an ordinance which, I have maintained, belonged to the conditions of 'fallen society' and no longer pertained to the status of woman in the redeemed community. Herein, certain scholars would find grounds to dispute my interpretation. Beckwith finds it noteworthy that Paul does not consider Eve's sentence to have been abrogated by Christ's redemption. 'This is doubtless because of his belief that female subordination did not begin at the Fall, but was only reinforced then.' In other words according to Paul's reading of the Old Testament, female subordination goes back to creation itself and extends throughout the whole gamut of male-female relations, not simply, Beckwith stresses, to those between husband and wife.[21] Furthermore, as Clark understands the passage, 'Paul instructs the woman to be silent because they are women, not because they are disorderly ... Paul is concerned with the subordination that is specifically part of being woman.'[22] Must we then agree with Whiteley's verdict?

It would appear that, according to even the least anti-feminist interpretation of 1 Corinthians which is at all plausible, St Paul did believe that women were inferior in status because of their sex, in addition to being functionally subordinate in marriage. Though the sex distinction no longer existed in Christ (Gal. 3.28) it was still important as part of the 'natural order'.[23]

Remarks such as these smooth over the fact that 1 Corinthians 14.33–6 is surrounded by a morass of some of the most intractable types of problem familiar to biblical study. First, there are textual difficulties and it is hotly debated whether or not these verses are authentically Pauline. Second, there are several exegetical problems arising from obscure references and uncertain vocabulary. Third, there are inconsistencies, in theology and practice, with other New Testament data.

(i) Regarding the *authenticity* issue, the suggestion that the passage is a non-Pauline interpolation made at a time when good order was thought more important than the freedom of the spirit, has much to be said for it.[24] Verse 33a links up well with verse 36, and the language of the intervening verses can be explained as a gloss. But, as Barrett admits, 'the textual evidence is not quite strong enough' to make this view compelling.[25] Furthermore, even if 1 Corinthians 14.33b–35 were a non-Pauline gloss, there is still the problem that it belongs to a document received by the Church as authoritative; it cannot simply be 'discarded'.

(ii) Having determined that the passage demands attention (even if it is non-Pauline), I turn to problems of *reference and vocabulary*. The opaque allusion to 'the law' has already been discussed; another crucial question is whether or not the writer referred only to married women. Moffatt, for example, thinks that the writer believed that 'the subordinate position of women to their husbands in the law of Genesis (3.16) extended to worship'.[26] Fiorenza believes that 'the injunction does not pertain to all women but solely to wives of Christians'.[27] The majority of commentators would agree with Barrett that while these verses contemplate married women whose husbands are Christians, '*a fortiori*, unmarried women and the wives of unbelievers will not speak in the assembly'.[28] Yet the picture is not sufficiently clear for anyone to be dogmatic here.

Again, there is uncertainty over the precise meaning of *lalein* in verse 34. In classical Greek the verb could bear the meaning 'to chatter'; therefore some commentators suggest that the inconsistency between 1 Corinthians 14.34 and 11.5 is removed if it is recognized that *lalein* does not refer to praying and prophesying but to uninspired discussion, or to gossip. 1 Corinthians 14.33–6 would then represent Paul's endeavours to restore order in a particular situation where women (who would not have received the same 'general education' as their menfolk and who were also probably ill-informed in 'Christian doctrine') had become very loquacious. The weakness of this interpretation, however, is that it rests upon taking *lalein* as 'to chatter', whereas in the New Testament generally and in Paul specifically, the verb normally does not have this meaning. Rather is is used throughout Chapter 14 (vv.2, 3, 4, 5, 6, 9, 11, 13, 18, 19, 21, 23, 27, 28, 29, 39) in the sense of inspired speech. As Barrett concludes, 'it is not impossible that Paul should now use it in a new sense (promptly reverting to the old in v.39), but it is unlikely'.[29]

(iii) The problem of *inconsistency* must now be considered. There is 'practical' inconsistency between the command that women should be silent in 1 Corinthians 14.34–5 and 1 Corinthians 11.5 where Paul clearly assumes that women will pray and prophesy (not to mention the many other New Testament references to women taking an active part in the Christian community without any impression that they were silent or subordinate). And there is 'theological' inconsistency in that the endorsement of female subordination in 1 Corinthians 14 seems to take no account of the renewal and liberation of the created order in Christ enunciated in such verses as Galatians 3.28 and 1 Corinthians 11.11–12.

Frequent attempts are made to account for these inconsistencies on the grounds of the non-Pauline authorship of 1 Corinthians 14.33–6. It is my belief, however, that whether the author was Paul himself or someone else, his words should be described as a reaction against various pressures which threatened to bring disorder and disgrace to the Church. This does not entail laying stress upon *lalein* meaning 'to chatter'; rather it takes seriously the context of the passage in the Corinthian correspondence. In chapters 11–14, as Fiorenza puts it: 'Paul seeks to persuade the Corinthians that decency and order should be more highly esteemed than the spiritual status and exercise of individual pneumatic inspiration . . . 14.26–36 is best understood as a church order with rules for glossolalists (vv.27ff), prophets (vv.29–33), and wives (vv.34–6).'[30] We do not possess sufficient background information to make categorical pronouncements, but it is likely that a group of female 'enthusiasts' had been over-asserting their new status in Christ. Such 'unedifying' behaviour was dangerous enough in a man (cf. v.26, 37f); it was disgraceful (v.35) in a woman in a society where the only female voices to be raised in public were those of debauched courtesans or cult fanatics. It must be recalled that in the synagogue a woman could neither read aloud nor speak, expound nor teach, could not even study the Torah. The traditional Roman sentiment against matrons speaking in public must also be remembered.[31] It is hardly surprising then that 'Paul' reacted to the Corinthian situation by retreating into a traditionally Jewish understanding of the place of women as taught by 'the law'.

Thus, in 1 Corinthians 14, as in the subordinationist verses 7–9 of 1 Corinthians 11, the statements are based upon contemporary cultural and Jewish ideas rather than on specifically 'Christian' principles. As Barrett points out, the appeal to 'the law' (*nomos*) (which appears in such verses as 1 Cor. 14.21; Rom. 3.19; John 10.34, 12.34, 15.25, as well as 1 Cor. 14.34) is 'rabbinic'.[32] It is significant that in 1 Corinthians 14.35, as at 11.13f, Paul appeals not only to the Old Testament but also to the common feeling of mankind. This suggests that the influence of background and culture upon him at that moment was intense.

I believe that to claim that 'Paul' in 1 Corinthians 14.33–6 was deliberately using a reference from the Old Testament to prove the inferior status of women, or to demonstrate that women must be silent just because they are women, is to misrepresent the aim of the passage. Paul's major concern was not so much the behaviour of women *qua* women (nor of men *qua* men) as the protection of the Christian community so that neither the quality of its worship nor of its missionary work should be impaired. Worship, Paul believed, should be 'spiritual' (cf. Rom. 12.1), free from disruptions, particularly those of a licentious nature (cf. 1 Cor. 5.1ff). Above all: 'everything should be done decently and in order' (1 Cor. 14.40). Without this guiding principle the Christian community might be mistaken for one of the orgiastic cults and outsiders might accuse Christians of 'religious madness'; then evangelism would be greatly hindered.

In these verses in 1 Corinthians 14, then, Paul (or whoever subsequently ascribed them to him) was governed by the overriding concern not to violate the rules of propriety that were generally observed at the time. This meant that in volatile situations a woman's personal freedom 'in Christ' might have to be suspended for the sake of the Body of Christ as a whole; (compare the principle behind 1 Corinthians 9, where Paul encourages the sacrifice of personal 'rights' to avoid putting obstacles in the way of the spread of the gospel). For wives to dare to question other women's husbands or point out the 'mistakes' of their own husbands during the congregational interpretation of Scripture and prophecy was against all traditional custom and law. Thus, these verses 'seem to be Paul's application of the Jewish etiquette whereby a wife could not address any man other than her husband outside her home'.[33]

This undoubtedly caused inconsistencies with theology and practice recorded elsewhere in the New Testament. It did represent a resort to conventional Jewish exegesis of the Old Testament regarding the place of woman. Yet, for the sake of orderly worship and effective missionary outreach, Paul (perhaps unconsciously) was prepared to be somewhat 'inconsistent' and 'culturally conditioned' on occasion. He cannot have disapproved on principle of contributions made by women to Christian worship and discussion or he would not have allowed 11.5 to stand in his epistle, but 'in the interests of peace and good order he could command the women to be silent, precisely as he could give orders for a male prophet to be silent if his continued speech was likely to prove unedifying (v.30)'.[34]

1 Corinthians 14.33–6 shows that Paul was prepared to use any method – including rabbinic-style reference to the Old Testament – to ensure that the Body of Christ was not injured by those whose first priority was the gratification of personal desire for status and authority. Thus, these verses should be understood as: 'a piece of specific advice given to certain Corinthian Christians whose behaviour had created a problem for the nascent church. Paul's counsel in this instance included what he evidently believed to be a necessary and legitimate accommodation to the social norms of that time and place'.[35]

2 Corinthians 11.3 and 1 Timothy 2.11–15

But I am afraid that as the serpent deceived Eve by his

cunning, your thoughts will be led astray from a sincere and pure devotion to Christ. – 2 Corinthians 11.3.
And Adam was not deceived, but the woman was deceived and became a transgressor. – 1 Timothy 2.14.

At first sight the similarity between these two verses seems considerable. In examining Genesis 3, it was ascertained that there is no authentication here for the belief that the female is by nature weaker and more gullible than the male; yet both these New Testament verses appear to use Genesis to demonstrate that woman is more easily deceived than man. They seem to be saying that the feminine nature is particularly vulnerable to temptation and therefore, according to 1 Timothy 2.11ff, women are not fitted to exercise authority over men in the Church. On closer examination, however, I believe it becomes clear that 2 Corinthians 11.3 and 1 Timothy 2.11–15 reveal different usages of the Old Testament within the New Testament regarding the question of woman's nature and role. When 1 Timothy 2.11–15 is taken as non-Pauline (following the majority of scholars), and contrasted with Paul's own hermeneutic of the Old Testament, a change in approach is discernible: the one usage is more reliant upon popular notions and Jewish exegesis than the other.

Analysis of 1 Timothy 2.11ff indicates that its author was strongly influenced by values and practices regarding womanhood found in Hellenistic and Jewish mores. In line with contemporary practice, he wrote that woman must be silent and submissive (v.11). In legalistic terms, he forbade woman to bear rule over man (v.12) – although it should be noted that there is increasing altercation over the exact meaning of the Greek verb *authentein*, which occurs nowhere else in the New Testament and which does not seem to have had the straightforward meaning, 'to exercise authority', in contemporary usage.[36] Again, the theme of Eve's deception by the serpent figured prominently in Jewish literature, which often placed full blame for the Fall upon woman. In Jewish elaboration of the story, Eve's deception was frequently posited not in an intellectual or a spiritual sphere but on a physical, sexual level; the temptation was to unchastity, the deception consisted in seduction.[37] Similar thinking seems to lie behind the interpretation of Eve's sin which is given by the author of 1 Timothy.

The extent to which such notions influenced Paul in 2 Corinthians 11.3 and 14 is debatable. It does seem likely that Paul was aware of the idea that Satan adopted various disguises. There is a possibility that the haggadic version of the Fall story, which interpreted Eve's seduction in a sexual sense, was known to Paul. But Paul's language in 2 Corinthians 11 is intelligible on the basis of Genesis 3 alone.[38]

Certainly, the nature and purpose of the use of Genesis in 2 Corinthians 11.3 and 1 Timothy 2.11–15 are significantly different. Paul, in 2 Corinthians 11, does not refer to the Old Testament in order to show that women are inherently untrustworthy and gullible because Eve, the common mother of all, was easily beguiled by the serpent. The intention of the statement is not to comment on femininity at all, but on the Christian community as a whole. Here the image of Eve *includes both women and men,* just as elsewhere, the image of Adam includes both men and women. 'As in Adam all die' (1 Cor. 15.22), does not mean that only males are susceptible to death; nor does 2 Corinthians 11.3 mean that only women are open to deception; in each case a single gender image embraces both sexes. 1 Timothy 2.13ff, by contrast, explicitly restricts the Adam image to men and the Eve image to women so as to emphasize the priority and fidelity of man over and against woman; and both the Adam and the Eve image are interpreted and applied in Jewish fashion and according to the cultural assumptions of the day.[39] In the final section of this chapter, we must ask what accounts for these different uses of the Genesis material and for the divergent views about its implications for Christian women. Before this, however, examination must be made of another New Testament reference to an Old Testament text regarding woman's status.

Galatians 3.27–9

Genesis 1.27 declares that God created mankind (Hebrew: *'ādām;* Greek: *anthrōpos*), in his image as 'male and female' (LXX: *arsen kai thēlu*). Galatians 3.28 proclaims that in Christ there cannot be 'male and female' (*arsen kai thēlu*). Does this imply a dichotomy between the 'order of creation' and the 'order of redemption' regarding the importance of sexual differentiation? Or are we misinterpreting the Old Testament or the New Testament – or both – if we find a contradiction between them here? These questions show why Galatians 3.28 presents a crux in the consideration of the use of Scripture in the debate about woman's status and ministry in the Church. On the one hand, it is the *locus classicus* of biblical texts for those who believe that, ultimately, Scripture does not discriminate between male and female and that it is therefore wrong for the Church to perpetuate such discrimination in its ordination practice. On the other hand, this text is dismissed as insignificant by those who allege that it does not mean what 'feminists' say it means or that even if it does have a 'liberationist' tenor, it is outranked by 'subordinationist' passages. Accordingly, a re-examination of Galatians 3.28 is called for here.

The probability that Galatians 3.28 does allude to Genesis 1.27 is high. There is a significant break in the symmetry of the three pairs when *kai*, 'and', rather than *oude*, 'nor', is placed between the third pair, 'male *and* female': 'there cannot be Jew nor Greek, there cannot be slave nor free, there cannot be male and female'. This is often glossed over in translation, but it indicates to discerning readers that 'this is intended as a conscious allusion to Genesis 1.27 in the LXX'.[40]

Why, then, does Paul echo Genesis 1.27 in Galatians 3.28? It seems wise to abandon all notions that Galatians 3.28 envisages some form of androgyny or obliteration of sexual distinctions. I share the view that Paul believed that for those who are in Christ distinctions between groups remain, while *values* and *roles* built upon such distinctions are destroyed.[41] But does this mean that male and female are equal only before God – *Coram Deo* – and that this 'equality' has no practical, social consequences? This is certainly the opinion of several writers. Beckwith, for example, denies that salvation and its blessings effect any change upon the relations of the sexes; female subordination is not annulled by Christ's redeeming work.[42]

Different attempts to explain Paul's meaning in Galatians 3.27f encounter different problems. On the one hand, those who hold that these verses were intended to herald a practical change of status for Gentiles, slaves and women in the Christian community often find themselves obliged to admit that this passage seems to contradict certain other passages in the New Testament. Galatians 3.28 represents 'the great breakthrough', whereas texts

such as the *mulier taceat in ecclesia* of 1 Corinthians 14.33ff have
to be regarded as 'limited' – in vision and in application. On the
other hand, those who argue that the statement about 'male and
female' in Galatians 3.28 does not affect the practicalities of daily
life then have to go to some lengths to explain that the first two
pairs in Galatians 3.28 are quite distinct from the last pair – in
order to demonstrate that one may not advocate the subordination of slaves and Gentiles if one argues for that of women.

It is true that in expounding the relation between the law and
the promise, which is Paul's main concern in Galatians 3, the
Apostle concentrates on the first pair, Jew and Greek, and does
not elaborate upon the status of women. It does not follow,
however, that while the consequences of baptism for Greeks were
fundamental and affected their total standing within the community of the redeemed, the consequences of baptism were
'incidental' for women and restricted solely to their standing
before God. On the contrary, the three pairs in verse 28 highlight
three fundamental areas of inequality manifested in the law,
where Gentiles, slaves and women were at best third-class
citizens, at worst 'non-persons'.

The religious privilege and superiority of the free male Jew was
exemplified in the *beraka*, the morning prayer in which he
thanked God for not making him a Gentile, a slave, or a woman.
Caird comments:

> The one thing these three pairs have in common is that they
> denote the three deepest divisions which split the society of the
> ancient world. What Paul is saying is that such divisions (and
> they are typical rather than exhaustive) can have no place in the
> thought of those who are united with Christ.[43]

In each case, their status under the law is contrasted with their
status in Christ – with no differentiation in the extent of their
emancipation. The idea that Galatians 3.28 assumes a dichotomy
between social order and life *Coram Deo* must be rejected.
'Whatever else may be called in question there can be no doubt
that Paul was a passionate advocate of liberty' (cf. Gal. 4.22; 5.1).
Therefore, those who assert that Galatians 3.27f calls for no
change in outward social patterns, just an impractical pietism, are
reducing Paul's career to a 'meaningless tragedy'.[44]

It is correct to say that 'freedom' was for Paul primarily a

spiritual rather than a political or legal liberty. Yet we grossly
misinterpret Paul if we imagine that this inner freedom does not
have immediate consequences for outward conduct, both personal and social (cf. Gal. 5.25). Bruce develops this truth that the
denial of discrimination which is sacramentally affirmed in baptism holds good for the new existence 'in Christ' in its entirety: 'If
in ordinary life existence in Christ is manifested openly in
Church fellowship, then, if a Gentile may exercise spiritual
leadership in church as freely as a Jew, or a slave as freely as a
citizen, why not a woman as freely as a man?'[45]

Lampe takes up the objection that in Galatians 3.28 Paul was
referring not to ordination but to baptism. He believes that such
verses express Christianity's 'remarkable advance beyond the
relative subordination of women in Judaism' by showing that
from the start women were admitted to full membership of the
Church. This fact has important implications for ministerial
priesthood,

> for if that priesthood is a representative nucleus ... of the
> priesthood of the whole body which consists equally of men
> and women, it is hard to see why the women members should
> be excluded from the ministerial priesthood which represents
> them ... In fact the more positive question arises, whether the
> ministerial priesthood can be properly representative of the
> priestly community unless it does include women.[46]

A word or two must be added here about New Testament
application of the principle of woman's new status in Christ.
Although Paul concentrated on putting into practice his teaching
regarding the new status of Gentiles, stressing that this must be
made manifest in the social dimensions of the Church (Gal. 2.11–
14), he did not ignore 'women's liberty'. In practice, Paul did not
neutralize the equality of male and female in Christ by confining
it to the *Coram Deo* dimension, unlike many subsequent ecclesiastics. If the Apostle had simply followed the Jewish interpretation of the Old Testament teaching on the place of women, it is
hardly likely that he would have greeted women as his 'fellow-
workers' in the gospel (cf. Phil. 4.3; Rom. 16, especially Phoebe, a
'deacon'). The evidence seems incontrovertible that women
worked alongside men in the Pauline churches, and there is
absolutely nothing in the text which would suggest that the work
was of a subordinate character.

Again, Fiorenza notes that the Pauline letters give us a glimpse of the egalitarian early Christian missionary movement. She laments the 'one-sided', 'androcentric' presentation of women's involvement, so that we see only 'the tip of an iceberg' – women generally being directly mentioned 'because they were exceptional women or because their actions had become a problem' (for example, 1 Cor. 11.2–16; Phil. 4.2f; cf. the 'problem-centred' passage on the Eucharist, 1 Cor. 11.17ff). Nevertheless, she does think that Acts shows women to have been 'involved in the Christian missionary movement at every stage of its expansion'.[47] The Book of Acts and even the Pastoral Epistles (for example, Acts 1.14; 9.36; 12.12; 21.9; 2 Tim. 4.19, 21) show women taking a very active part in the life and work of the Church.

As an example of the application of the theory of male–female equality in the treatment of practical problems in the Christian community, 1 Corinthians 7 may be instanced. In this chapter, Paul carefully lays down the equality of duties and rights for both sexes. Analysis of the structure shows that Paul in almost every instance addresses himself explicitly to *both* men and women in order to show that each sex has the same freedom and the same responsibility. Paul does not merely say that the wife's body belongs to the husband; he goes on to say that the husband's body belongs to the wife. Barrett comments:

> It is the exact parallelism that is most striking here. Conjugal rights are equal and reciprocal. If the husband has authority over his wife, his wife has equal authority over him. This striking assertion must be borne in mind as we follow Paul's arguments about the relations between man and woman.[48]

It is, indeed, unjust to condemn Paul as allowing equality to remain an abstract ideology where women are concerned.

'There cannot be male and female' is a difficult phrase to interpret because on one level it appears to be a denial of the human biology established in Genesis 1.27f. It raises the question: was Paul suggesting that God has now improved on his original design by producing a homogenized society devoid of distinguishing characteristics? I believe that the context of Galatians 3.28 within Paul's discourse on the law belies this idea. It is the condition of male and female *as they existed under the law* which is abrogated in Christ, not the original 'order of creation'.

As was shown in Chapter 4, much of the Old Testament bears

witness to the subordinate position of women. This subordination was authorized by the Torah (cf. Gen. 3.16) as a means of
regulating the disharmony between male and female consequen-
tial upon human disobedience to God (cf. Gal. 3.19f). What Paul
says in Galatians 3 about the position of Jew and Greek also
applies to male and female. 'Before faith came, we were confined
under the law, kept under restraint . . .' (v.23), and women, it
might be said, felt this restraint and confinement even more
keenly than men. With the advent of the Christian faith, however,
women need no longer be in the custody of the law (v.25). Men
and women alike may experience the responsibilities and privi-
leges of being 'sons of God through faith in Christ' (v.26). In
Christ, women as well as men are heirs of the promise (v.29), for
women and men have equal status before God and in the
Christian community; both sexes share full citizenship in the
Kingdom of God. Christ restores men and women in the image of
God.

It is, then, male and female as the oppressive custody of the law
ordered their relationship which is transcended in Christ, not sexua-
lity as it was intended to be when God 'from the beginning made them
male and female' (Matt. 19.14). Herein lies the essential harmony
between the various Pauline statements on the subject. In spite of
the superficial differences between 1 Corinthians 11.2–16 and
Galatians 3.27f, Paul's deepest thoughts on male–female relations
and woman's status are the same in both passages. In both he
strives to convey the truth that 'in the Lord' (1 Cor. 11.11), 'in
Christ' (Gal. 3.26f), men and women are equal and interdependent. Neither sex is more privileged than the other, neither is
bound in subjection to the other; together they are released from
past restrictions to worship and serve God freely and responsibly.

Nowhere, however, does the Apostle indicate that all this
means that human sexuality in itself is evil or redundant in the
new order, or that the process by which men and women become
one in Christ requires women to deny their femininity. Christianity does not obliterate the real distinction between maleness and
femaleness on the human level, nor does it extol maleness above
femaleness. Rather, woman's new power and equality under
Christ is related to her being fully woman.

This contrasts strikingly with other attitudes towards sexuality, especially female sexuality. Various patristic texts betray a

distorted understanding of the value of femaleness within the order of creation and the order of redemption. For example, Jerome wrote: 'When she wishes to serve Christ more than the world, then she will cease to be a woman and will be called man.' And Ambrose declared: 'She who does not believe is a woman and should be designated by the name of her sex, whereas she who believes progresses to perfect manhood.'[49] As Fiorenza summarizes the situation, Gnostic and patristic writers who demanded that a woman aspiring to be a disciple should become 'male' did so because they assumed that 'the male principle stands for the heavenly, angelic, divine, realm, whereas the female principle represents either human weakness or evil'.[50] Texts like Galatians 3.27f show that Paul's attitude towards sexuality in general and femininity in particular involved no such aberration.

What Galatians 3.27f affirms, then, is that all the baptized are one in Christ. 'In Christ', racial, social and sexual distinctions are transcended and transformed. What is good and God-given in them is retained, but those aspects which have become distorted or perverted – including male dominance – are to be removed, in theory and in practice, from the Christian community.

Moreover, as several commentators point out, it is probable that these verses represent a pre-Pauline liturgical (baptismal) formula. The text does not simply preserve a theological 'breakthrough' achieved by Paul; rather it provided insight into the theological understanding of the early Christian community.[51] The early Christians understood themselves as freed by the Holy Spirit to a new life of egalitarian discipleship. Over against the patriarchal patterns of 'the world', over against the commonly accepted ratification of sexual discrimination in Judaism and Hellenism, they set the equality and freedom of the children of God.

'But now we are discharged from the law, dead to that which held us captive, so that we serve not under the old written code but in the new life of the Spirit.' Galatians 3.28 shows that verses such as this (Romans 7.6) apply to women as well as to men. It proclaims that in Christ women are freed from subservience; women, long oppressed by the sexual discrimination of the Torah, are set at liberty by the gospel (cf. Luke 4.18).

Subordination and Equality

In this chapter I have surveyed principal New Testament texts which incorporate Old Testament concepts and terminology associated with the question of woman's nature and role. These texts reveal an underlying dependence upon ideas derived from Genesis 1–3. The survey also reveals, however, significant differences in the way in which themes from Genesis are taken up. It appears that Scripture embodies variant views on woman's status and function – views which may loosely be termed the *subordinationist* and the *equalitarian*. The question must now be considered: why are there variant uses of the Old Testament in New Testament teaching about woman's place in the Church? What factors contributed to the formation of differing Christian views on woman?

I believe that various pressures combined to precipitate the Church in an 'anti-feminist' direction. These pressures arose out of the particularity of the New Testament situation: the time and place in and for which the correspondence was penned, the cultural situation, the specific strengths and weaknesses of the congregations to whom the letters were addressed. For example, the Church would have been under pressure to dissociate itself from contemporary forms of licentiousness. The fertility cult threat to pure religion – which, I have maintained, greatly influenced the Yahwistic attitude towards women – had not vanished by the first century AD. In the Graeco-Roman world, early Christianity was in competition with a resurgence of Goddess-worship – from the devotion to the Phrygian *Mater Magna* throughout Asia Minor and Rome to the cult of Isis and her veneration under many other names (for example, Demeter, Athena, Venus).[52]

Goddess worship encouraged the equal participation of men and women in cultic leadership, but the rites of the Great Goddess were not devoid of promiscuity and perversion. Even if reports were exaggerated, there was enough evidence to give Christians a negative view of female activities in cultic leadership. In a society where voices raised in support of 'women's liberation' were frequently the same voices which condoned immorality, homosexuality and lesbianism, it is understandable that Christians were wary of laying too much stress upon female equality. Instead, they returned to the security of time-honoured Jewish teaching on female submissiveness.

Some scholars are of the opinion that anxiety over the suspect sexuality of proto-Gnosticism exerted a powerful influence upon Christian leaders. For instance, it is said that the reason for Paul's insistence on distinctive hairstyle at worship as a visible sign of the distinction between the sexes (1 Cor. 11.2–16) was that 'at Corinth a dualist Gnosticism tended to deny any distinction between a man and a woman, on the grounds that sex belongs to flesh and matter, and is, therefore, indifferent to the spirit'.[53] Again, W. Schmithals believes that it was a Gnostic-type distorted emphasis on sexual equality which led Paul to react as he did in 1 Corinthians 14.33b–6. In assessing Paul's views, writes Schmithals, 'one must keep in mind the special cause which compelled him, in the last analysis against his intention, to limit Christian freedom in this way'.[54]

After Paul's death, the need for the Church to dissociate itself from Gnostic-type sexuality increased. Some of Paul's radical statements (for example, Gal. 3.27f) could be misunderstood or twisted in a Gnostic direction; the Apostle himself was no longer on hand to rectify abuses; and the Gnostic ethos was developing and gaining strength. Thus, even within the New Testament there is evidence of attempts to combat the problem by retreating into the rigid patriarchal framework for male–female relations. Hanson believes that the author of the Pastoral Epistles was a Church leader who wished to use all the material at his disposal in order to attain his great aim, 'the instruction of contemporary church leaders in how to deal with the false teaching (probably incipient Gnosticism) with which they were faced'.[55]

Much of this 'material' was drawn from the Old Testament, particularly the Genesis Creation narratives. Such material was apposite because 'if we look at the speculations associated with Gnostic sects, it is remarkable how many of them could be explained as arising from reflections upon the early chapters of Genesis'. For example, many Gnostics were fascinated by the serpent's relation to Eve (Gen. 3).[56] When early Church leaders became aware that some of their scriptural source-material could be manipulated by those with Gnostic leanings, it is understandable that they should have reacted by using Scripture polemically

in a way in which they might not have used it had they not been
endeavouring to counter their opponents' tactics.

Of course, we do not possess enough information to recon-
struct an exact picture of the detailed circumstances within and
without the Church. Yet we do know that the early days of the
Church were fraught with challenge and danger as the first
Christians sought above all to proclaim Christ crucified in a
hostile environment. The primary aim was the dissemination of
the gospel and 'secondary' issues such as the social emancipation
of slaves and women were subordinated to the missionary cause.
In situations where overt emphasis upon woman's new status in
Christ might bring reprisals from those offended by the disruption of the *status quo*, Paul and other Church leaders urged the
cautious approach exemplified in the *Haustafeln* (household
codes) (cf. 1 Tim. 2.8–15; Col. 3.18f; Eph. 5.21–6.9; 1 Peter 2.13–
3.7). As Caird advises, the subordinationist passages in the New
Testament must be read in the light of the practicalities of the
contemporary situation: Christian slaves were frequently in bondage to pagan masters, Christian wives often had pagan husbands. Most Church leaders were sensitive enough not to court
reprisals by launching over-rapid reforms. Barriers could be
broken down only gradually, and only where people were united
to Christ – 'where the Spirit is, and only there, is liberty' (cf. 2
Cor. 3.17).[57]

It may be concluded, then, that several problems combined to
dim the Christian vision of liberating woman from her 'fallen'
position and restoring her to equality with man in Christ. St Paul
was well aware of the problems of implementing this vision in a
society where, heretofore, fear of sexual impropriety had resulted
in a policy of avoidance of women. Assessing the needs of each
situation, Paul sometimes attempted to deal with the problems by
urging his readers to stand firm. In their Christ-given freedom
(cf. Gal. 5.1), at other times by counselling compromise and
acquiescence with Jewish understanding of Old Testament
teaching about woman's status and function (cf. 1 Cor. 14.33ff).
Diversity was a common feature of the early Church – as of the
Church today – and the fact that different books in the New
Testament, and even the same author addressing different circumstances, should adopt differing approaches when using

Scripture to address the subject of woman's role should not surprise us.

The Christian ideal, then, frequently manifested in practice in the earliest days of the Church, was equalitarian and counter-cultural. Membership in the Body of Christ was defined by 'faith commitment', not by sexuality. But internal and external pressures upon the Church, pressures which were largely culturally conditioned, led Christian leaders to resort to Jewish interpretations of Old Testament teaching on woman's place and to reimpose ancient subordinationist views about family order and rules of conduct for females. Much of the equalitarianism of primitive Christianity was lost.[58] As Christians, finding themselves in a vulnerable position, took refuge in the adoption of the institutional forms of the surrounding patriarchal culture, 'subjection' rather than 'authority' (*exousia*) again characterized womanhood and women were more and more excluded from Christian leadership.

NOTES

1. N. Fuchs-Kreimer, 'Feminism and Scriptural Interpretation: A Contemporary Jewish Critique', *JES*, 20 (1983), p. 540.
2. F. Zerbst, *The Office of Woman in the Church* (St Louis 1955), p. 68.
3. S. Bedale, 'The Meaning of *kephalē* in the Pauline Epistles', *JTS*, New Series, 5 (1954), pp. 211–15.
4. C. K. Barrett, *A Commentary on the First Epistle to the Corinthians*, 2 (London 1971), p. 248.
5. Note that the sequence in verse 3 further undermines the theory that Paul intended to depict a hierarchy with God the Father as the chief authority figure and woman occupying the lowest position. cf. M. Evans, *Woman in the Bible* (Exeter 1983), p. 86.
6. H. L. Goudge, *The First Epistle to the Corinthians* (London 1903), p. 96.
7. Beckwith, 'The Bearing of Holy Scripture', p. 51.
8. Tavard, *Woman*, pp. 28–9.
9. Caird, *Principalities and Powers* (Oxford 1956), p. 20.
10. On the Jewish angelology reflected in v.10, see for example, Moffatt, *1 Corinthians* (London 1947), p. 152; W. Trompf, 'On Attitudes Toward Woman in Paul and Paulinist Literature: 1 Corinthians 11:3–16 and Its Context', *CBQ* 42 (1980), p. 207; J. A.

Fitzmyer, 'A Feature of Qumran Angelology and the Angels of 1 Corinthians 11:10', *NTS*, 4 (1957–8), pp. 48–58.

11. Barrett, op. cit., p. 250.
12. J. Murphy-O'Connor, 'Sex and Logic in 1 Corinthians 11.2–16', *CBQ*, 42 (1980), p. 497.
13. M. D. Hooker, 'Authority on her head: an examination of 1 Corinthians 11.10', *NTS*, 10 (1964), pp. 416, 412.
14. R. Scroggs, 'Paul and the Eschatological Woman', *JAAR*, 40 (1972), p. 302.
15. E. S. Fiorenza, *In Memory of Her* (London 1983), pp. 227–8.
16. Scroggs, op. cit., pp. 293, 283 n. 1. See also 'Paul and the Eschatological Woman: Revisited', *JAAR*, 42 (1974), p. 534.
17. Murphy-O'Connor, 'Sex and Logic', pp. 485–90.
18. Murphy-O'Connor, 'Sex and Logic', p. 498.
19. cf. Lev. 5.18; M. Kelim 24.16; M. Sotah 3.8; M. Ketuboth 7.6; M. Kiddushin 1.7.
20. Caird, 'Paul and Women's Liberty', *BJRL*, 54 (1971–2), p. 278.
21. Beckwith, op. cit., pp. 53–4.
22. Clark, *Man and Woman in Christ*, pp. 185–6.
23. D. E. H. Whiteley, *The Theology of St Paul*, 2nd edition (Oxford 1974), p. 225.
24. For example, Scroggs, 'Eschatological Woman' (1972), p. 284.
25. Barrett, op. cit., pp. 332–5.
26. Moffatt, op. cit., p. 233.
27. Fiorenza, op. cit., p. 231.
28. Barrett, op. cit., p. 331.
29. ibid., p. 332.
30. Fiorenza, op. cit., p. 230.
31. cf. for example, H. van der Meer, *Women Priests*, p. 39. On the particular pressures which were likely to have influenced the early Church to restrict women's liberty see below, pp. 104ff.
32. Barrett, op. cit., p. 322. cf. W. G. H. Simon, *The First Epistle to the Corinthians* (London 1959), p. 136; S. Aalen, 'A Rabbinic Formula in 1 Corinthians 14.34', *St Ev*, 87 (1964), pp. 513–25.
33. J. M. Ford, 'Biblical Material Relevant to the Ordination of Women', *JES*, 10 (1973), p. 681.
34. Barrett, op. cit., p. 332.
35. T. R. W. Longstaff, 'The Ordination of Women: A Biblical Perspective', *ATR*, 57 (1975), p. 326.
36. cf. M. Evans, *Woman in the Bible* (Exeter 1983), pp. 102ff.
37. cf. 1 En. 69.6; 2 En. 30.18, 31.6; Ecclus. 25.24; vita Ad. 3.2; Apoc. Moses 8.2, 11. See also Scroggs, *The Last Adam* (Oxford 1966), p. 38; N. P. Williams, *The Ideas of the Fall and of Original Sin* (London 1927), pp. 58, 122, 227, 304.

38. cf. F. F. Bruce, *1 and 2 Corinthians* (London 1971), p. 235.
39. cf. A. T. Hanson, *Living Utterances*, pp. 137f.
40. B. Witherington, 'Rite and Rights for Women – Galatians 3.28', *NTS*, 27 (1981), p. 597.
41. cf. Bruce, *The Epistle to the Galatians* (Exeter 1982), p. 189.
42. Beckwith, op. cit., p. 56; see also J. I. Packer, 'Thoughts on the Role and Function of Women in the Church', *Evangelicals and the Ordination of Women*, ed. C. Craston, 1973, p. 23.
43. Caird, 'Paul and Women's Liberty', pp. 273–4. cf. Talmud b Menakhoth 43 b; Tosephta Berakoth 7.18.
44. Caird, op. cit., pp. 271–3.
45. Bruce, *Galatians*, p. 190.
46. Lampe, 'Women and the Ministry of Priesthood', p. 94.
47. Fiorenza, op. cit., pp. 167–8.
48. Barrett, *1 Corinthians*, p. 156.
49. Jerome, *PL* 26, c. 567; Ambrose, *PL*, 15, c. 1844.
50. Fiorenza, op. cit., p. 218.
51. See, for example, R. J. Karris, 'The Role of Women according to Jesus and the Early Church', *Women and Priesthood*, ed. C. Stuhlmueller (Minnesota 1978), p. 50.
52. See for example, Acts 19.23ff. cf. Swidler, *Biblical Affirmations*, p. 355.
53. R. Gryson, *The Ministry of Women in the Early Church* (Minnesota 1976), p. 5.
54. W. Schmithals, *Gnosticism in Corinth* (New York 1971), pp. 239, 244.
55. Hanson, *Living Utterances*, p. 134.
56. cf. A. D. Nock, 'Gnosticism', *Essays on Religion and the Ancient World*, ed. Z. Stewart (Oxford 1972), pp. 947–8; R. M. Grant, *Gnosticism and Early Christianity*, 2 (London 1966), p. 104.
57. Caird, 'Paul and Women's Liberty', pp. 279–80.
58. There are even signs that the prominence of women in the Christian community, as recorded in the New Testament, was deliberately modified by textual scribes. For example, on Acts 17.12, 34; 18.26, see Bruce, *The Acts of the Apostles*, 2 (London 1952), pp. 329, 341, 352.

8

Biblical Criticism, Christian Woman and the Church

It has become clear that the Bible does not provide unequivocal answers to our questions about the status and role of woman. Scripture presents two views of womanhood: the subordinationist and the equalitarian. The problem now before us, then, is how to determine which, if either, of these views should be taken as authoritative for modern doctrine. There is need for a method which will help us to discern how to interpret the various scriptural pronouncements in the light of the issues facing women and men in the Church today.

> The general consensus of Biblical scholarship holds that Paul's instructions to the Corinthians, and the teaching of the Pastoral Epistles, were related to the particular social and religious situation in which Christians of the first century found themselves in the Hellenistic world. The Apostle is following and endorsing ... a custom which was highly desirable in the circumstances of the time but which 'may be changed according to the diversities of countries, times and men's manners'. The unchanging truth implicit in the gospel, but which could not be completely translated into practice in Paul's own day, is contained in ... Galatians 3:28.[1]

The principle which Lampe outlines is that the biblical writings, like all literature, were to some extent dependent on the cultural milieux from which they emanated and certain aspects of the Bible are so *culturally conditioned* that they may not simply be transferred to present-day issues. (The term cultural *relativism* will be used sparingly because of its association with the extreme liberal position which I do not wish to espouse.) Other aspects, however, are said to transcend their particular cultural setting and so to constitute 'unchanging truth' of eternal relevance for the Church. Critical examination of the text is necessary in order to determine whether a passage embodies 'indispensable divine law' or 'mutable church law'. Several exegetes have applied this principle to the problem of discerning the New Testament's authoritative position on women's ministry. Typical of these is R. W. Howard, who says of certain injunctions: 'St. Paul was surely only making local rules for a particularly volatile Christian community.' Verses like Galatians 3.27–8, on the other hand, are said to manifest the higher principle of liberty.[2]

This approach to biblical teaching on women, which, for convenience, I shall refer to as *the culture-critical method*, is not welcomed by all scholars. Clark, for example, dismisses the attempt to distinguish the 'timeless' elements of scriptural teaching on male–female roles from the conditioned application of it; he calls this 'a hazardous approach to interpretation which can subtly lead to various pitfalls'.[3] The practical consequences of the rejection of the culture-critical method are made explicit by such writers as Hurley. Maintaining that Christian women are still bound by biblical subordinationist teaching, he says that St Paul taught that the appointive headship of the man applied in worship as well as in the home: 'The basis of Paul's view of the headship of men was not in an area which is culturally relative.'[4] Clark concludes that woman's headship is anathematized in *all* spheres, not simply in the Church. Family and community structures must reinforce one another; when a woman is allowed to exercise authority in any area this undermines the authority of the males in her family. Thus Clark exhorts Christians to try to organize society so that woman is oriented towards fulfilling her proper roles in the household.[5]

When examination is made of the methods by which such conclusions are reached, however, it may be shown that they manifest intractable problems, whereas the apparent weaknesses of the culture-critical method may be overcome. In this chapter, I shall outline the 'pitfalls' which are said to lie in the culture-critics' path. I shall endeavour to show that an abuse or distortion of the culture-critical method does not, in fact, negate its proper use.

The Culturally Conditioned and the Trans-Cultural

The first 'pitfall' into which culture-critics are often alleged to descend is that of *distinguishing between the culturally conditioned and the transcultural on highly subjective and arbitrary grounds.*[6]

The attempt to avoid this pitfall by finding objective guidelines for the categorization of New Testament material led, in some quarters, to the assumption that literary style is significant. Where a New Testament writer adopts a notably formal manner this is said to indicate that the content of the pronouncement is of lasting importance for the Church. Such a criterion is patently inadequate! Certainly, in 1 Timothy 2.12, woman is forbidden to exercise authority over man in forthright terms; but the writer is no less firm in admonishing women not to braid their hair or wear jewellery at public worship (1 Tim. 2.9f), or in directing the recipient of the letter to drink a little wine (1 Tim. 5.23), or in exhorting slaves to honour their masters (1 Tim. 6.1). Again, in 1 Corinthians, Paul argues just as much on principle that a believer should have no contact with a fallen brother (1 Cor. 5), or that Christians should never take one another to a civic court (1 Cor. 6) – injunctions which the Church no longer sees fit to endorse – as he does that women should be subordinate (1 Cor. 14). As van der Meer comments, 'the style of argumentation can scarcely be a decisive principle' in determining whether a certain scriptural passage contains 'divine law' (permanent) or 'ecclesiastical law' (mutable).[7]

Clark purports to offer a viable method of interpreting the New Testament teaching on women, but on examination it is his approach which may be shown to be arbitrary and subjective. At times he modifies his rigorous rejection of culture-criticism with the admission that 'there is, of course, some evidence of cultural adaptation in the New Testament teaching on the roles of men and women . . . the teaching on headcoverings for women is one likely example of such an adaptation'. Clark gives no satisfactory explanation of the process whereby he finds it legitimate to place the teaching about headcoverings in one category and other New Testament teaching about male–female roles in another. When he does raise the question of how we decide when to acknowledge that a passage no longer applies, or that only certain elements of it apply, his answer is ambiguous and unworkable: 'Those who believe the authority of Scripture to be supreme and submit themselves to it will find the answer in Scripture itself as far as Scripture gives guidance.'[8]

The authority of biblical sayings is not blind. The Bible must be interpreted according to certain principles because the risk of subjective arbitrariness cannot be eliminated through any simple claim of 'faithfulness to the Bible'. In my view, the antithesis set up between 'faithfulness to Scripture' and 'modern critical methods' is a false one. The Church must combine biblical faith with biblical criticism. When carefully applied, the expertise of modern scholarship can help precisely to avoid arbitrariness and subjectivity and produce an interpretation which is true to the meaning of the scriptural text in a way that fundamentalism cannot be. I believe that, in looking to Scripture for guidance on the women's ministry question, adherence to three principles will prevent decisions about the applicability of New Testament teaching for the twentieth-century Church from being arbitrary and subjective. These principles are based, as will become apparent, upon conclusions reached in foregoing chapters.

The *first principle* is that *Church order*, including specific directives on woman's place within the worshipping community, *should always be designed to meet the interdependent objectives of glorifying God and edifying the whole congregation.* The early Church was characterized by variety – including variety in its doctrine and practice regarding ministry. 'There is no such thing as *the* New Testament Church Order. Even in New Testament times circumstances were very varied.'[9] This variety was healthy and legitimate; the Church, as a living, growing organism, developed its ministries under the guidance of the Holy Spirit and in response to the particular demands of the ever-changing patterns of social evolution. The objective was constant: to glorify God and edify the congregation; but the methods of meeting the objective had to be flexible enough to satisfy the needs of different situations. With regard to women, in some churches – for example, in Galatia – where legalism threatened to hinder the glorifying of God and the edifying of the congregation, the baptismal ideal of freedom and equality needed to be exemplified. In places like Corinth, on the other hand, where the opposite danger – libertinism – threatened the same objective from a different angle, restraint and caution were needed ('let all things be done for edification', 1 Cor. 14.26c), so that the 'God of peace' might be glorified (v.33, cf. vv.3, 4, 5, 12, 17, 40, and Eph. 4.12). When it is said in this context that the woman should be silent, 'then this commandment is certainly meant for other times and circumstances only if in these other circumstances it is also true that the speaking of women works against the "edification of the congregation" '.[10]

Thus, the New Testament does not present a single, fixed, normative pattern for woman's place in church order. It does, however, provide the principle that the Church today, like the New Testament Church, must endeavour, under the guidance of the Holy Spirit, to order itself in a way which will be glorifying to God and edifying for all its members. Church order must not be made an end in itself nor must it be absolutized. As Schillebeeckx points out:

> With a shift in the dominant picture of man and the world, with social and economic changes and a new social and cultural sensibility and set of emotions, a church order which has grown up through history can in fact hinder and obstruct precisely what in earlier generations it was intended to ensure: the building up of a Christian community.[11]

Church order, then, must not be rigid and inflexible, but adaptable to local conditions. Adherence to this principle might well incline Church leaders in the East, for example, to the view that it would be inappropriate to press ahead with full-scale women's ordination at present; whereas an increasing number of Western Churches might decide that the ordination of women to priesthood and episcopate would indeed facilitate the glorifying of God and the building up of congregations.

The *second principle* is that *everything in the life of the Church*, including the status and function of women, *should be designed to promote the proclamation of the Gospel*. The first Christians saw their *raison d'être* in evangelism (for example, Matt. 28.19; Luke 24.47; Acts 1.8). In Chapter 7, reference was made to the New Testament practice of subordinating personal interests to the primary concern of 'discipling'. Anything, including the 'rights' of an individual, which might prove to be a serious stumbling-block to another person's faith, must be sacrificed (for example, 1 Cor. 10.23–11.1; Rom. 15.1–3). Everything, including personal liberty, must be counted as loss for the surpassing worth of knowing Christ as Lord and the privilege of sharing that knowledge with others (Phil. 3.8, 1.7; Eph. 3.1; Paul, 'a prisoner for Christ Jesus', gave up his freedom in a very practical, literal sense). If, therefore, in a given instance, the practical expression of a woman's new status in Christ so disrupted the *status quo* that it might hinder the spread of the Gospel – for instance, to her pagan husband (1 Peter 3.1f) – then the traditional pattern of female subordination must be followed. If the abuse of their new-found freedom by Christian women threatened to discredit the Church and its message then this freedom must be (temporarily) curtailed.

This New Testament principle holds good for the Church today. In each different cultural setting Christians must try to discern what pattern of man–woman relations in the Church, what teaching about woman's status and function, will bear most effective witness to the transforming power of the gospel and the attractiveness of the Christian way of life. St Paul sometimes appealed to what his readers would find most natural and in accord with common sense to support his arguments (for example, 1 Cor. 11.13f). Today, quite different customs might not only seem to be consonant with common sense but also be required for the furtherance of the gospel. In our society, which naturally accepts women's leadership and male–female equality, many people feel alienated from the Church by the attitude of ecclesiastics who still demand woman's subordination.

Some conservative thinkers tend to censure any adaption by the Church to contemporary moves, even when the adaptation is prompted by such a motive as evangelism. Yet it is misguided to dismiss adaptability for the sake of evangelism as capricious compromise with worldly standards. St Paul himself defended the principle: 'I have become all things to all people, that I might by all means save some' (1 Cor. 9.22–3). It is a principle to which Christian apologists have always adhered. Applying the principle to the question of women's ministry, Lampe states that in our society the ordination of women is the natural conclusion to the changes in female roles that the socio-economic revolution has brought about during the last century and a quarter:

> We should be cautious about using the word 'secular' to describe these changes. They do not come about without God's providence. God speaks to the Church through the world as well as through the Church, and it is through the interaction of the Church with the world that we may, if we listen, hear God's word.[12]

The *third principle* is that, when confusion arises about what aspects of scriptural teaching on women are most applicable today, *guidance may be found by examining the relation between New Testament anthropology and Christology*. Dunn maintains that early Christians interpreted the Jewish Bible '*in the light of the revelation of the Christ event*'. Faith *in Christ* was the cohesive focal point which united the '*many different expressions of Christianity within* the New Testament'. Even in the first century, Christianity had to adapt itself to the diverse cultural contexts of the different environments to which it spread. Therefore, the actual outworking of Christian faith resulted in 'different concepts and practices of mission, ministry and worship' in response to the needs of particular situations. Yet in the final analysis 'the unity of first century Christianity focuses (often exclusively) on Jesus the man now exalted, Christ crucified but risen'.[13]

In my view, then, scriptural anthropological teaching which is not tied to local rule-giving but is most clearly integrated with Christology provides the most constant and the highest principle for the Church's formulation of doctrine and practical guidelines on woman's position and male–female relations in diverse times and places. The doctrine of the work of Christ shows that within the sphere of redeemed humanity sexual differentiation may not be used as a basis for the domination, superiority or privilege of one sex over the other. In Christ, sexual divisions and antagonism are overcome. The cross of Christ brings reconciliation between God and mankind (cf. 2 Cor. 5.18f) which opens the way to reconciliation between men and women as individually they are restored to the *Imago Dei*. The recreation of male and female in God's image begins at baptism (Gal. 3.27) and is gradually accomplished in the lives of believers to the extent to which they allow the Holy Spirit to exercise his transforming power (for example, Rom. 12.2; 2 Cor. 3.17–18). Sent in Christ's name (John 14.26), the Holy Spirit does not discriminate between men and women in the distribution of his gifts (cf. Joel 2.28–9; Acts 2.16–18). There is no indication in the lists of Romans 12, 1 Corinthians 12 or Ephesians 4 that the *charismata* of prophecy, teaching ministry, evangelism, healing and the like are bestowed according to the recipient's sex.

God deals with the human race, male and female, as a unity; He does not treat the male half in one way, the female half in another. Biblical terms such as 'saint', 'disciple', 'believer', 'witness', do not pertain to men only. Men and women together are invited to 'put on the new nature, which is being renewed in knowledge after the image of its creator' (Col. 3.10); there is no secondary *Imago Dei* for woman, no special treatment for man, because 'Christ is all and in all' (Col. 3.11: certain manuscripts include a reference to 'male and female' here, as in Gal. 3.28). Christ is the pattern for all creatures (Col. 1.15–19), woman included, so that in Christ there is a new Eve as well as a new Adam (using the terms 'Adam' and 'Eve' here as 'representative male' and 'representative female'). Through Christ the tragic human story of the Fall – of wholeness broken into domination and submission – is turned around.[14]

Essentially, then, New Testament writers, following the example of Jesus himself, treat men and women equally. 'No one can read the New Testament without immediately being aware that it thrills with the sense of barriers longstanding being broken down.' Nationalism, class, sex – the divisive factors of history – these 'in Christ' and in his Church in the New Testament are transcended.[15] Sometimes, in particular limited situations, New Testament writers record specific directives to women – directives which, in order to deal with *sui generis* problems, resorted to legalistic interpretations of the Old Testament and traditional patriarchal societal structures. But when these structures are set against the christological teaching which posits freedom and equality for men and women in Christ, then they are clearly distinguished as secondary, mutable, culturally conditioned instructions and not the highest expression of an unchanging divine plan for male–female relations.

Many Christians feel confused when faced by the two scriptural perspectives on women. Those who wish to decide, on objective and consistent grounds, whether the subordinationist or the equalitarian position should govern their belief and conduct would do well to ask these questions: Which view lies nearer to the centre of Christian doctrine? Which comes closest to expressing the highest ideals of the Christian faith? Three principles have been outlined above, namely:

  (i) that the Church should be ordered in a way that will glorify God and edify the whole congregation;
 (ii) that everything in the life of the Church should be designed to promote the proclamation of the gospel;
(iii) that Christology puts anthropology in its proper perspective.

In the light of the application of these principles, I believe that there can be no doubt which of the two views on women's status and function should govern modern doctrine and practice.

Relativism and the Relevance of the Bible

A second 'pitfall' into which culture-critics are said to descend is that of *undermining scriptural authority by relegating the entire Bible to the realm of the interesting but outmoded religious literature of man's primitive past.*

Nineham is convinced that people of different periods differ 'in some cases so widely that accounts of the nature and relations of God, men and the world put forward in one culture may be unacceptable, as they stand, in a different culture'. He believes that patriarchal, medieval and Reformation scholars interpreted the Bible according to their own cultural presuppositions – which were different from both those of the biblical writers and of our own post-Enlightenment culture. Therefore, the biblical teaching and its interpretations, upon which much Christian doctrine is established, are alien to our own situation. Nineham questions the 'relevance' not only of statements like Paul's in 1 Corinthians 11 about the duty of women to cover their heads in church, but also of passages relating to fundamental Christian doctrines: for example, creation, the idea of divine intervention and the life, death and resurrection of Christ.[16] In sum, extreme cultural relativists like Nineham hold that twentieth-century human beings respond to reality very differently from the men and women of the Bible and that therefore little if anything in the Bible can be transcultural. Obviously, if this position were to be widely accepted then the idea that the Bible can serve as the dominant criterion for Christian faith and ethics would soon be dismissed as absurd.

It is true that extreme cultural relativism involves a drastic diminution of scriptural authority; but the culture-critical method should not be confused with radical relativism. The majority of scholars who wish to distinguish between timeless and culturally conditioned elements of biblical teaching on women's ministry are not radical relativists of Nineham's ilk. They engage in the painstaking endeavour to sift the supratemporal from the timebound precisely because they want to avoid the 'kind of critical nihilism according to which texts from the past are simply inscrutable'.[17] In order to affirm scriptural authority, biblical study must involve estimative weighing of the data, not mere passive acceptance of it. In fact, it is those who sidestep or decry the struggle to distinguish the transcultural from the culturally conditioned who undermine the authority of Scripture.

Two examples may be adduced to show that approaches to Scripture which reject critical methods make a nonsense of biblical authority. First, critical scholars do not see Genesis 3.16 as expressing God's permanent ideal for womankind, and do not find it endorsed in the New Testament. If their method is rejected and it is said that female subordination is built into the order of creation because Genesis 3.16 expresses God's abiding purpose for women, then, as H. van der Meer shows, 'the extremely conservative Dutch Calvinists would also have been correct in declaring on the basis of Genesis 3.16 that the modern methods of painless childbirth are not permitted'. Second, 1 Timothy 2.14 seems to foreclose the ministerial offices of preaching and exercising authority to women because Eve was deceived and became a transgressor. The critical approach recognizes that archaic notions have influenced this passage and it refuses to employ the argument that woman's 'original sin' affects her eligibility for ministry. If the critical approach is abandoned and the reasoning of 1 Timothy 2.14 is taken as authoritative for today, then logically, as H. van der Meer puts it, one would have to deny the priesthood to males on the basis of Romans 5; for Adam was also seduced, sin came into the world through him.[18] Clearly, therefore, Scripture is as much abused by the failure to read it critically and intelligently as it is by an idolatrous confidence in the technical competence of scholars to sit in judgement on the biblical texts.

Most theologians would agree that it is unlikely that God wants us to assume that little or nothing in the Bible is transcultural; it is also highly doubtful that God wants us to play 'first-century Semites' by treating the New Testament as a detailed blueprint for our situation here and now. Museum-minded conservatism no more enables the dynamic truth of Scripture to challenge the men and women of our age than do the circumventions of liberalism. As Barr states tersely, 'it never should have been our view of biblical authority, that it meant that all the cultural baggage of past ages should be loaded upon the unfortunate bearer of the twentieth century'.[19]

Scriptural Tradition and Traditional Interpretations of Scripture

A third 'pitfall' into which culture-critics are said to descend is the 'spiritual peril' of *breaking with scriptural tradition and traditional interpretations of Scripture.*

A central tradition which those who support women's ordination are said to contravene is that of the male-only ordained ministry initiated by Jesus when he appointed an all-male apostolate. The Roman Catholic *Declaration* on the question of the admission of women to ministerial priesthood points to the practice of Jesus who 'did not call any women to become part of the Twelve' or 'entrust the apostolic charge to women'. This is said to be a deliberate choice on his part, not an example of sociocultural conditioning, for Jesus showed that he was quite capable of 'deliberately and courageously' breaking with the customs of his time regarding women in other respects.[20] Thus, as one scholar puts it, if Christ did not call women 'either to the apostolate proper or to any kind of apostolic ministry, it must have been as a matter not of chance, nor of lack of practical and actual opportunity, but of principle'.[21]

This argument from tradition also appeals to the practice of the Apostles, stressing, for example, that the apostolic community chose a man to replace Judas and the Apostles and Peter did not confer ordination on women. Evidence of the continuing practice in subsequent Church history is called upon to complete the argument. Although the practice of ordaining women is found in the more recent tradition of Protestant churches and amongst 'heretical' groups in patristic times, this has not been accepted by Orthodox, Roman Catholic and Anglo-Catholic leaders as an 'orthodox' part of the received tradition. Traditionalists conclude that the non-ordaining of women is an unbroken and unbreakable tradition originating from the Father's plan for the Church, expressed in Jesus' own practice and perpetuated by the faithful. Mascall asks:

When we find our Lord and the primitive Church restricting the ministry to males *in spite of the emphasis laid by both alike on the absolute equality of women and men as members of the New Israel which is the Body of Christ*, is it not natural to assume that there must be some very deep and significant reason in the nature of things for this restriction?[22]

Yet those who base their opposition to women's ordination on arguments from scriptural tradition and traditional interpretations of Scripture do not themselves consistently manifest an exemplary attitude towards tradition. Those who state categorically that unbroken tradition forbids the ordination of women often fail to provide an adequate definition of their usage of the term 'tradition'. There are two classes of scriptural and, more especially, of ecclesiastical tradition. Sometimes, the term denotes the accumulated deposit of doctrine, with its conscious and deliberate interpretation and re-interpretation of fundamental tenets of the faith. This is primary, class-one Tradition. At other times, the term is used in a secondary sense to signify customs in the life and worship of the Church, matters of ecclesiastical discipline which have developed almost imperceptibly and in haphazard fashion over the years.

If it could be demonstrated that Jesus deliberately excluded women from the apostolate in order to teach that the Church must permanently exclude women from priesthood, then the tradition of male-only ordained ministry could be considered as class-one Tradition. In fact, however, the case is by no means as clear as some writers imply. Even the *Declaration*, in referring to Jesus' attitude towards women and his choice of an all-male apostolate, admits that 'it is true that these facts do not make the matter immediately obvious'.[23]

Schillebeeckx sharply criticises the *Declaration* for attaching so much theological significance to Jesus' choice of twelve *males* and yet according no theological significance to the *married* state of most (perhaps all) of these men. The fact that the maleness of the apostolate is stressed whilst the law of celibacy ignores the marital status of the Twelve, leads Schillebeeckx to believe that 'two standards are used, depending on the particular interest'. This 'mutually conflicting arbitrarily selective biblical hermeneutic' shows that here 'non-theological themes unconsciously play a decisive role, while being presented on the authority of the Bible'.[24]

In my view, of the possible explanations suggested to account for the fact that none of the Twelve was a woman, the notion that Jesus thereby intended to establish the primary Tradition of the exclusion of women from priesthood is the least plausible. Indeed, I would agree with Lampe that Scripture is misused 'when it is said that since Jesus included no women among the Twelve, the Church must follow his example and ordain no women to the priesthood'.[25] The fact that Jesus deliberately broke with Jewish custom regarding the status and role of women does not automatically or necessarily imply that he would have included women in the apostolate if he had wanted them to stand on a par with men in the Church's subsequent Ministry. The strength of socio-cultural prejudice against women would have made it practically impossible even for Jesus, with his revolutionary attitude towards them, to commission women to the original apostolate.[26]

This point is made most persuasively by Rahner. He makes the preliminary observation that 'A practical rule of action can be culturally and sociologically conditioned and be open to change and actually changed as a result of a changed cultural and sociological situation and yet at an earlier stage . . . may even have been morally binding.' For example, Rahner recalls polygamy and the laws of war in the Old Testament, the institution of slavery during the first Christian centuries, and the Church's prohibition of usury until well into the eighteenth century: 'In all these cases it is decisively important to observe that a concrete rule of action co-existed with more general moral principles, while being really "in the abstract" opposed to the latter, although this basic contradiction could not in practice be perceived in the earlier sociological situation.' Rahner then demonstrates that in the cultural and sociological situation at the time it was both practically impossible and morally inappropriate for Jesus and the early Church after him to appoint female congregational leaders. They could not have observed a contradiction 'as such' and in the abstract between their general appreciation of women (in which they dissociated themselves from the mentality of their time) and their concrete practice with the concrete rules that this implied. Thus, the conclusion seems 'inescapable' that the attitude of Jesus and his Apostles 'is sufficiently explained by the cultural and sociological milieu' in which they had to act; their behaviour 'did not need to have a normative significance for all times – that is, for the time when this cultural and social milieu had been substantially changed'.[27]

Furthermore, as many theologians have agreed, it seems most likely that the Twelve were all men for the same reason that they were all Jewish – namely, to emphasize the correspondence between the old and the new Israel. Jesus' messianic vocation included the task of forming a new Israel through whom he would extend his redemptive activity to all nations (Matt. 28.19). The Twelve constituted the reformed patriarchate, the counterpart to the original patriarchs of Israel (Matt. 19.28; Luke 22.30; cf. Eph. 2.20). Thus, the masculinity of the apostolate may be understood theologically more as a fulfilment of God's promise to Israel than as a divine law governing the future of the Church. In the Twelve the structure of the old Israel, with its patriarchs and tribes, was represented and fulfilled. There is no indication that the preservation of an apostolic ministry should forever exclude women (or Gentiles).[28]

A further point must be made here. The tradition of the male character of ordained ministry is said to be primary and normative because it goes back to the Lord's manner of acting which reflected God's abiding plan to restrict priesthood to men. Leaving on one side the discussion over whether Jesus' choice of twelve male apostles from amongst his disciples (Luke 6.13f) was determined by a conscious desire to restrict the original apostolate to men or whether it may be understood in terms of sociocultural influence, historical expediency and the symbolic intention that the Twelve should represent the ancient patriarchate – still another problem remains. The difficulty centres upon the implicit equation of apostolic ministry in New Testament times with ordained ministry as later found in the threefold orders of bishop, priest and deacon. Very few New Testament scholars who have studied the development of ministry would lend support to this equation. R. E. Brown, for instance, questions the idea that Jesus foresaw the whole future of the Church, vocalized God's intention for an all-male priesthood, and provided a 'blueprint ecclesiology' which ruled out forever the possibility of ordaining women.[29] On the contrary, it is naïve and dangerous to

suppose that some teaching of Jesus, which is absolutely normative for priesthood, may simply be read off the pages of the New
Testament and applied to the Church today. Hodgson castigates
those who read back into the gospels the detailed circumstances
of our own time and imagine Jesus consciously deciding upon
modern formulations of questions such as the admissibility of
women to priesthood: 'Arguments based on such a way of using
the New Testament cannot be accepted as theologically sound.'[30]

Again, J. P. Meier highlights as 'the most fundamental problem' of the *Declaration* a weakness also found in several other
writings on the subject of ministry and women's ordination,
namely the presumption that Jesus and the New Testament
writers were concerned about Catholic priesthood as it is now
understood: 'This fundamental flaw of anachronism ... invali-
dates a good deal of this Declaration. To the question, What does
the New Testament have to say about women becoming Catholic
priests? the answer must be *nothing*, because the New Testament
does not operate with our conception of the ordained Catholic
priesthood.'[31] Whilst it might be said that Meier overstates the
case when he proclaims that the New Testament has 'nothing' to
say about women and priesthood, nevertheless the essence of his
argument is surely valid. The Church must be very careful how it
looks to scriptural tradition for guidance on questions with which
biblical writers were not themselves directly concerned. To argue
from the 'maleness' of the original apostolate to the exclusion of
women from ordained ministry today is a *non-sequitur*. The status
and function of the Twelve was unique and unrepeatable. Therefore, as Craston concludes, 'no necessary deductions from the
appointment of ministers after Pentecost may be drawn from the
choice of the Twelve'.[32]

Does the rest of the New Testament provide a normative
Tradition excluding women permanently from priesthood?
Several scholars assert that it does. But when the hermeneutical
procedure by which they reach this conclusion is analysed, it
appears that they have not taken historical-critical exegesis very
seriously. For instance, in referring to 1 Corinthians 11.2–16, the
Declaration notes that certain New Testament ordinances, 'such
as the obligation imposed upon women to wear a veil', were
'probably inspired by the customs of the period'; they 'concern
scarcely more than disciplinary practices of minor importance ...

such requirements no longer have normative value'. The *Declaration* then moves on swiftly to say that the 'the Apostle's forbidding of women "to speak" in the assemblies (cf. 1 Cor. 14.34–5; 1 Tim. 2.12) is of a different nature'.[33]

Meier suggests that the *Declaration* quickly dismissed 1 Corinthians 11.2–16 because 'the more one examines the content, presuppositions and arguments of Paul in 1 Corinthians 11.2–16, the more one opens a Pandora's box about historical conditioning, a box the *Declaration* prefers to keep shut'. Meier also complains that whilst the document contains plenty of learned footnotes, it does not follow through the historical-critical method – and 'one cannot be just a little bit critical'.[34] I would endorse Meier's judgement, and would add that it may be extended to indict the methods of writers like Hurley and Clark. As Barr comments:

> In biblical research one can use 'modern methods' or even 'critical methods', without being in the least touched by the spirit of criticism; criticism means the freedom, not simply to *use* methods, but to follow them wherever they may lead ... The freedom to come to exegetical results which may differ from, or even contradict, the accepted theological interpretation.[35]

In my view, a properly critical approach does not uncover in the New Testament a normative Tradition excluding women permanently from priesthood. The New Testament does not encourage Christians to think that nothing must be done for the first time. Granted that silence and subordination were enjoined upon women to overcome a particular problem at a particular place, this does not mean that an unrepealable code restricting priesthood to men is being enunciated. Paul was a man passionately concerned to emancipate religion from a written code; the last thing he would have desired is that his advice should be fossilized and applied to the vastly different circumstances of other ages and other cultures.[36] It was vital for Christian communities to remain faithful to the central tenets of the faith, to the unifying, primary tradition concerning Jesus Crucified and Risen. Yet, in changing socio-cultural situations, rigid and inflexible adherence to secondary traditions could result in ossification and infidelity to the living Lord. True faithfulness to the primary

Tradition might well entail changes in matters of ecclesiastical discipline and secondary traditions, such as those governing women's roles. Paul wanted Christians to be constantly alert to the fresh guidance of the Spirit (cf. 2 Cor. 3.17b; Gal. 5.25) for the maintenance of a live interchange of tradition and freedom. The New Testament gives evidence that the Spirit guided the Church to adapt to diverse circumstances – a principle of adaptation which is surely valid today.

When traditional interpretations of Scripture on this subject are examined it becomes clear that here, again, there is no firm support for the view that the exclusion of women from ordained ministry is a Tradition of the first class. Those who argue to the contrary are in danger of fossilizing prejudice. The Vatican *Declaration*, for example, concedes that 'it is true that in the writings of the Fathers one will find the undeniable influence of prejudices unfavourable to women'. With reference to medieval theology, it admits that the scholastic doctors often present arguments on this point that modern thought would rightly reject. Two sentences later, however, the *Declaration* concludes that the Catholic Church should maintain its practice of not ordaining women because 'the Church's tradition in the matter has ... been so firm',[37] – as if the fact that the non-priesting of women might be based upon bigotry and anachronistic reasoning is rendered insignificant by the antiquity and pervasiveness of these obsolete prejudices. Meier aptly reminds us of Cyprian's dictum: '*Traditio sine veritate vetustas erroris*'.[38]

Is it right for the Church to uphold a tradition which can be shown to rest upon inaccurate biology and misguided philosophy? The inferiority of women to men was believed to reflect an 'order of creation' which more advanced biological and sociological knowledge has shown to be rather the order of a particular economic and social system in one part of the world in one period of its history. To expose and expunge unsound assumptions is not to launch a negative attack on scriptural tradition and traditional interpretations of Scripture. It is rather to serve the genuine Word of God by making sure that we are preaching the divine Word and not antiquated human notions. It is the refusal to re-examine tradition which risks infidelity to our Lord (Mark 7.8).

When all these factors are considered, they strongly support

Lampe's conclusion that the tradition of the non-ordination of women 'most certainly belongs to those traditions which the Church is free to alter under the Spirit's guidance'.[39] Lampe demonstrates that the tradition of the Church is 'solidly against the ordination of women, not in the sense that it has followed negative rulings given after full consideration of the matter, but that this has never been done and it has always been assumed that it was out of the question'. Some people insist that the Vincentian Canon – *quod semper, quod ubique, quod ab omnibus* – precludes all possibility of change. Yet, as Lampe points out, this canon applied to faith rather than practice and

> if we were really bound to exclude from our thought and life everything that has not been thought and lived out 'always', 'everywhere', 'by all Christians', we should rule out the possibility of all change in the church, nothing could ever happen in it for the first time. This is manifestly absurd, and is contradicted by history. There have been great and frequent changes in the church's belief, ethics, worship and structures.[40]

Misconceptions about the meaning of tradition and misjudgements which categorize a matter of ecclesiastical discipline as a primary Tradition will, if uncorrected, stultify Christian doctrine. There is abundant theological justification for the belief that the time has come for the Church to move beyond the secondary tradition governing woman's admissibility to priesthood in order to respond to God's guidance and to the needs of his people in the twentieth century. Instead of over-indulging in the negative exercise of castigating past generations for their apparent myopia regarding women and their role in ministry, Christians today should respond positively to fresh insights and apply them to their own new situations. Fidelity to the primary Tradition about Jesus Crucified and Risen entails adaptation even of long-standing secondary traditions.

Synthesis and Selection

Finally, and embracing aspects of the three previous 'pitfalls', the culture-critical approach is attacked by those who object that *it undermines scriptural authority by refusing to accept the Bible as it stands.*

Conservative writers who try to maintain the equal authority of every verse in the Bible protest that 'liberal' theologians adhere only to selected elements of Scripture. This is said to be tantamount to an attempt to establish a new canon, an attempt which destroys the authority of the true canon. Clark deplores the trend to value 'an oppositional or contrasting rather than a synthetic style of thought', leading scholars to stress the differences between various New Testament 'theologies' and 'church orders'. Where most critical scholars purport to find one part of Scripture counterbalanced by another part and maintain that intellectual integrity forbids a glossing over of inconsistencies, Clark declares that 'such contradictions arise from the interpretations of modern writers, not from the Scripture'.[41]

This assertion – that modern critics undermine scriptural authority by their so-called 'oppositional' or 'selective' approach to scriptural teaching about women's status and function – may be countered by the claim that it is in fact the over-synthetic approach, a trait of fundamentalism, which weakens the challenge of the Bible. In the public eye, as Barr notes, 'the fundamentalist point of view often appears to be the genuine manifestation of what a truly *biblical* Christianity would have to be'.[42] Actually, this stance produces a hotchpotch in which the distinctive emphasis of texts like Galatians 3.28 and 1 Corinthians 11.11–12 has been so absorbed and neutralized that the *biblical* message is received as something different from that which was set down by the writers.

It is right that one text should be allowed to illuminate another, that cross-reference and counterbalance should be made in the search for the 'wholeness of the truth revealed in Scripture'. Indeed, there is a sense in which it is proper for theologians to synthesize – when synthesis involves a consideration of biblical unity in diversity, an equilibration of the integral message – so long as the systematists remember that the truth is larger than our capacity to perceive it at any particular moment. This, however, does not appear to be the kind of synthesis which writers like Clark have in mind. Such people cannot allow the theologies of the Bible to stand in dialectical relation to each other because they do not, in the first instance, admit the pluralism of Scripture. Denying the rich diversity of Scripture, they manufacture a conflation, thereby eliminating the positive value of paradox and tension within Scripture which criticism, by contrast, seeks to explore.

'The diversity of theological views implied in Scripture defies brief description or easy synthesis . . . if we try to distil out what they all have in common, the result is very thin milk.'[43] To avoid the insipid dilution that results from over-harmonization, alternative means of ordering the material must be found, and this is what the critical method tries to do. Conservative writers who dismiss this as equivalent to the formation of a new canon are ignoring the self-evident principle that all theological thinking involves some kind of selection and ordering within the Bible.

There are ancient precedents for this principle. The Hebrew Bible is characterized by a threefold gradation, and although it is inaccurate to say that this corresponds exactly to decreasing degrees of importance between the Torah, the Prophets and the Writings, the dominance of the Torah and its influence upon the interpretation of the other parts is beyond question. Again, a strong element of critical selection is incorporated within the New Testament documents, for the New Testament use of the Old Testament is highly selective. Moreover, the principle was accepted, albeit often unconsciously, by very conservative biblicistic people. As Barr observes: 'Even those who thought women must wear hats in church because it was commanded in the Bible did not obey the entire law of Moses, though that also was commanded in the Bible; at the most they obeyed a precarious selection from within the requirements of that law.'[44]

I am not defending the adoption of an elaborate 'inner canon'; the term itself is misleading and involves a metaphorical use of the word 'canon'. But clearly, since the Bible is not a systematic doctrinal textbook, theologians are bound to delineate some sort of nodal points around which other statements are arranged. Serious hermeneutical naïveté is betrayed in the anti-critical claims that everything in Scripture stands on the same authoritative level and that contradictions arise only in the minds of modern interpreters. As Brunner writes, 'we cannot maintain that everything that is Biblical . . . is in the same way, or to the same extent, the "bearer" of the word of God'.[45] Critical and estimative weighing of biblical material is not a deathblow to scriptural authority. Rather, we come closer to objectivity 'as a result of scholars putting alongside of one another their various readings of the evidence' and attempting to discern what God is now using the Bible to teach us.[46]

Summary

As scholars like Brunner recognize, 'a certain depreciation of women', derived from pre-Christian Judaism and general attitudes towards woman in antiquity, casts a shadow over the New Testament. 'Along with other elements this forms part of the garment in which the message of the New Testament is clothed.'[47] It is an aspect of the scandal of particularity – of which the incarnation itself is the supreme instance – that the words of the Bible emanate from particular historico-cultural settings. Some of the New Testament directives on woman's position are timebound, culturally conditioned, relevant only for particular historical circumstances, rather than being supra-temporal decrees. The very 'particularity' of the scriptural documents demands that we acknowledge the economic, social and political differences between those circumstances and our own and then that we read the text with critical respect, in order to distinguish the timeless truths of Scripture from its more culturally conditioned aspects.

Naturally, this process is not easy, and much time, energy and sensitivity is required to work out a balance between ultra-radical cultural-relativism and conservative fundamentalism. But a realistic and relevant interpretation of Scripture demands such effort, and the awareness of 'pitfalls' along the way should not dissuade us from the course. Those who assert that female-subordinationist teachings are binding upon the Church today reach their conclusions by minimizing critical methods or by using them erratically. Yet, critical study of Scripture is not an optional extra to faith, which can be employed so long as it is convenient and helpful but otherwise ignored. 'On the contrary, it is the Bible itself which makes criticism inevitable and defends its freedom in practice.' As Muddiman advises, unless we apply our critical faculties to our Bible study, many passages come across as 'patent nonsense',[48] whereas sensitive application of critical methods can, in fact, re-establish the authority of the Bible for today. I believe that application of the culture-critical method enables it to be clearly demonstrated that the equalitarian position on womanhood – propounded in verses like Galatians 3.27f, frequently maintained in practice by the early Church, and derived from Jesus himself – is the scriptural position which should be taken as authoritative for modern doctrine.

NOTES

1. Lampe, 'Church Tradition and the Ordination of Women', p. 124. He quotes from Article 34 of the 'Articles of Religion', *BCP*.
2. R. W. Howard, *Should Women be Priests?*, pp. 19, 20.
3. Clark, *Man and Woman in Christ*, p. 552.
4. Hurley, *Man and Woman in Biblical Perspective*, p. 184.
5. Clark, op. cit., pp 134ff, 198, 211. Note that Hurley does not think that male headship applies outside the family and the Church, op. cit., p. 241.
6. Clark, op. cit., pp. 358–9.
7. Van der Meer, *Women Priests*, p. 30.
8. Clark, op. cit., pp. 266–7, 562.
9. E. Schweizer, *Church Order in the New Testament* (London 1961), p. 13.
10. Van der Meer, op. cit., p. 21.
11. E. Schillebeeckx, *Ministry* (London 1981), p. 75.
12. Lampe, 'Women and the Ministry of Priesthood', p. 102. cf. J. A. Baker, 'The Right Time', *Feminine in the Church*, ed. M. Furlong, pp. 168ff.
13. J. D. G. Dunn, *Unity and Diversity in the New Testament* (London 1977), pp. 369, 371ff.
14. cf. C. F. Parvey, ed., *The Community of Men and Women in the Church* (Geneva 1983), p. 167.
15. W. D. Davies, *Christian Origins and Judaism* (London 1962), pp. 222–3.
16. D. Nineham, *The Use and Abuse of the Bible* (London 1978), pp. 1, 37, 180ff, 212, 223ff.
17. J. Barton, *Reading the Old Testament* (London 1984), p. 29. cf. 'Reflections on Cultural Relativism', *Theology*, 82 (1979), pp. 103–9, 191–9; J. Barr, *Explorations in Theology 7* (London 1980), pp. 56ff.
18. Van der Meer, op. cit., pp. 28–9.
19. Barr, *Explorations 7*, p. 58.
20. Sacred Congregation for the Doctrine of the Faith, *Declaration 'inter insigniores' on the Question of the Admission of Women to the Ministerial Priesthood* (London 1977), pp. 6, 7.

21. L. Bouyer, 'Christian Priesthood and Women', *Man, Woman, and Priesthood*, p. 63.
22. Mascall, 'Women and the Priesthood of the Church', *Why Not?*, p. 102.
23. *Declaration*, p. 7.
24. Schillebeeckx, *Ministry*, p. 97.
25. Lampe, 'Women and the Ministry of Priesthood', p. 100.
26. cf. Jewett, *Male and Female*, p. 169.
27. K. Rahner, *Theological Investigations 20* (London 1981), pp. 41, 42, 44–5.
28. cf. Muddiman, *Women, the Bible and the Priesthood*, pp. 11ff.
29. R. E. Brown, *Biblical Reflections on Crises Facing the Church* (London 1975), pp. 52ff. Note that Brown thinks it possible that women presided at the Eucharist in NT times, 'Roles of Women in the Fourth Gospel', *TS*, 36 (1975), pp. 688f, n. 2.
30. Hodgson, 'Theological Objections', p. 211.
31. J. P. Meier, 'On the Veiling of Hermeneutics (1 Cor. 11.2–16)', *CBQ*, 40 (1978), p. 226.
32. Craston, *Evangelicals and the Ordination of Women*, p. 15. cf. R. Hanson, *Christian Priesthood Examined*, pp. 11, 111.
33. *Declaration*, p. 10.
34. Meier, op. cit., pp. 214, 226.
35. Barr, *Holy Scripture* (Oxford 1983), pp. 33f.
36. cf. Caird, 'Paul and Women's Liberty', p. 280.
37. *Declaration*, pp. 5, 6.
38. Meier, op. cit., p. 213, n. 4. 'Tradition without truth is error grown old.'
39. Lampe, 'Church Tradition', pp. 124–5.
40. Lampe, 'Women and the Ministry of Priesthood', p. 98.
41. Clark, op. cit., pp. 359, 361f.
42. Barr, *The Bible in the Modern World* (London 1973), p. 11.
43. J. Muddiman, *The Bible: Fountain and Well of Truth* (Oxford 1983), pp. 90–1, 17, 89.
44. Barr, *Modern World*, pp. 164–5.
45. Brunner, *Revelation and Reason*, p. 129.
46. L. Hodgson, 'God and the Bible', *On the Authority of the Bible* (London 1960), pp. 8, 10.
47. Brunner, *Man in Revolt*, p. 358, footnote.
48. Muddiman, *The Bible*, pp. 12, 14.

Conclusion

The investigation of the use of Scripture in the debate about women's ministry encompasses a multiplicity of issues. In this study these issues have been considered under two main headings: first, the question of sexuality in God and its bearing upon the sexual characterization of priesthood; second, the question of woman's theological status and her eligibility to bear the authority of an ordained minister. It is not my purpose here to make detailed recapitulation of every conclusion drawn in the foregoing chapters. Rather, I wish to elucidate briefly the overall implication of those conclusions for future discussion and action.

Many people approach the debate about women's ministry with the *a priori* assumption that the Bible forbids the ordination of women. It is asserted that, as far as sexuality can be predicated of divine Being (and some people predicate further than others), God must be described in terms of maleness, not femaleness. Since the God of the Bible is masculine, those who represent him as priests and religious leaders must also be masculine. Furthermore, it is presumed that women, being of lower theological status than men, assigned from the moment of creation to a place of submission to male dominance, are incapable of receiving the charism of ministerial leadership, unsuited for priestly office – in the new covenant as in the old. Thus, exponents of women's ordination are said to be denying scriptural authority and distorting the faith upheld by orthodox believers in the old Israel and in the new.

I hope to have set forth cogently my own conviction that this view fails to do justice to the message of Scripture; it is unworthy of clear-thinking Christians. The Old Testament does not link the sexual characterization of Yahwistic priesthood with beliefs about the maleness of God. Those – whether radical feminist or ardent anti-feminist – who allege that the God of the Bible is male and that his masculinity determines the male priesthoods of Judaism and Christianity are misinterpreting biblical teaching about both God and priesthood. Nor does Scripture endorse the depreciation of womanhood nor declare that woman is inherently unfit for the ordained ministry of the Church. Only a faulty hermeneutic can make the texts suggest that male dominance has an eternally significant place in the Kingdom of God.

In bringing this study to a conclusion, it must be reiterated that the Bible does not constitute a manifesto for opponents of the ordination of women any more than it provides a manual for supporters of women priests and bishops. In fact the Bible contains verses which have been quoted in support of both the 'subordinationist' and the 'equalitarian' positions. It is, however, only on the level of impassioned generalization and partisan rhetoric that it can be claimed either that Scripture confirms every woman's *right* to be ordained or that Scripture for ever excludes woman *qua* woman from ministry. By contrast, patient exegesis and careful analysis of the relevant texts in openness to the mind of Christ does, I have maintained, enable us to discern the essential scriptural directive on women and ministry for the Church today.

It is not that the Bible provides the 'last word' for or against women's ministry. Such finality is unlikely, since biblical writers were not concerned with the question in the form in which it must be considered by modern ecclesiastics and scholars. Rather, as Dodd put it: 'if the Bible is indeed "the Word of God", it is so not as the "last word" on all religious questions, but as the "seminal word" out of which fresh apprehension of truth springs in the mind of man'.[1]

I believe that the moment is at hand for fresh apprehension of the unique liberating power of the gospel to lead men and women to a new and deeper expression of the truth of their co-equal creation in the *Imago Dei*. According to the 'seminal word' of Scripture, the all-important factor is not whether a person is male or female but whether or not he or she believes and trusts in God the Creator and Redeemer of mankind. When a person is a man or woman of faith then, if God the Holy Spirit chooses to bestow gifts which equip that person for ministerial priesthood, the Church should encourage free and full use of these gifts.

In and through Christ, woman's theological status is no longer one of inferiority and of submission to male dominance. Eve in Christ becomes a new creation, no longer bound by the subordinating rubrics of the Law, set free to enjoy the glorious liberty of the children of God (cf. Rom. 8.21; 7.6; 2 Cor. 5.17). In the freedom which the Spirit of the Lord imparts and with his authority, men and women together are called to share Christ's own ministry of proclaiming release to those still in bondage, of setting at liberty those who remain in the thraldom of the fallen world. The liberty of the new Eve in Christ is a freedom which is neither self-assertive nor careless of others' needs (cf. Luke 4.18f; Mark 10.43ff). It is a freedom which facilitates the priestly service of all God's people – to his greater glory (cf. 1 Pet. 2.5, 9).

NOTE

1. C. H. Dodd, *The Authority of the Bible, ?* (London 1938), p. 300.

Bibliography

Aalen, S., 'A Rabbinic Formula in 1 Corinthians 14:34', *St Ev*, 87 (1964), pp. 513–25.

Ackroyd, P. R., 'The Old Testament in the Christian Church, *Theology*, 66 (1963), pp. 46–52.

Ahlström, G. W., *Aspects of Syncretism in Israelite Religion* (Lund 1963).

Albright, W. F., *Archaeology and the Religion of Israel*, 3rd edition (Baltimore 1953).

Albright, W. F., *From Stone Age to Christianity* (first published Baltimore 1940).

Albright, W. F., *Yahweh and the Gods of Canaan* (London 1968).

Aquinas, T., *Summa Theologiae*, ET, T. Gilby *et al.* (London 1964f).

Bailey, S., 'Woman and the Church's Lay Ministry', *Theology*, 57 (1954), pp. 322–30.

Baker, J. A., 'The Right Time', *Feminine in the Church*, ed. M. Furlong (London 1984).

Barnhouse, R. T., 'Is Patriarchy Obsolete?', *Male and Female*, ed. R. T. Barnhouse and U. T. Holmes (New York 1976).

Barr, J., *The Bible in the Modern World* (London 1973).

Barr, J., *Escaping from Fundamentalism* (London 1984).

Barr, J., *Explorations in Theology 7* (London 1980).

Barr, J., *Holy Scripture: Canon, Authority, Criticism* (Oxford 1983).

Barr, J., 'The Image of God in the Book of Genesis – a Study of Terminology', *BJRL*, 51 (1968), pp. 11–26.

Barr, J., *Old and New in Interpretation*, 2nd edition (London 1982).

Barrett, C. K., 'The Bible in the New Testament Period', *The Church's Use of the Bible Past and Present*, ed. D. Nineham (London 1963).

Barrett, C. K., *A Commentary on the First Epistle to the Corinthians*, 2nd edition (London 1971).

Barrett, C. K., *A Commentary on the Second Epistle to the Corinthians* (London 1973).

Barrett, C. K., 'The Interpretation of the Old Testament in the New'. *CHB* I, pp. 377–411.

Barth, K., *Church Dogmatics*, I.1–IV.4, ET (Edinburgh 1936–1981).

Barton, J., *Reading the Old Testament: Method in Biblical Study* (London 1984).

Barton, J., 'Reflections on Cultural Relativism', *Theology*, 82 (1979), pp. 103–9 and 191–9.

Beauvoir, S. de, *The Second Sex*, ET (Middlesex 1972).

Beckwith, R. T., 'The Bearing of Holy Scripture', *Man, Woman, and Priesthood*, ed. P. Moore (London 1978).

Beckwith, R. T. (ed.), *Why Not? Priesthood and the Ministry of Women*, revised and augmented edition (Abingdon 1976).

Bedale, S., 'The Meaning of *kephalē* in the Pauline Epistles', *JTS* (new series), 5 (1954), pp. 211–15.

Berdyaev, N., *The Destiny of Man* (London 1937).

Betz, H. D., *Galatians* (Philadelphia 1979).

Bevan, E., *Symbolism and Belief* (London 1938).

Bird, P., 'Images of Women in the Old Testament', *Religion and Sexism*, ed. R. R. Ruether (New York 1974).

Blomfield, F. C., *Wonderful Order* (London 1955).

Boer, P. A. H. de, 'The Counsellor', 'Wisdom in Israel and in the Ancient Near East', *SVT*, 3 (Leiden 1955), pp. 42–71.

Boer, P. A. H. de, *Fatherhood and Motherhood in Israelite and Judean Piety* (Leiden 1974).

Bonhoeffer, D., *Creation and Fall*, ET (London 1959).

Bonner, D., 'Church Law and the Prohibition to Ordain Women', *Women and Priesthood: Future Directions*, ed. C. Stuhlmueller (Minnesota 1978).

Boucher, M., 'Some Unexplored Parallels to 1 Corinthians 11·11–12 and Galatians 3.28: The New Testament on the Role of Women', *CBQ*, 31 (1969), pp. 50–8.

Bouyer, L., 'Christian Priesthood and Women', *Man, Woman, and Priesthood*, ed. P. Moore (London 1978).

Bouyer, L., *Woman and Man with God*, ET (London 1960).

Brandon, S. G. F., '"In the Beginning": the Hebrew Story of the Creation in its Contemporary Setting', *HT*, 11 (1961), pp. 380–7.

Brandon, S. G. F., *Creation Legends of the Ancient Near East* (London 1963).

Bratsiotis, N. P., *'ish, 'ishshah*, *TDOT*, pp. 222–35.

Briffault, R. S., *The Mothers: A Study of the Origins of Sentiments and Institutions* (London 1927).

Bright, J., *The Authority of the Old Testament* (London 1967).

Brockett, L., *The Ordination of Women: A Roman Catholic Viewpoint*, MOW, Occasional Paper No. 4 (London 1980).

Brooks, B. A., 'Fertility Cult Functionaries in the Old Testament', *JBL*, 60 (1941), pp. 227–53.

Brown, E. F., *The Pastoral Epistles* (London 1917).

Brown, R. E., *Biblical Reflections on Crises Facing the Church* (London 1975).

Brown, R. E., 'Roles of Women in the Fourth Gospel', *TS*, 36 (1975), pp. 688–99.

Bruce, F. F., *The Acts of the Apostles*, 2nd edition (London 1952).

Bruce, F. F., *1 and 2 Corinthians* (London 1971).

Bruce, F. F., *The Epistle to the Galatians* (Exeter 1982).

Bruce, M., 'Heresy, Equality, and the Rights of Women', *Why Not?*, ed. R. T. Beckwith (Abingdon 1976).

Brunner, H. E., *The Christian Doctrine of Creation and Redemption: Dogmatics II*, ET (London 1952).

Brunner, H. E., *The Divine Imperative*, ET (London 1937).

Brunner, H. E., *Man in Revolt: A Christian Anthropology*, ET (London 1939).

Brunner, H. E., 'The New Barth', *SJT*, 4 (1951), pp. 123–5.

Brunner, H. E., *Revelation and Reason*, ET (London 1947).

Buber, M., *The Prophetic Faith*, ET (New York 1949).

Burrows, M., *The Basis of Israelite Marriage* (New Haven 1938).

Caird, G. B., *The Language and Imagery of the Bible* (London 1980).

Caird, G. B., 'Paul and Women's Liberty', *BJRL*, 54 (1971–2), pp. 268–81.

Caird, G. B., *Principalities and Powers: A Study in Pauline Theology* (Oxford 1956).

Cairns, D., *The Image of God in Man*, revised edition (London 1973).

Callahan, S., 'Misunderstanding of Sexuality and Resistance to Women Priests', *Women Priests*, ed. L. and A. Swidler (New York 1977).

Calvin, J., *Commentaries on the First Book of Moses called Genesis*, trans. J. King (Edinburgh 1847).

Carey, G., *I Believe in Man* (London 1977).

Carroll, E., 'Women and Ministry', *TS*, 36 (1975), pp. 660–87.

Clark, S. B., *Man and Woman in Christ* (Michigan 1980).

Clines, D. J. A., 'The Image of God in Man', *TB*, 19 (1968), pp. 53–103.

Cody, A., 'A History of Old Testament Priesthood', *AB*, 35 (1969).

Concerning the Ordination of Women, Department on Faith and Order and Department on Co-operation of Men and Women in Church, Family and Society, WCC Symposium (Geneva 1964).

Conzelmann, H., *1 Corinthians*, ET (Philadelphia 1975).

Conzelmann, H., 'The Mother of Wisdom', *The Future of our Religious Past*, ET, ed. J. M. Robinson (London 1971).

Cope, L., '1 Corinthians 11:2–16: One Step Further', *JBL*, 97 (1978), pp. 435–6.

Cowley, A. C. (ed.), *Aramaic Papyri of the Fifth Century BC* (Oxford 1923).

Craig, C. T. and Short, J., '1 Corinthians', *The Interpreter's Bible*, 10 (New York 1953).

Cranfield, C. E. B., *The Epistle to the Romans*, I (Edinburgh 1975).

Craston, C. (ed.), *Evangelicals and the Ordination of Women*, Grove Booklet on Ministry and Worship No. 17 (Bramcote 1973).

Cross, E. B., *The Hebrew Family* (Chicago 1927).

Crouch, J. E., *The Origin and Intention of the Colossian Haustafel* (Göttingen 1972).

Culver, E. T., *Women in the World of Religion* (New York 1967).

Daly, M., *Beyond God the Father: Toward a Philosophy of Women's Liberation* (Boston 1973).

Daly, M., *The Church and the Second Sex* (London 1968).

Davidson, R., *Genesis 1–11* (Cambridge 1973).

Davidson, R., *Genesis 12–50* (Cambridge 1979).

Davies, D., 'An Anthropological Perspective', *Why Not?*, ed. R. T. Beckwith (Abingdon 1976).

Davies, W. D., *Christian Origins and Judaism* (London 1962).

Davies, W. D., *Paul and Rabbinic Judaism* (London 1965).

Daube, D., *The New Testament and Rabbinic Judaism* (London 1956).

Declaration 'inter insigniores' on the Question of the Admission of Women to the Ministerial Priesthood, Sacred Congregation for the Doctrine of the Faith, ET (London 1977).

Demant, V., 'Why the Christian Priesthood is Male', *Women and Holy Orders*, Appendix C (London 1966).

Denzinger, H., *Enchiridion Symbolorum: Definitionum et Declarationum de Rebus Fidei et Morum*, 34th edition, ed. A. Schönmetzer (Herder 1967).

Dibelius, M. and Conzelmann, H., *The Pastoral Epistles*, ET (Philadelphia 1972).

Dillistone, F. W., 'Male–Female Symbolism', *Yes to Women Priests*, ed. II. Montefiore (Oxford 1978).

Doctrine in the Church of England, The Report of the Commission on Christian Doctrine Appointed by the Archbishops of Canterbury and York in 1922 (London 1938).

Dodd, C. H., *The Authority of the Bible*, 2nd edition (London 1938).

Dodd, C. H., *The Old Testament in the New* (London 1952).

Dowell, S. and Hurcombe, L., *Dispossessed Daughters of Eve* (London 1981).

Driver, G. R. and Miles, J. C., *The Babylonian Laws* (Oxford 1955).

Driver, S. R., *The Book of Genesis* (London 1904).

Driver, S. R., *Deuteronomy*, 3rd edition (Edinburgh 1902).

Dumas, A., 'Biblical Anthropology and the Participation of Women in the Ministry of the Church', *Concerning the Ordination of Women*, WCC Symposium (Geneva 1964), pp. 12–40.

Dunn, J. D. G., *Unity and Diversity in the New Testament: An Inquiry into the Character of Earliest Christianity* (London 1977).

Eichrodt, W., *Theology of the Old Testament*, I and II (London 1961 and 1967).

Éliade, M., *Patterns in Comparative Religion*, ET (London 1958).

Eller, V., *The Language of Canaan and the Grammar of Feminism* (Grand Rapids 1982).

Ellis, E. E., *Paul's Use of the Old Testament* (Edinburgh 1957).

Emerton, J. A., 'New Light on Israelite Religion: The Implications of the Inscriptions from Kuntillet 'Ajrud', *ZAW*, 94 (1982), pp. 2–20.

Epstein, L. M., *Sex Laws and Customs in Judaism* (New York 1948).

Evans, M., *Woman in the Bible* (Exeter 1983).

Farrer, A., *The Glass of Vision* (London 1948).

Fiorenza, E. S., 'Feminist Theology and New Testament Interpretation', *JSOT*, 22 (1982), pp. 32–46.

Fiorenza, E. S., *In Memory of Her: A Feminist Theological Reconstruction of Christian Origins* (London 1983).

Fiorenza, E. S., 'Word, Spirit and Power: Women in Early Christian Communities', *Women of Spirit: Female Leadership in the Jewish and Christian Traditions*, ed. R. R. Ruether and E. McLaughlin (New York 1979).

Fitzmyer, J. A., 'A Feature of Qumran Angelology and the Angels of 1 Corinthians 11:10', *NTS*, 4 (1957–8), pp. 48–58.

Fitzmyer, J. A., 'The Use of Explicit Old Testament Quotations in Qumran Literature and in the New Testament', *NTS*, 7 (1961), pp. 297–333.

Ford, J. M., 'Biblical Material Relevant to the Ordination of Women', *JES*, 10 (1973), pp. 669–94.

Frazer, J. G., *Folk-lore in the Old Testament*, I (London 1919).

Frazer, J. G., *The Golden Bough*, I (London 1922).

Friedmann, M., 'Mitwirkung von Frauen beim Gottesdienste', *HUCA*, 8–9 (1931–2), pp. 511–23.

Fuchs-Kreimer, N., 'Feminism and Scriptural Interpretation: A Contemporary Jewish Critique', *JES*, 20 (1983), pp. 534–48.

Fuller, R. H., 'Pro and Con: The Ordination of Women in the New Testament', *Toward a New Theology of Ordination: Essays on the Ordination of Women*, ed. H. M. Micks and C. P. Price (Virginia 1976).

Furnish, V. P., *The Moral Teaching of Paul: Selected Issues* (Abingdon, Nashville 1979).

Geffré, C., '"Father" as the Proper Name of God', 'God as Father?', *Concilium* (March 1981), pp. 43–50.

Goldenberg, N., *Changing of the Gods* (Boston 1979).

Gordon, C. H., *Ugaritic Manual* (Rome 1955).

Goudge, H. L., *The First Epistle to the Corinthians* (London 1903).

Graham, W. C. and May, H. G., *Culture and Conscience* (Chicago 1936).

Grant, R. M., *Gnosticism and Early Christianity*, 2nd edition (London 1966).

Gratian, *Decretum Gratiani*, ed. J. H. Boehmer and E. L. Richter, *PL* 187 (Paris, 1855).

Gray, G. B., *Sacrifice in the Old Testament: Its Theory and Practice* (Oxford 1925).

Gray, J., *Archaeology and the Old Testament World* (London 1962).

Gray, J., *1 and 2 Kings*, 3rd edition (London 1977).

Gray, J., 'The Legacy of Canaan', *SVT*, 5 (Leiden 1957).

Grosheide, F. W., *Commentary on 1 Corinthians* (Grand Rapids 1979).

Gryson, R., *The Ministry of Women in the Early Church*, E T (Minnesota 1976).

Haenchen, E., *The Acts of the Apostles*, E T (Oxford 1971).

Halkes, C., 'The Themes of Protest in Feminist Theology against God the Father', 'God as Father?', *Concilium* (March 1981), pp. 103–10.

Hanson, A. T., *The Living Utterances of God: The New Testament Exegesis of the Old* (London 1983).

Hanson, A. T., *The New Testament Interpretation of Scripture* (London 1980).

Hanson, A. T., *The Pastoral Letters* (Cambridge 1966).

Hanson, A. T., *Studies in the Pastoral Epistles* (London 1968).

Hanson, A. T., *Studies in Paul's Technique and Theology* (London 1974).

Hanson, P. D., 'Masculine Metaphors for God and Sex-discrimination in the Old Testament', *ER*, 27 (1975), pp. 316–24.

Hanson, R., *Christian Priesthood Examined* (Guildford and London 1979).

Harvey, A. E., *Priest or President?* (London 1975).

Hempel, J., *Gott und Mensch im Alten Testament*, 2nd edition (Stuttgart 1936).

Héring, J., *The First Epistle of St. Paul to the Corinthians*, E T (London 1962).

Heyob, S. K., *The Cult of Isis Among Women in the Greco-Roman World* (Leiden 1975).

Higgins, J. M., 'The Myth of Eve: The Temptress', *JAAR*, 44 (1976), pp. 639–47.

Hobson, R. F., 'Psychological Considerations', *Women and Holy Orders*, Report of the Archbishops' Commission (London 1966), pp. 45–73.

Hodgson, L., 'God and the Bible', *On the Authority of the Bible, Some Recent Studies* (London 1960); article reprinted from *CQR*, 159 (1958), pp. 532–46.

Hodgson, L., 'Theological Objections to the Ordination of Women', *Exp T*, 77 (1965–66), pp. 210–13.

Holmes, U. T., 'The Sexuality of God', *Male and Female*, ed. R. T. Barnhouse and U. T. Holmes (New York 1976).

Hooke, S. H., 'Myth and Ritual: Past and Present', *Myth, Ritual and Kingship* (Oxford 1958).

Hooke, S. H., 'Traces of the Myth and Ritual Pattern in Canaan', *Myth and Ritual* (Oxford 1933).

Hooker, M. D., 'Authority on her head: An examination of 1 Corinthians 11:10', *NTS*, 10 (1964), pp. 410–16.

Howard, R. W., *Should Women be Priests?* (Oxford 1949).

Hurley, J. B., *Man and Woman in Biblical Perspective* (Leicester 1981).

Hvidberg, F., 'The Canaanitic Background of Genesis 1–3', *VT*, 10 (1960), pp. 285–94.

Jacob, E., *Theology of the Old Testament*, ET (London 1958).

James, E. O., 'An Anthropologist's Comments', Appendix to the Church Union's publication of E. L. Mascall's *Women and the Priesthood of the Church* (London 1960).

James, E. O., *The Cult of the Mother-Goddess* (London 1959).

James, E. O., *The Nature and Function of Priesthood* (London 1955).

Jastrow, M., *The Religion of Babylonia and Assyria* (Boston 1898).

Jenson, R. W., *The Triune Identity* (Philadelphia 1982).

Jeremias, J., *Jerusalem in the Time of Jesus*, ET (London 1969).

Jeremias, J., *New Testament Theology*, I, ET (London 1971).

Jeremias, J., *The Prayers of Jesus*, ET (London 1967).

Jewett, P. K., *Man as Male and Female* (Grand Rapids 1975).

Jewett, P. K., *The Ordination of Women* (Grand Rapids 1980).

Johnson, A. R., *The One and the Many in the Israelite Conception of God*, 2nd edition (Cardiff 1961).

Kapelrud, A. S., *The Ras Shamra Discoveries and the Old Testament*, ET (Oxford 1965).

Kapelrud, A. S., *The Violent Goddess* (Oslo 1969).

Karris, R. J., 'The Role of Women According to Jesus and the Early Church', *Women and Priesthood*, ed. C. Stuhlmueller (Minnesota 1978).

Kaufmann, Y., *The Religion of Israel*, ET (London 1961).

Keel, O. (ed.), *Monotheismus im Alten Israel und Seiner Umwelt* (Freiburg 1980).

Kemp, E. W., *N. P. Williams* (London 1954).

Kerkhofs, J., 'From Frustration to Liberation?: A Factual Approach to Ministries in the Church', *Minister? Pastor? Prophet?: Grass-roots Leadership in the Churches*, ET (London 1980).

Kirk, K. E., 'The Ordination of Women', *Beauty and Bands* (London 1955).

Kittel, G., '*abba*' *TDNT*, I, 1964, pp. 5–6.

Knierim, R., 'The Role of the Sexes in the Old Testament', *LTQ*, 10 (1975), pp. 1–10.

Köhler, L., *Hebrew Man*, ET (London 1956).

Köhler, L., *Old Testament Theology*, ET (London 1957).

Lagrange, M.-J., 'La Paternité de Dieu dans L'Ancien Testament', *RB* (1908), pp. 481–99.

Lampe, G. W. H., 'Church Tradition and the Ordination of Women', *Exp T*, 76 (1965), pp. 123–5.

Lampe, G. W. H., 'Women and the Ministry of Priesthood', *Explorations in Theology*, 8 (London 1981).

Landtman, G., *The Origin of Priesthood* (Finland 1905).

Lefkowitz, M. R. and Fant, M. B. (eds.), *Women in Greece and Rome* (Toronto 1977).

Lewis, A. E. (ed.), *The Motherhood of God*, A Report by a Study Group appointed by the Women's Guild and the Panel on Doctrine on the invitation of the General Assembly of the Church of Scotland (Edinburgh 1984).

Lewis, C. S., 'Priestesses in the Church?' (1948), reprinted in *God in the Dock* (London 1979).

Longnecker, R. N., *Biblical Exegesis in the Apostolic Period* (Grand Rapids 1975).

Longstaff, T. R. W., 'The Ordination of Women: A Biblical Perspective', *ATR*, 57 (1975), pp. 316–27.

Lossky, V., *In the Image and Likeness of God*, ET (New York 1974).

Luther, M., 'Lectures on Genesis', *Luther's Works*, I, ed. J. Pelikan (St Louis 1958).

MacCulloch, J. A., 'Serpent-Worship', *ERE*, 11, pp. 399–411.

Mace, D. R., *Hebrew Marriage* (London 1953).

Macquarrie, J., *Principles of Christian Theology*, revised edition (London 1977).

Manson, T. W., *The Sayings of Jesus* (London 1949).

Manson, W., *The Gospel of Luke* (London 1930).

Mare, W. H., '1 Corinthians', *Expositor's Bible Commentary*, 10 (London 1976).

Marrett, R. R., *Sacraments of Simple Folk* (Oxford 1933).

Martin, W. J., '1 Corinthians 11:2–16: An Interpretation', *Apostolic History and the Gospel*, eds. W. W. Gasque and R. P. Martin (Exeter 1970).

Mascall, E. L., *Christ, the Christian, and the Church* (London 1946).

Mascall, E. L., 'Some Basic Considerations', *Man, Woman, and Priesthood*, ed. P. Moore (London 1978).

Mascall, E. L., *Whatever Happened to the Human Mind?* (London 1980).

Mascall, E. L., 'Women and the Priesthood of the Church', *Why Not?*, ed. R. T. Beckwith (Abingdon 1976); article previously published separately by the Church Union (London 1960).

Mays, J. L., *Hosea* (London 1969).

Mead, M., *Male and Female: A Study of the Sexes in a Changing World* (London 1949).

Meek, T. J., *Hebrew Origins*, revised edition (New York 1960).

Meeks, W. A., 'The Image of Androgyne: Some Uses of a Symbol in Earliest Christianity', *History of Religions*, 13 (1974), pp. 165–208.

Meer, H. van der, *Women Priests in the Catholic Church? A Theological Investigation*, ET (Philadelphia 1973).

Meier, J. P., 'On the Veiling of Hermeneutics (1 Cor. 11:2–16)', *CBQ*, 40 (1978), pp. 212–26.

Meshel, Z., 'Did Yahweh Have a Consort?', *BAR*, 5 (1979), pp. 24–35.

Miller, J. M., 'In the "Image" and "Likeness" of God', *JBL*, 91 (1972), pp. 289–304.

Miller, P. D., 'Genesis 1–11: Studies in Structure and Theme', *JSOT*, Supplement Series 8, 1978.

Moberly, E. R., *Homosexuality: A New Christian Ethic* (Cambridge 1983).

Moffatt, J., *The First Epistle of Paul to the Corinthians* (London 1947).

Moltmann, J., 'The Motherly Father: Is Trinitarian Patripassianism Replacing Theological Patriarchalism?', 'God as Father?', *Concilium* (March 1981), pp. 51–6.

Moss, R. (ed.), *God's Yes to Sexuality*, BCC Report (Glasgow 1981).

Moule, C. F. D., *The Birth of the New Testament*, 3rd edition (London 1981).

Moule, C. F. D., 'God, NT', *IDB*, E–J, pp. 430–6.

Moule, C. F. D., *Worship in the New Testament* (London 1961).

Muddiman, J., *The Bible: Fountain and Well of Truth* (Oxford 1983).

Muddiman, J. and G., *Women, The Bible and the Priesthood*, MOW paper (London 1984).

Murphy-O'Connor, J., 'The Non-Pauline Character of 1 Corinthians 11:2–16?', *JBL*, 95 (1976), pp. 615–21.

Murphy-O'Connor, J., 'Sex and Logic in 1 Corinthians 11:2–16', *CBQ*, 42 (1980), pp. 482–500.

Neumann, E., *The Great Mother*, ET (London 1955).

Nineham, D., *The Use and Abuse of the Bible: A Study of the Bible in an Age of Rapid Cultural Change* (London 1978).

Nock, A. D., 'Gnosticism, *Essays on Religion and the Ancient World*, ed. Z. Stewart (Oxford 1972).

Norris, R. A., jun., 'The Ordination of Women and the "Maleness" of the Christ', *Feminine in the Church*, ed. M. Furlong (London 1984).

Oddie, W., *What Will Happen to God? Feminism and the Reconstruction of Christian Belief* (London 1984).

Oddie, W., 'Why Women Priests could be a Step Towards a New Religion', *Daily Telegraph*, 5 May 1982.

Oesterley, W. O. E., 'Early Hebrew Festival Rituals', *Myth and Ritual*, ed. S. H. Hooke (Oxford 1933).

O'Faolain, J. and Martines, L. (eds.), *Not in God's Image: Women in History* (London 1973).

Ogden, C. K. and Richards, I. A., *The Meaning of Meaning* (London 1923).

The Ordination of Women to the Priesthood, A consultative document presented by ACCM, GS, 104 (London 1972).

Orr, W. F. and Walther, J. A., *1 Corinthians* (New York 1976).

Osiek, C., 'The Ministry and Ordination of Women According to the Early Church Fathers', *Women and Priesthood: Future Directions*, ed. C. Stuhlmueller (Minnesota 1978).

Ostdiek, G., 'The Ordination of Woman and the Force of Tradition', Women and Priesthood, ed. C. Stuhlmueller, *Women and Priesthood*, q.v.

Otwell, J. H., *And Sarah Laughed: The Status of Women in the Old Testament* (Philadelphia 1977).

Packer, J. I., 'I Believe in Women's Ministry', *Why Not?*, ed. R. T. Beckwith (Abingdon 1976).

Packer, J. I., 'Thoughts on the Role and Function of Women in the Church', *Evangelicals and the Ordination of Women*, ed. C. Craston, q.v.

Pagels, E. H., 'Paul and Women: A Response to Recent Discussion', *JAAR*, 42 (1974), pp. 538–49.

Pagels, E. H., 'What Became of God the Mother? Conflicting Images of God in Early Christianity', *Signs*, 2 (1976), pp. 293–303.

Parvey, C. F. (ed.), *The Community of Women and Men in the Church: The Sheffield Report 1981* WCC (Geneva 1983).

Patai, R., *The Hebrew Goddess* (New York 1967).

Peacocke, A. R., *Creation and the World of Science* (Oxford 1979).

Pedersen, J., *Israel: Its Life and Culture*, volumes I–II and III–IV (Copenhagen 1926 and 1940).

Peritz, I. J., 'Women in the Ancient Hebrew Cult', *JBL*, 17 (1898), pp. 111–48.

Perry, M., 'Why Not Now?', *Yes to Women Priests*, ed. H. Montefiore (Oxford 1978).

Phillips, A. C. J., *Deuteronomy* (Cambridge 1973).

Phillips, A. C. J., 'The Ecstatics' Father', *Words and Meanings*, eds. P. R. Ackroyd and B. Lindars (Cambridge 1968).

Phillips, A. C. J., *Lower Than the Angels: Questions Raised by Genesis I–II* (Oxford 1983).

Philo, 'Questions and Answers on Genesis', ET, *Philo* Supplement I, Loeb Classical Library (London 1953).

Porter, J. R., *Leviticus* (Cambridge 1976).

Pritchard, J. B. (ed.), *Ancient Near Eastern Texts Relating to the Old Testament*, 2nd edition (New Jersey 1955).

Quell, G., '*patēr*', *TDNT*, V, pp. 959–74.

Rad, G. von, '*eikōn*', *TDNT*, II, pp. 390–2.

Rad, G. von, *Genesis*, ET, revised edition (London 1972).

Rad, G. von, *Old Testament Theology*, I, ET (London 1975).

Rahner, K., *Concern for the Church: Theological Investigations 20*, ET (London 1981).

Ramsey, I. T., *Religious Language* (London 1957).

Reed, W. L., *The Asherah in the Old Testament* (Texas 1949).

Richardson, A., *Genesis I–XI* (London 1953).

Ringgren, H., ''*ābh*', *TDOT*, I, pp. 1–19.

Ringgren, H., *Israelite Religion*, ET (London 1966).

Ringgren, H., *Religions of the Ancient Near East*, ET (London 1973).

Robbins, I. M., 'St. Paul and the Ministry of Women', *Exp T*, 46 (1934–5), pp. 185–8.

Robertson, A. and Plummer, A., *The First Epistle of St Paul to the Corinthians* (Edinburgh 1911).

Rowley, H. H., *The Faith of Israel* (London 1956).

Ruether, R. R., 'The Female Nature of God: A Problem in Contemporary Religious Life', 'God as Father?', *Concilium* (March 1981), pp. 61–6.

Ruether, R. R., *Religion and Sexism* (New York 1974).

Ruether, R. R., *Sexism and God-Talk* (London 1983).

Russell, G. and Dewey, M., 'Psychological Aspects', *Man, Woman, and Priesthood*, ed. P. Moore (London 1978).

Sabourin, L., 'Priesthood: A Comparative Study', *SN*, 25 (Leiden 1973).

Sacks, J., 'The Role of Women in Judaism', *Man, Woman, and Priesthood*, ed. P. Moore (London 1978).

Saggs, H. W. F., *The Encounter with the Divine in Mesopotomia and Israel* (London 1978).

Sapp, S., *Sexuality, the Bible, and Science* (Philadelphia 1977).

Saward, J., *Christ and His Bride* (London 1977).

Schillebeeckx, E., 'A Creative Retrospect as Inspiration for the Ministry in the Future', *Minister? Pastor? Prophet? Grassroots Leadership in the Churches*, ET (London 1980).

Shillebeeckx, E., *Ministry – A Case for Change*, ET (London 1981).

Schlier, H., *'kephalē'*, *TDNT*, III, pp. 673–81.

Schmid, H. H., *Altorientalische Welt in der alttestamentlichen Theologie* (Zürich 1974).

Schmithals, W., *Gnosticism in Corinth*, ET (New York 1971).

Schrenk, G., *'patēr'*, *TDNT*, V, pp. 948–59; 974–82.

Schweizer, E., *Church Order in the New Testament*, ET (London 1961).

Scroggs, R., *The Last Adam: A Study in Pauline Anthropology* (Oxford 1966).

Scroggs, R., 'Paul and the Eschatological Woman', *JAAR*, 40 (1972), pp. 283–303.

Scroggs, R., 'Paul and the Eschatological Woman: Revisited', *JAAR*, 42 (1974), pp. 532–7.

Segal, J. B., 'The Jewish Attitude Towards Women', *JJS*, 30 (1979), pp. 121–37.

Sethe, K., *Urgeschichte und älteste Religion der Aegypter* (Leipzig 1930).

Simon, W. G. H., *The First Epistle to the Corinthians* (London 1959).

Skinner, J., *Genesis*, 2nd edition (Edinburgh 1930)

Smail, T. A., *The Forgotten Father* (London 1980).

Smith, D. M., jun., 'The Use of the Old Testament in the New', *The Use of the Old Testament in the New and Other Essays*, ed J. M. Efird (Durham N.C. 1972).

Smith, S., 'The Practice of Kingship in Early Semitic Kingdoms', *Myth, Ritual and Kingship*, ed. S. H. Hooke (Oxford 1958).

Smith, W. Robertson, *The Religion of the Semites*, 3rd edition (London 1927).

Stendahl, K., *The Bible and the Role of Women*, ET (Philadelphia 1966).

Stuhlmueller, C., 'Bridegroom: A Biblical Symbol of Union, not Sepa ration', *Women Priests: A Catholic Commentary on the Vatican Declaration*, ed. L. and A. Swidler (New York 1977).

Swidler, L., *Biblical Affirmations of Woman* (Philadelphia 1979).

Tavard, G. H., 'Sexist Language in Theology?', *TS*, 36 (1975), pp. 700–24.

Tavard, G. H., *Woman in Christian Tradition* (Notre Dame 1973).

Terrien, S., 'Toward a Biblical Theology of Womanhood', *Male and Female*, eds. R. T. Barnhouse and U. T. Holmes (New York 1976).

Thielicke, H., *How the World Began: Man in the First Chapters of the Bible*, ET (London 1964).

Thomas, W. D., 'The Place of Women in the Church of Philippi', *Exp T*, 83 (1971–2), pp. 117–20.

Thrall, M. E., *1 and 2 Corinthians* (Cambridge 1965).

Thrall, M. E., *The Ordination of Women to the Priesthood: A Study of the Biblical Evidence* (London 1958).

Thurian, M., *Priesthood and Ministry*, ET (London 1983).

Trible, P., 'Depatriarchalizing in Biblical Interpretation', *JAAR*, 41 (1973), pp. 30–48.

Trible, P., *God and the Rhetoric of Sexuality* (Philadelphia 1978).

Trompf, G. W., 'On Attitudes Towards Woman in Paul and Paulinist Literature: 1 Corinthians 11:3–16 and Its Context', *CBQ*, 42 (1980), pp. 196–215.

Ulanov, A. B., *The Feminine in Jungian Psychology and in Christian Theology* (Evanston 1971).

Vaux, R. de, *Ancient Israel*, 2nd edition (London 1965).

Vawter, B., *On Genesis: A New Reading* (New York 1977).

Vermes, G., *Jesus and the World of Judaism* (London 1983).

Vogels, W., 'It is not good that the *Mensch* should be alone; I will make him/her a helper fit for him/her (Gen.2:18)', *E et T*, 9 (1978), pp. 9–35.

Vos, C. J., *Woman in Old Testament Worship* (Amsterdam 1968).

Vriezen, Th. C., *An Outline of Old Testament Theology*, ET, 2nd edition (Oxford, 1970).

Vriezen, Th. C., *The Religion of Ancient Israel*, ET (London 1967).

Walker, W. O., '1 Corinthians 11:2–16 and Paul's Views Regarding Women', *JBL*, 94 (1975), pp. 94–110.

Ware, K., 'Man, Woman, and the Priesthood of Christ', *Man, Woman, and Priesthood*, ed. P. Moore (London 1978).

Watson, V. E. and Brett, W., *Women Priests Impossible?* (London 1973).

Weber, M., *Ancient Judaism*, ET (Illinois 1952).

Weiser, A., *The Psalms*, ET (London 1962).

Westermann, C., *The Genesis Accounts of Creation*, ET (Philadelphia 1964).

Westermann, C., *Isaiah 40–66*, ET (London 1969).

Westermann, C., *What does the Old Testament say about God?* (London 1979).

Whiteley, D. E. H., *The Theology of St Paul*, 2nd edition (Oxford 1974).

Widengren, G., 'Early Hebrew Myths and their Interpretation', *Myth, Ritual and Kingship*, ed. S. H. Hooke (Oxford 1958).

Williams, J. G., 'The Prophetic Father', *JBL*, 85 (1966), pp. 344–8.

Williams, J. G., *Women Recounted: Narrative Thinking and the God of Israel* (Sheffield 1982).

Williams, N. P., *The Ideas of the Fall and of Original Sin* (London 1927).

Wilson, R. McL., *Gnosis in the New Testament* (Oxford 1968).

Witherington, B., 'Rite and Rights for Women: Galatians 3:28', *NTS*, 27 (1981), pp. 593–604.

Wolff, H. W., *Anthropology of the Old Testament*, ET (London 1974).

Women and Holy Orders, Report of a Commission appointed by the Archbishops of Canterbury and York (London 1966).

Zerbst, F., *The Office of Woman in the Church: A Study in Practical Theology*, ET (St Louis 1955).

Index of Biblical References

Old Testament

New Testament

Index of Names and Subjects